Sia alma Thomas
524 Highway 43
Jefferson, Tx

Pd Merrill David AT&T pd 152, + 70.
4/15/12

A Channel Of Blessing

Other books by New Authors Publications

Parenting In The '90s
Where Have We Gone Wrong?
By Dr. Trevor and Karen Crabtree

The Checkerboard Triangle
By John Richard Small

Bittersweet: The Story of the Heath Candy
Company
By Richard J. Heath with Ray Elliott

Fall of the House of Gacy
By Harlan H. Mendenhall

Where Have You Gone Thomas Jefferson?
By Michael J. Bakalis

Love The Town Couldn't Stop
By Chicago Alderman Ed H. Smith

A Channel
Of Blessing

*The inspiring story of a divine promise fulfilled
and the role of Danny & Linda Shelton*

Bob Ellis

With A Foreword By
Kenneth J. Gray
U.S. Congressman (Ret.)

New Authors Publications

West Frankfort, Illinois

For permission requests or to order books, write to:

Three Angels Broadcasting Network
Post Ofice Box 220
West Frankfort, IL 62896

For Visa or MasterCard orders call
(618) 627-4651
Ask for "Call Center"

Discount on volume sales for church or educational purposes

Published by New Authors Publications
P.O. Box 10, West Frankfort, IL 62896
(618) 937-6412   FAX-(618) 932-3848

This book is dedicated to
God's greatest gift to me, my wife, Kay.

Contents

Foreword

Ralph Waldo Emerson once said, "Make the most of yourself because that's all there is to you." Danny and Linda Shelton have surely lived up to that credo. If ever there were two people who have pulled themselves up by their bootstraps, it is this couple. They have raised themselves up by using inspiration, perspiration and prayer, to create a worldwide ministry that is universally recognized today and is still reaching out into the farthest and darkest corners of the globe to bring people to God.

From its inception 3ABN struggled to exist, to grow, and then to blossom. How it was conceived and its ongoing expansion into today's astounding proportions is the stuff that legends are made of.

While serving in the United States Congress I closely followed the remarkable story of the growth of 3ABN. In fact, I was pleased to be able to play a small role in the development of the network by working with the Federal Communications Commission in regard to their first satellite. This effort involved more than just helping a constituent. It became obvious early on that 3ABN was unique, special and blessed with a destiny which is yet unfolding. Also, the endeavor of the Sheltons speaks of the hardy spirit, work ethic and ingenuity of the citizens of southern Illinois, a district where I had the great privilege of serving the people for more than 20 years.

From a humble beginning, Danny Shelton rose to greatness as he and his wife, Linda, have created a ministry now known everywhere in the world that television reaches. Yet they have retained their personal humility. I am proud to call them my friends and I am pleased that, through this book, everyone can now know their incredible story.

Kenneth J. Gray, U.S. Congressman (Ret.)
Ken Gray was a 12-term member of the U.S. House of Representatives from Illinois, and a decorated World War II hero who flew missions over Germany.

Preface

The genesis of my association with Danny Shelton and Three Angels Broadcasting Network (3ABN) was most ordinary. It began as a routine newspaper assignment to "cover" a local man who was achieving what appeared to be a modicum of success at building a television ministry, and to write a feature story about that enterprise. Thus assigned I was a bit disgruntled because I felt I was the wrong newsman for the task.

First of all, I preferred writing hard news such as that reflecting activity in the always intense and interesting political arena. Second, my qualifications for this particular assignment were suspect because, as a "skeptic," I knew nothing of religion, per se. Third, and perhaps most importantly, if the truth be known, theologically I was an outright doubter. This "Doubting Thomas" attitude went beyond the mandatory suspicious demeanor congenital to my particular craft. I have read the Bible with the same interest and curiosity as other classic works. Furthermore, I have sought out and held riveting discussions with learned theologians, at every opportunity, actually. I tried to absorb their meaning and messages. Only a fool would not want to "believe." I tried. I really tried. But I have learned in the course of more than 60 winters that the Devil, too, can quote scriptures. Therefore all theologians were suspect in my mind. The then recent fall from prominence of the likes of Jim and Tammy Bakker, Jimmy Swaggert, et al, had reinforced and brought to the surface my long-dormant feeling that there was nothing within religion, for me. To my way of thinking, their shame eroded the entire religious community, not just my personal confidence.

So, wearing my preconceived notions of bias and cynicism like the press tag I so often attached to my lapel in order to gain entrance into areas where the average citizen is not allowed to tread, I set out to fulfill my journalistic obligation to the best of my ability. However, in my drudgery, the strangest thing happened on the way to writing my routine story.

I discovered that I did not need an imposing press pass to get into the area where Danny Shelton works. Even though I admittedly entered this assignment with doubt in my heart, objectivity is supposed to be my stock in trade and I was determined to keep an open mind. That professional attitude was soon to dissolve, unneeded as it were. I was visited by awe for the enticing environment of 3ABN. My self-imposed objectivity proved to be superfluous and melted away, and the investigation that ensued would become instrumental in changing my life, unequivocally for the better. The worst thing that can happen to a journalist occurred. The story worked me.

I have observed remarkable things during my subsequent involvement with Danny and Linda Shelton, and the wondrous place that is 3ABN. Words like "miracle" do not easily flow from the pen of this writer. But I am keenly challenged to tell the story of 3ABN by using lesser terminology. I felt compelled to tell the story of 3ABN.

My fascination of the network began in 1989, when I covered their first trip to Romania, at the end of a bloody revolution. Armed soldiers still patrolled the streets. We met with Christians whose churches had been destroyed by a despotic regime, and who had gone underground to avoid imprisonment or death. It continued through many other ventures into Europe, Russia, Honduras and the like. Early on I continued making these trips for the pure joy of it, unencumbered by any journalistic responsibility.

What follows, however, is not so much about how this adventure has affected me and added new dimension to my life. That is personal. Rather it is how Danny Shelton, through his own personal divine inspiration and faith and joined by his wife, Linda, has impacted the world. Literally, the entire world. 3ABN is now an international television network sending signals to every inhabited continent in the world via five different satellites twenty-four hours a day, seven days a week. 3ABN owns and operates 88 UHF stations throughout the United States with 26 new ones under construction as well as a number of full power FM and AM radio stations. 3ABN can also be seen twenty-four hours a day, seven days a week on hundreds of cable stations around the world with new cable systems being added weekly. They own new full power stations in both Manilla, Philippines and Port Moresby, Papua New Guinea and can be seen in nearly 190 cities in the ex-Soviet Union. 3ABN receives letters and emails daily from around the world from those who view 3ABN over the Internet via Internet-streaming. 3ABN's potential viewership is well over 100 million and growing by leaps and bounds – and this doesn't include the multiple millions of Internet users who are able to access 3ABN throughout the world.

The story told in large measure by Danny Shelton himself, and Linda, is the remarkable story of 3ABN. My fervent prayer is that I can relate it to you with unerring fidelity.

Bob Ellis, May 16, 2002

Chapter 1

It was no surprise when Danny Shelton telephoned me in West Frankfort, Illinois, from Hong Kong, China. He had done that from time to time from various places around the world, while traveling the globe spreading the Word through Three Angels Broadcasting Network (3ABN), of which he is the president and protagonist.

He would keep me up to date on his various projects, especially if I had been personally involved at some level.

Danny poignantly spoke to me about his trip. He described how beautiful Hong Kong is and how much he and his wife Linda appreciated its enchanting qualities as well as its bustling human activity. But I could tell from Danny's voice that his heart was heavy with a burden of some sort. Likewise, I knew he would eventually bring it out, vocalize it without any prompting from me. And so he did.

He described in detailed heart-wrenching anguish the stark contrast between the tranquil beauty of Hong Kong, and the horrific reality of the previous several days that he and his traveling companions had spent in the "killing fields" of Cambodia and in hunger-ridden Bangladesh.

The Sheltons were traveling with Garwin McNeilus, founder and former owner of the McNeilus Companies in Dodge Center, Minnesota, the world's premier manufacturer of cement trucks and other vehicles. Also in the group were McNeilus' son and daughter-in-law, Denzil and Donna.

They were undaunted by such dangers as civil unrest and the aftermath of a war which left an untold number of uncharted land mines about the landscapes. The group was traveling through that troubled part of the world searching for locations to build schools, churches and medical facilities for the impoverished people. They also sought to help bring economic relief to people in dire need.

The McNeilus family has, as has the Seventh-day Adventist Church, been active in bringing aid and comfort to brutalized civilians in that region, just as 3ABN steadfastly strives to do throughout much of the world. Danny Shelton's description of the grotesqueries he witnessed on that trip was grim and graphic. Inevitably his telephonic conversation turned to the foundation of his grief. I made notes for the eventual use in this book.

In Danny Shelton's own words: "Bob, I have never seen such abject poverty or deplorable living conditions as those in Bangladesh. Most of this third-world population is struggling just to exist—to stay alive. It is horrible to witness people surviving by foraging through garbage cans for food. Often, dried manure is used as a combustible for cooking purposes and, in this modern technological society, as we move into the 21st Century, oxen still help till the soil there.

"Women are second class citizens and treated dreadfully by the men. Many women are literally thrown out of their homes for offenses real or imagined and must resort to prostitution or any other frantic means to sustain life. The McNeilus family, and other dedicated volunteers, are doing the work of God there. They are helping these women raise themselves up and gain self-pride through the fruits of their own labor, and by applying the basic principles of the free enterprise system. They have formed groups to make crafts to sell to Americans and other western markets, and often these women end up earning more money than their belligerent, dominating male counterparts.

"The sights and sounds of these people touched Linda and me. Also, it is inspiring to meet the missionaries struggling there who have abandoned all thoughts of self and personal comfort and well-being, to bring sustenance to those in such great need. Their labor of love is complicated by the fact that they are in an area of the world where the truth of God's Word is known only by the minority.

"In this third world atmosphere, nutritious food and clean water are seldom available and the blessing of proper medical care is often non-existent. We were constantly reminded that God has given 3ABN the unique and blessed opportunity to assist similar worthy ministries around the world by making the multitudes aware of the needs through our programming, and in turn channeling our viewers' love gifts to those ministries.

"One incident in Bangladesh is etched in Linda's memory forever. We wanted to observe a typical local family in their natural home surroundings, so we sloshed through a muddy field to reach a thatched hut. Due to intense inclement weather from torrential rains that never seem to quit, dealing with mud is a constant factor.

"Although Linda tried to balance carefully and stay on the rocks and pieces of wood that were thrown haphazardly over the mud to provide a crude sidewalk, her skills as a tightrope walker proved to be lacking. By the time she arrived at the hut, her feet up to the ankles, were covered with mud and grime. That was uncomfortable, but help from an unexpected source was about to present itself.

"A Bangla girl, whom we had never met, smiled (the universal language) at Linda's dilemma and motioned for her to stop. Armed with a bucket of water and before Linda realized what was happening, the girl was on her knees washing Linda's feet.

"Although we have often experienced foot-washing services at church, this was the first time Linda had ever encountered it spontaneously from a total stranger in a remote field far from home, and with her feet so blackened with mud and so repulsive in appearance.

"It was a touching, heartfelt moment for Linda and she could not help but reflect on the words of Christ—'If I then your Lord and Master have washed your feet, ye also ought to wash one another's feet... the servant is not greater than his Lord...'

"In other words, love each other enough to deal with dirt. Don't avoid it, deal with it!

"In Cambodia, a place where it is estimated that millions of people were murdered by their government, we could almost hear the cries and feel the agony of the victims of some of the worst human rights violations in history. One area is universally and quite properly referred to as 'The Killing Fields.' The dastardly Khmer Rouge regime forced most Cambodians into virtual slavery by taking multitudes of them from the cities to labor in what can only be described as state-run agriculture co-ops. It is estimated that as many as two million people died of starvation, overwork, disease and executions during that dark period of a communist-imposed policy of genocide.

"We entered one building that housed human skulls and chilling photographs of the tortured people and of mass murder. It was almost like a monument to remind future generations of the potential for human depravity and a corrupt government run amok.

"We then went into an area of unspeakable horror made infamous in Hollywood. It is called 'The Killing Fields.' Aptly named, it is full of cavernous graves that were forcibly dug by the murdered victims themselves. There are still human bones and clothing visibly protruding above the ground in some places. It epitomizes man's inhumanity to man. I've never seen anything like it.

"As bad as the shadow of evil was, though, we found inspiration there too. God's work is evident everywhere. In Dacca, Bangladesh, we boarded a rented bus for a six-hour journey that ended with an uplifting experience.

"We visited a place where SDA Global Missions and the

4

McNeiluses have built a church, schools and an orphanage. In a place where waifs had previously slept on dirt floors with holes in the ground for toilets there are now dormitories, plumbing facilities and modern cooking areas. The orphanage has approximately 150 residents where children are well cared for; they are little ones who are nurtured and can be visited regularly by parents and family. These are children who would not have lived long under the ill-fated conditions they were born to.

"While at this sanctuary, Linda and I witnessed 125 people being baptized. We were also blessed to meet the unselfish volunteers who live and work with these unfortunate human beings.

"It was equally rewarding to learn that by next spring, through the Seventh-day Adventists' Global Mission, and organizations like Maranatha, some 200 schools and churches would be built in the country, employing up to 600 people in the process. It inspires an intense emotion in me watching people of great wealth, like our companions, helping the poorest of the poor. They are not just giving money, but literally getting into the mud trenches and working to build a better life for those who are struggling to survive. It was an awesome testimony to Christianity and invigorating for the soul.

"The trip, in part, was grueling and unpleasant by virtue of witnessing human cruelty. But Linda and I agreed that we had to go there, to see firsthand the pressing need for the light of the Word to invade the utter darkness, and for the wretched condition of human suffering to be eased.

"It became our burden to help."

Chapter 2

It became our burden to help! Those words from Danny Shelton pose no surprise to those who know him, and Linda. For years many thousands of people around the world who tune in to 3ABN every day have watched the couple bear that "burden" graciously. Those viewers and the throngs of people, who meet them in person during their travels and personal appearances, find comfort in talking to the couple and often have their concerns and fears assuaged by such an encounter.

Sometimes Danny's recognizable personage and the rapport the Sheltons both have with viewers can actually prove to be inopportune. When you are traveling with Danny, anywhere in the world, it is not uncommon to have people approach him in public and begin a conversation as though they had known him all of their lives. Most of these admirers even forego the typical, "Say, aren't you…?" approach. They just feel like they know him, and recognize a kindred spirit.

More than once the not-as-compassionate me has become agitated when, in the rush of making a connecting flight on time, or attending to some other pressing agenda responsibility, Danny was intercepted by a member of what he (and they) think of as the "3ABN Family."

No matter what the circumstance is or where he happens to be at the moment, Danny always takes time to engage in conversation with the admirer. He modestly fields their enthusiastic compliments, or takes special interest in problems they bring up. As often as not a follower will ask Danny to pray for an ailing loved one. He always accommodates them regardless of the surroundings.

I recall a typical incident that took place at JFK Airport in New York. Danny and I were exhausted after a flight from Moscow and were inconspicuously grabbing a welcome and needed repose while awaiting a connecting flight to St. Louis.

I noticed a woman with a laser-like stare zero in on Danny from across the Delta boarding gate area. I recognized the look immediately and braced for the inevitable. She scurried over to us and, without fanfare, in broken English, explained to Danny that she was from Bucharest, Romania, and had seen him on television.

To underwrite her claim she cited chapter and verse a specific Bible quote that Shelton had spoken on the air recently. (We had been in Romania twice in the most recent years and 3ABN was making arrangements for expansion into that revolution-torn nation.)

As it turned out, this woman was taking a circuitous route to Houston, Texas, through St. Louis, to visit a friend in that Lone Star city. She was going to retrace her steps back through the Arch City on her return to Bucharest. Danny wearily listened to her tale and then took out a business card and wrote his personal telephone number on it. He told her to contact him during her return trip, when she touched down in St. Louis.

He said he would make arrangements to have her picked up at the airport and driven the 100 miles south, to West Frankfort, Illinois, to tour the 3ABN complex and to meet Linda. The woman was enthralled at what she inferred would be an adventure of unprecedented proportion in her lifetime.

This was quintessential "Sheltonese." I've witnessed it many times. In fact, I've learned to yield to the inevitability of such occurrences anywhere, at any time. It seems to be the manifest will of members of the vast 3ABN family to presume this familiarity with Danny Shelton, and Linda.

And indeed, the Sheltons unequivocally deem it their

(the viewers) just due. I'm genuinely intrigued by this. No matter how many times I've witnessed this phenomenon I'm still captivated by the power and influence, the force for good that is 3ABN. That fascination is the prime motivation in the conception of this document.

When I began covering 3ABN for my newspaper, *The Daily American*, in West Frankfort, Illinois, I did not belong to any church. Nor did I adhere to any formal religion. Theologically, I listlessly took the meandering path of least resistance, all too often straying this way or that. When you don't know where you are going every road will take you there. I fashioned an emotional compensatory facade, rationalizing that as long as I believed in God, I needed no earthly congregational reinforcement.

Then I took on the Shelton/3ABN assignment.

It would be high drama and a spectacular twist to this story to reveal at this point that through our association I was converted, baptized, and will live blissfully with the Lord, forever. The storyteller in me yearns for such a happy ending. But I cannot do so even though I fervently long for such a blessing. However, I will reveal one personal truth. Being involved with the Sheltons and 3ABN has changed my life for the better.

This adventure has extended far beyond the initial professional assignment, and filled me with a great resolve to seek out the ultimate experience of knowing Him. Some fortunate day, perhaps.

I vividly recall observing a 3ABN Seventh-day Adventist baptism involving over 50 Russians. It was a beautiful ceremony that took place at a lake located just outside of Nizhny Novgorod (formerly Gorky). I experienced a longing deep within me as I witnessed the new Christians, mostly former communists and atheists, emerge from the water smiling and with a new inner glow.

I mention all of this simply to establish this writer's frame of mind while pursuing the incredible story of

3ABN. Despite all of these pleasant diversions, I truly believe I have managed to maintain my journalistic equilibrium.

Frankly, I am awed by all that I survey when it comes to 3ABN and the ministry of the Sheltons. Everything about the network's development almost defies description when I attempt to equate it within the parameters generally accepted by my profession.

Admittedly, I was predisposed to not believe that anything miraculous is involved in conjunction with this organization. Luck, coincidence, right timing? Take your pick. But in the final analysis I'm hard-pressed to otherwise coherently explain certain aspects of what has transpired.

From 3ABN's inception to becoming the recognized worldwide force for good that it is today— the network has been forged into an extraordinary entity that is gaining global recognition by leaps and bounds. Millions of people see 3ABN's emergence as a true miracle. Those who know the story intimately are convinced that divine intervention has played a role in this ministry from the start.

Whether or not you are inclined to embrace that theory after reading this book, one indisputable fact is that there are mountains of mail and a constant flow of daily telephone contacts emphatically documenting the following revelations. Also, television network moguls of world renown, even political leaders of nations, have, and continue to negotiate with the Sheltons concerning the potential of airing the 3ABN programming package. Such high-ranking personage has even appeared on live television shows with the Sheltons.

After years of covering this story and contemplating the subject, let me make a righteous proposition to you, the reader. I'll lay it straight out and forthright and issue it to you in the form of a personal challenge.

I suggest that the way 3ABN was created and how it grew into what it is today can not be explained through conventional wisdom. The theory of on-going coincidence is simply not applicable here, as you will see. Pure luck? That theory too is unacceptable. Therefore, after you read this account and preferably check out the facts of the network for yourself, I challenge you to produce an alternate explanation for the advent and development of this profound ministry!

Does such a revealing alternate answer lie in Shelton's past? Like, maybe he was born rich and with friends in high, influential places? Not really.

In preparation for the newspaper assignment I did my homework by checking the Sheltons' background. If anything, that probe tends to enhance the theory that the Sheltons' success is difficult to describe in logical terms.

For openers, Danny Shelton was the most unlikely prospect to create a worldwide television religious agency. In southern Illinois, folks have an expression which is, "dirt poor." The virtual demise of the once king coal industry in that area brought on an Appalachian-type communal poverty.

By any standard applied, as a child, Shelton qualified for that dubious economic classification. As a toddler, while trying to help his family eke out a living by gathering and smashing discarded glass bottles to sell for recycling, a flying splintered shard of broken glass claimed one of his eyes. Although totally unnoticeable in his appearance (most people are shocked to learn of it), this blinding handicap alone would have impeded most people's road to success.

Furthermore, his career was unremarkable during his early years, at least by comparison to his current stature. He made a living laboring as a carpenter and construction contractor. Also, he and his daughter, Melody gained a praiseworthy reputation as gospel singers after his first wife was killed in a tragic automobile accident. He lived a respectable lifestyle, but hardly the stuff that one would expect worldwide television personalities are made of.

11

But, as the Nobel Prize winning Russian writer, Boris Pasternak, said, "Surprise is the greatest gift life grants us." Lo and behold, Boris was correct!

The cardinal rule of journalism is to present the facts and allow the readers to draw their own conclusions, and so I shall. Bear in mind too, that this is not a formal news report. My colleagues would probably even call it a "puff piece." I offer those critical scribes the same challenge as other readers, to come up with an alternate explanation. After an in-depth study of the organization and the principals and principles involved, I felt compelled to disseminate the story of 3ABN and specifically to solicit the readers' evaluation.

So I extend to you a most reasonable entreaty. Read in the following chapters Danny and Linda Shelton's own words as they describe their astonishing personal stories and the genesis, growth, and maturation of 3ABN. All of which became the foundation for their personal and eloquent concept of, "Mending Broken People." Then judge for yourself, if therein lies a miracle.

Chapter 3

It happened on November 14, 1984. Going by precise chronology, perhaps it was on November 15. That blurry timetable is historically noted simply because what happened came about between late evening and the following early morning hours. It was a monumental event that forever changed Danny Shelton's life, and in due course, the lives of everyone close to him.

What could easily be interpreted as a divine revelation unleashed a series of mind-boggling incidents that would eventually propel a soft-spoken carpenter and sometimes gospel singer into a self-made lay evangelist known worldwide for his television ministry.

Danny readily acknowledges his own reluctance to speak in public about that momentous lifestyle-altering event. Even now he relates the details in simple terms when others might be inclined to shout it from the rooftops. This laid-back manner stems naturally from his childhood, and sometimes when he relates this startling story his simple acceptance on faith of what transpired softens the impact of the significance of what took place.

"If you are nervous about being preached to, relax," Danny now calmly tells audiences when answering requests for personal appearances. "I'm not a preacher. I'm a talker. I love to talk."

But such a quiet approach can detract from the true meaning of what took place, at least in the ears of the beholder who might be more attuned to the imposing, haranguing style of many of today's prominent television theologians.

Danny's propensity to be "a talker" is somewhat amazing considering his family history. Many years ago the Shelton family used a bus to travel the "circuit" and perform music at various churches around the country. Previous to that, his parents, professionally known as the Melody Kings, had sung country music on a regular radio show. Thus explains the siblings' natural evolution toward musical talents.

However, later on, when the Shelton ensemble traveled, Danny would get so nervous that when they appeared before a congregation he would clam up, and it was his brother Tommy who had to pick up on the commentary. That would surely surprise anyone who knows both of them today because Danny is outgoing and has tremendous stage presence while Tommy, although a world-class pianist, is more reserved.

What happened to transform that reticent young gospel singer/carpenter into a television personality of international stature? A performer that can articulate in such a relaxed, yet compelling manner as to bring throngs of people to accept Jesus as their Savior? The absorbing answer to that question is narrated here in Danny Shelton's own words. The following first-person account reveals the dramatic details of that momentous nocturnal event that occurred in November of 1984, and which changed his life. And, more importantly perhaps, altered the lives of throngs of other people since then through an ongoing process.

"It had been a long day and after saying goodnight to my daughter, Melody, I had a long telephone conversation saying goodnight to Linda. As we are all inclined to do at times I was reading and only half-listening to the religious program that was airing. However, even by catching only a word here and there my brain began telling me to tune in and pay closer attention to what was being said. Then, I realized why.

"It was because what the minister was saying was not biblically true!

"I wasn't completely naive about this type of programming. For years I had traveled with my family singing, and I had personally made guest appearances on a number of television shows. Often on these programs I had heard and seen things from other singers and preachers, comments that bothered me. But I had no idea as to how to offset or dispute those errant messages.

"Yet, for some reason, on the particular night in question, at that specific time in my life, the old grievance that had haunted me for so long hit me hard. How could they do this? I asked myself. How could God be so blatantly misrepresented on national television, to millions of viewers? Didn't anyone care?

"After all, His message is not so complex. It is pure and free to anyone who will open their heart. As a Seventh-day Adventist Christian I know that God really only told us to do two basic things and they are not at all difficult to comprehend. He told us to come, and to go. To come to the foot of the Cross and dedicate our life to Him, as our Savior, and then to go out and tell the entire world what God has done for us.

"Yet here, on national television, I was seeing and hearing a totally distorted and misleading message, and that really bothered me. But even though I was greatly disturbed by what I was hearing I still had no forewarning of what was yet to come to pass that very night. But surely my being upset in such a manner must have sparked it. Fully awake and interested now I became more absorbed in the ongoing program.

"And the more I watched it the more determined I was that the word being telecast was fraudulent, according to my studies of the Bible, and contrary to what I consider the truth. All of this also made me ask myself a pertinent question: 'Where were we, as a church?' Why was our Bible-based Seventh-day Adventist message not being televised to offset this misleading programming? Shouldn't the Seventh-day Adventist Church have a television network to share with the world our biblical persective?

"For example, I had tuned into a Christian program broadcast from California. The president of the network was there on the set and he was telling people that after the Rapture, Jesus Himself will come down, John the Baptist and Moses, and they'll be preaching to all those left behind. The Rapture theory is that when the Lord comes, he comes secretly and all of a sudden people will be driving along in their cars and pilots will be flying planes, and they'll be gone and the poor saps left on the plane will go down because their pilot went to heaven and they weren't ready. So the plane crashes and they are killed. I was hearing this kind of thing on this program, and I had heard things like this, and worse, before. Then the man on the program was saying how one could be saved during this seven-year period, but it's more difficult so everyone needs to be saved now.

"Well, first of all, you never put off something like salvation. The other thing is that the Bible says of Christ's coming, (1st Thess. 4:16,17) he dead in Christ shall rise first and they'll be blowing the trumpets. It will be a huge climactic event, which will be literally heard and seen around the world. (Rev. 1:7 'Every eye shall see him. . . ')And here these people were saying on TV that this is a secret Rapture because the Bible says he comes as a thief in the night. But what that actually means is that He comes suddenly, and takes you by surprise. So He is saying get ready today because you never know when this event is happening. But the people misuse it. So it's not only the fact that they misrepresent that, but it teaches people falsely that you don't really have to be saved now, you can wait until after the second coming and you'll have seven years.

"That's the type of thing that I have heard on Christian TV that bothers me. I've also heard preachers say that if you are good, Jesus will take you to heaven forever in eternal bliss. But if you are bad, and you don't serve Him, He'll

16

burn you forever and ever. If that's true, then God is a torturer worse than Hitler was. That's a lie. It's not Biblical. When you really study the Bible you'll find out that God is a God of love. He loves you forever. Sin is destroyed, but nobody burns forever as punishment. You can't love and torture at the same time.

"Those are a sample of things I had been hearing and viewing on television. But I know that what people needed to know is that God is love. If I were not a Christian and somebody told me that God would torture me forever, I wouldn't serve him simply because I would feel like anyone capable of that, could not really love. I want people to know that we should serve God out of love, not out of fear. As I pondered all of this, the fact hit me that there were no Seventh-day Adventist television networks broadcasting to get our word out to people everywhere. There was no way to offset these erroneus messages. Where were we, as a church, in the media?

"Where were we, indeed? I know we have an end times message to give to an end times people. And since we do, shouldn't that message be given loud and clear? Revelation: 18 tells us that the earth will be lighted with the glory of God, and then Jesus can come back. Surely this message must go forward with great power. But could I become a part of it? If so, how? I was only positive about one thing. Our voices must somehow ring out clearly and eloquently. I'm certainly not a psychologist, but perhaps it was this frame of mind that set into motion what was to follow that very night.

"Later, these thoughts burdened me as I lay in bed. They were deep-rooted, and they bothered me to the point that I couldn't sleep. I was burdened with the false messages that were being delivered in the name of Christianity. I knew those words, a distortion of God and His character, would do great harm to millions of people if allowed to go unchallenged.

"As I lay awake I began to mentally wrestle with this problem and suddenly a vivid impression overwhelmed me. It was totally foreign to my regular thoughts and emotions. I know myself better than anyone and this was something I'd never before experienced. It simply wasn't me. But I heard it as clearly as I would the peal of the most beautiful bell in the world, and even though it was not in an audible voice, I heard it nonetheless. It was impressed in my mind, and it distinctly said, 'I want you to build a television station that will reach the world with an undiluted Three Angels message. One that will counteract the counterfeit.'

"'Counteract the counterfeit?' I didn't even know what that meant. I don't even talk like that. To be perfectly honest I had no idea what that kind of project, building a television station, would even require. Later on, after I was actually into the project for a few years, I thought I was beginning to grasp what it took to build a station.

"But even today, after more than seventeen years at it, I am still learning more every day about what it involves. Probably only in eternity will I comprehend the full meaning of that beautiful message that night. But at that moment, it was baffling.

"Unashamedly I say that at the time I was confused. Frankly, I wasn't even sure what the term 'undiluted' meant in this context. And the overall concept of me, of all people, building a television station seemed preposterous.

"One thing it did accomplish was to bring me fully awake and alert. Such an experience is not the kind of thing you ignore. It was one of the strongest emotions I had, or have, ever experienced. I was thinking very alertly and clearly, but I was also a bit cautious. There was no doubt that it had happened. It was an absolute fact.

"Aloud I said, 'Lord, I can't do this. But if this is really You, I will go forward. God, You know that I don't have any money to put toward any television station. And beyond that, I have no degree or technical education that would even remotely qualify me for this project.

"In fact, I hardly have an education at all. And my expertise, if I have any, is in building houses. Also, since such an experience was unprecedented in my life, I couldn't help but be a little careful. Just because we are impressed with something doesn't guarantee it is Word from God. The Devil is out there to deceive and he sometimes comes sneaking up deviously, as a pretender, as an angel of light. He, the Devil, could just be trying to lure me into trouble by getting me to go into debt or attempting something that I wasn't capable of doing and would therefore fail and maybe hurt others in the process.

"So, I decided to approach it from a different angle. That was to evaluate the viability of the message in and of itself. I began to think, if there was a television station that would reach around the world twenty-four-hours a day with the undiluted Three Angels messages, would that be in God's plan? Would this be something that God would support? That thought was electrifying. And yes, instantly I knew unequivocally that it would be His way. It was a moment of total enlightenment. Isaiah: 8:20 says, 'To the law and to the testimony, if they speak not according to this Word, there is no light in them.' I knew this would be according to God's plan.

"It seemed to me that it was the right game plan but the wrong coach. This would obviously become an enormous undertaking. Not just for me, of such limited means, but for anyone. I thought, 'Lord, this is wonderful and great. But you picked the wrong guy. I can't do any of this.' Just as quickly as I had mentally expressed that self-doubt it came back to me as distinctly as if I had spoken aloud and was receiving the answer, 'You are right, you can't do this. But I can!'

"Praise the Lord! I was beginning to get very excited about what was taking place. To put it mildly, it was thrilling beyond description. My mind turned to the Bible and I thought about Moses. What an unlikely person to be chosen to lead the children of Israel. At age eighty, and with a speech impediment, or a lack of ongoing communicative skills, why would anyone at that time point to Moses to lead the multitude of men, women and children? But people would eventually see through the ages of time that it was really God who was leading the children of Israel, not Moses alone. I also began to think about Daniel, another unlikely hero, and how he faced the ferocity and terror of the lion's den to become a great leader. It wasn't difficult at all, in that sense to grasp that it was God working through these individuals that really prevailed.

"These thoughts began to encourage me and I mentally traced all the way down through the stream of time, and I remembered a lady named Ellen White, one of the early founders of the Seventh-day Adventist movement. Since the eighteen-forties she has inspired millions of people, and continues to do so, after overcoming a lack of formal education and poor health, as well as the tyrannical male chauvinism that dominated the Nineteenth Century.

"I suddenly realized that God's true message here was that He could show the world that His Word and Work can be carried out by anyone who is motivated by truthful intent, and who was willing to go forward in God's ability. The true beacon in these people was Jesus. That is what made them remarkable, and it was His influence that should readily, and without fear or trepidation, now be embraced. He was simply repeating His poignant message to me, 'Go ye into all the world!'

"I was very excited embracing these thoughts like a warm blanket. They gave me great confidence. It was about three o'clock in the morning by now and I said aloud, 'God, if this is really You, I'll go forward if You will supply all the needs.

" That order, that specific sequence, is very important.

20

All too often we say to God that if He supplies the needs we'll go forward. There's a distinct difference. There are inherent problems in such hesitation, such a lack of confidence. We mustn't sit back and wait for Him to provide the needs. I believe the Lord helps those who help themselves. When the cause is just, we must first go forward and then look to God, who will assuredly supply the wherewithal to accomplish our task, if it is really worthy of Him.

"As I contemplated all of this I was weary, but exhilarated as I had never previously been in my life. Then and there I made a solemn vow, a total personal commitment and I shared it with Him. I told God, 'I will go forward as you provide the needs!'"

Chapter 4

I will go forward. It was a total personal commitment to God, made by Danny Shelton on that chilly predawn November morning in 1984, and it was a pledge that would ultimately affect the lives of hundreds of thousands of people. And in this case, it was also the precursor of proving once again the fact that the power of faith can move mountains!

Although already hooked on the project emotionally, he had no idea whatsoever as to how all of this was going to come about.

One doesn't just jump up in the morning and say to one's self, "Hey, I think I'll build a television station today!"

But Danny was convinced that it was truly God that wanted him to perform this laborious task and he was determined to have a go at it, even though the outlook for success at that time seemed to range from bleak to impossible.

He didn't even know where to begin. But as he is accustomed to doing, Shelton plunged in with the same zest and tenacity that had made him a better-than-average athlete and team leader in the amateur sports he had played during his youth and young adult years. He had competed in softball and basketball and was even a bit of a gymnast with acrobatic skills that were still a few Olympic games before their time. Until recent years Danny could easily stand flat-footed and do a back flip on request. However, organizing a winning softball team was one thing. Building a television station that would carry the Word, no matter how precious that message is, to the entire world, was quite another matter. But that "morning after," the great adventure began in earnest.

His first thought the night before (at three a.m., actually) had been to telephone his best friend and soon-to-be wife, his beloved Linda. Since their first meeting, related elsewhere in this book, they had been working together on writing songs as well as singing as a trio, along with Melody, at various churches, and she was destined to become an integral part of his life and the future television network. If his betrothed found it extraordinary to receive a phone call at three a.m. the previous night, from an inspired Danny Shelton, she didn't reveal it.

"I was living in a two-story apartment and my phone was downstairs, in the kitchen," Linda said. "The phone rang, and rang, and rang and didn't stop. I couldn't imagine what it was but I got up and half staggered down the stairs and picked it up. It was Dan and he was very excited. Without even saying hello he blurted out, 'Linda, you won't believe it. But the Holy Spirit has just impressed me to build a television station that will reach the world!' I was still half-asleep and still trying to absorb this so I told him that was good."

Linda is well known for becoming a virtual sleepy zombie after ten p.m. and when Dan first began talking about God telling him to build a television station to reach the world she tried to figure out if she was dreaming or if it was really happening.

"I guess I really didn't comprehend it all until the next day," Linda said. "Anyway, he finally slowed down enough to realize that I wasn't mirroring his excitement and he recognized my sleepy state. Although fuzzy-headed, I immediately believed this was really going to happen."

Linda listened to Danny enthuse about his wondrous experience for a few minutes longer. "That's great," she finally said.

He decided to show mercy to a sleepy girl and said, 'Honey, you're sleepy. Let's talk some more about this in the morning.'"

Why did Linda calmly take in stride a call in the middle of the night that could be considered strange by any standard? That is because she had seen it happen before and remembered the successful outcome. Several months prior to this incident, Danny had been impressed to build a recording studio.

"This was on my mind when I took his call about the TV station," she explains. "On the other occasion, he had felt for a long time that southern Illinois had needed a recording studio. There were none in the area and people had to go to Nashville or St. Louis to record. In a very similar incident, Danny was impressed to build a studio. Not for him, but for anyone to use to create music to His glory. He had a three-sided barn where it would fit. He thought about this project and told me that the Lord wouldn't bless this project if we didn't first use everything we have. He added that he only had one piece of lumber out in the barn. He went out and got that board and nailed it up to begin covering the barn. After that, in just a couple of months, he had the needed funds to build the very simple studio. So that's what I had in my mind when I received Dan's call about building a TV station, and why I took it so seriously."

That early recording studio was not the high-tech modern studio that 3ABN recently built at the network complex, which is one of the best in the Midwest, and is described in a later chapter. But at the time, this earlier makeshift facility was a Godsend for many local artists who could not afford to pay "Nashville" costs.

As to the impression to build the TV station, Dan's family was also destined to give him support and encouragement.

"We're behind you. We'll support you. Do what God has told you to do," they urged. So far, so good. If he expected anyone to scoff at his dream or tell him it was impossible he could forget it. In fact, the main encouragement for Danny was that no one seemed to be awed by this prospect. Nobody laughed or ridiculed the idea. It was almost as if they were saying, "You can do it." But mostly, they believed in "Him." And that made all things possible.

And so it began.

What followed makes for an inspiring story. Enough so, to inspirit anyone, regardless of his or her religious or philosophical disposition. Many people are reluctant to believe in miracles. Probably more so than not. Those types might be inclined to attempt to pick holes in this upcoming account. So be it. That's fine. Any close observation of 3ABN is welcomed by the network, and encouraged. In fact, guided tours of the complex can be arranged by request. People have come from around the world to visit the 3ABN home.

A special warm welcome goes out to true seekers. And just as it is on the air, and on the 3ABN television programs, you will encounter no "hard sell." Only a warm welcome.

But even the most ardent of flaw-finders would be hard-pressed to suggest that the emergence and growth of 3ABN, after that fateful first night, could alternatively be attributed to blind luck, coincidence or accident. The history herein logged is a matter of record at virtually every turn. Especially easy to trace is the pathetic financial status of the founder at that time, as it pertained to the looming project, and his personal lack of technical skills in this field.

The doubters, those of limited faith, might also astutely perceive that this author leans in a biased manner toward the "miracle" explanation. If so, those same skeptics must also acknowledge the other side of that coin. That is that such a conclusion by me came about only after ten years of intensely, professionally observing 3ABN at its inner-most levels. This investigative work has even included ten trips abroad to observe expansion activities of the network, such as those into Russia and Romania. During this same period I spent no time whatsoever at any Adventist church.

26

The point being is that there was never an attempt from any quarter to proselytize me. In fact, to this day, I have no church affiliation whatsoever. Furthermore, my having originally entered the investigation with the standard pessimistic expectation, which is the hallmark of most journalists, should count for something when contemplating all of this.

Step-by-step what followed his night of divine manifestation is pertinent. Here, in his own words, Danny Shelton describes how his covenant with God, as it pertains to 3ABN, began:

"You will have to supply the needs."

"I was still aglow after the long memorable night neared its end. After I phoned Linda, I also called other friends who, despite being awoken in the middle of the night, were very encouraging and even said that they would visit the next day and help me however they could. Before I finally drifted off to sleep I said to God that I would do it— 'I'll go forward, but You will have to supply the needs because I have nothing.'

"Still, the next morning (November fifteenth, nineteen-eighty-four) I didn't know what to do, or where to begin. I figured it would be best to visit an expert on life, one who would know how to approach a major chore. I went to see mom.

"We had a good talk and she encouraged me, as my parents always had, that we kids could do anything if we set our minds to it. The degree of difficulty of what I proposed didn't seem to bother her in the least. I got further encouragement that afternoon when I visited my brother, Kenny, and his wife, Emma Lou. Instead of scoffing at the idea they simply said that they would help all they could.

"This was all well and good, but this was all family and they were expected to encourage me. That's their job. But what would an outsider think of this concept? I decided to go see my friend. Hal Steenson, a charismatic pastor, owned some television equipment, and had been doing television work for local ministries. So I did pay brother Hal a visit the next day, Friday, and asked if I might look at his television equipment and check out things like sets, lighting and how it all coordinated for broadcasting. I realized that this was pretty basic and fundamental, but I had to start somewhere.

"I'd always taken these things, this type of equipment, for granted. I had appeared on television several times before, but had never been behind a camera, and that's a different world. Things sure look different from that end and, for the first time, I realized the kinds of intricate skills and expertise we would need to operate all of this technical equipment properly. This only added to the degree of difficulty in the task ahead.

"I told Hal about the stirring event I had experienced which had impressed me to build a television station that would be seen around the world carrying the Three Angels message.

"He patiently listened to this account and then called for his wife, Mollie, to join us. 'Come in here and hear this,' he said.

"When I repeated the same story for her she just smiled knowingly and walked away without making a comment. Her reaction was a little confusing to me but I soon found out that it wasn't at all that she was laughing at or belittling my story. In fact, I felt better when Hal explained Mollie's unusual reaction. As it turned out, the equipment in question had been much on both their minds recently.

"'This is very interesting,' he told me. 'We have about one-hundred-thousand dollars worth of equipment here. Last week a man visiting from Indiana offered to buy this equipment but I told him no. After he left I felt bad because he had really wanted the equipment. I wondered if I had made a mistake by denying him. But the Lord impressed me that I was right in not selling it and I felt good about that. We had worked hard to get this equipment and that apparently meant that I could keep it. But no, Danny, that wasn't the final answer on what to do because I was further impressed that I shouldn't keep it either,' he said. 'Well, if I shouldn't sell it or keep it, what was I to do? Give it away? Then it came to me very clearly that, yes, I think this is the right answer. To give it away to the right person at the right time. I also am terribly impressed that this is the right day, and you are the right person to give it to.'

"Even though he didn't make a final commitment then and there this was amazing. I can't describe how much encouragement this gave me. Imagine, one-hundred-thousand dollars worth of equipment! I had never even seen one-hundred-thousand dollars before at one time. But that wasn't really the point. If it had been worth only seventy-five thousand dollars or five-thousand dollars, here was this pastor, brother Hal, not even a Seventh-day Adventist like me, who would consider doing something so generous for me. I wasn't even sure he was authorized to make such a decision.

"That night I couldn't sleep due to thinking about it. I dared to think that maybe right off the bat the Lord was going to do something much greater than I intended, or could even imagine. Finally, I couldn't contain these thoughts any longer. At about eleven p.m. I picked up the phone and called brother Hal. I was becoming a regular night owl. I told him that since our meeting that afternoon I was so excited that I couldn't sleep. I added that it seemed logical to me that since I couldn't sleep, and since he caused the excitement in the first place, I might as well just phone him every hour and talk about it. He responded in words I will never forget.

"He said, 'Go to sleep, Danny, rest and sleep. During the afternoon the Lord impressed me that we should support your ministry and donate this equipment to you to help you get your message into the world.'

"I couldn't believe it. I can't explain the kind of encouragement this gave me. I know Hal. He is our friend and was very soon, in his official capacity, to marry Linda and me. Hal is a godly man, even though we didn't believe everything in the same way. And the real significance of what had just taken place didn't escape me. I initially thought I would have to go to people in my church alone, to raise money for our needs. But did this generous act mean that God had people everywhere, among Methodists, Baptists, Pentecostal, and others, who would help make His will be done? Apparently it did. God had won the first round."

Chapter 5

I t had begun! And in a rather spectacular fashion at that! Steenson's board eventually voted that Shelton could have the television equipment if and when his station was built and the studio was ready to make use of the gift. Of course, some disbelievers at that time might have thought, "So what?" That the seemingly out-of-reach goal of starting a television ministry no doubt still appeared, at best, to be light years away— if indeed it was ever to come about at all. But a first step had at least been taken, albeit a small one.

The reality of the unfolding drama however was that the unexpected acquisition of this vital equipment was just a start. Inexplicable developments began to follow, rather quickly too. Inexplicable that is, unless you are prepared to use the "M" word.

Not yet? Okay. But as I've stated previously, luck simply cannot explain the events that followed. One after the other they came about in parade-like fashion, almost as if predestined. At each juncture of the network's formation, when a specific need arose precise help would arrive. Mind you, not general help, but precise help.

It was the type of aid that eased a particular isolated problem at that very moment in time when it was needed. As you shall see.

Sometimes said help arrived in a subtle manner, but often it thundered forward in spectacular fashion, as if the struggle to build the television network was being under-written by a higher power. Of this, of course, Danny and Linda, and those close to them, never had a doubt. But even to them at times these amazing episodes seemed akin to manna from heaven.

For one thing, the remoteness and total lack of connection between problems that arose and the people and/or events that ultimately solved them were stunning. A compelling cloak of conspicuous inevitability was slowly settling over the project. That is fact, not fancy.

Truth, as in receiving the gift of the television equipment at precisely that time when encouragement was most needed is a good example of the theory. But there were more, many more such incidents to follow. Miraculous? All right, already! I know I'm being too pushy on the "M" word, so I'll back off for the moment.

But for those readers who think I overwrite, and who absolutely refuse to accept that other word, let it suffice to say that numerous following incidents defy conventional logic.

Even the most avid skeptics, ye of little faith, will have to agree that these events, described here by Danny Shelton, and elsewhere historically recorded, are extraordinary and difficult to explain.

"I did need to know that this was God's project"

In Danny's own words: "When I was told of this most generous (TV camera) gift, I realized that I didn't need the (television) equipment at once since I had no studio. But I did need to know that God was behind this project. This incredible development gave me enormous encouragement and an added incentive to move ahead. And as a result I got so excited that the following week I called a couple of my brothers, Tommy, and Kenny, and asked them to go with me to visit this television station in Marion, Illinois. I had sung there several times, but I had never paid any attention to any of the television equipment. I just knew that it worked. Now, all of a sudden, that unawareness disappeared and I had a keen interest in all of the tools of the television trade. So, we Sheltons three made the trip together.

"After we arrived at the local Christian TV station I ran into a fellow that I had met before, named Clarence Larson. I introduced my brothers and myself to him and Clarence responded that he remembered me from the several times that my daughter, Melody, and I had sung at the station. I asked him if he would show me around and give me a little technical insight as to the operation of the station.

"He was most receptive and cooperative. However, he is an excellent engineer and here I am a rookie would-be TV station operator not knowing anything about the technical aspect of this business. Therefore I wasn't intending to tell him that the Lord had impressed me to build a television station.

"Clarence, of all people, being a professional, would surely laugh at such a lofty ambition coming from a rank amateur, or so I imagined. So we set out on a tour of the station and, as we moved about, our guide described each piece of apparatus and its function. Today, I'm basically familiar with all of this equipment but back then, given my lack of knowledge, he might as well have been describing the components of a space shuttle. But we looked at everything, my seeing things with a new interest and paying much more attention than I had on previous visits.

"More enlightened after finishing the tour of the facility, we were getting ready to leave when Clarence, who, incidentally, was then a Baptist who worked at that time at a charismatic station, said to me, 'Can I talk to you, Danny? I need to speak to you privately.'

"I have to admit that I was intrigued by his request and could just picture in my mind's eye him telling me to stay away from the television business because of my obvious limited knowledge. But nothing could have been further from the truth.

"We went upstairs into an isolated area where they were

building on a new room and I must admit that my curiosity was tweaked. But if I'd made a thousand guesses I would have never correctly anticipated what he had in mind to say to me.

"'I feel compelled to tell you something,' Clarence said. 'I generally think of you Sheltons as carpenters and singers, so I don't even know why I'm saying this to you other than the fact that I feel compelled to tell you. I believe that a satellite station could be built here in southern Illinois out near the Thompsonville area.' (At this time Clarence had no idea, or way of knowing what Danny had in mind. But, when Clarence made this unsolicited comment, Danny shared the entire story with him, too.)

"Reflecting the level of my knowledge of the television industry at that time, I said to him that that's really great, but then followed up his optimistic technical evaluation with what I felt was an appropriate question. Namely, what's a satellite station?

"If Clarence's confidence in me was shaken by such a sophomoric question he didn't show it at the time. Although much later he did laughingly admit that he was taken aback with the simplicity of the question. At the moment, however, he simply explained in effect that the satellite establishes the boundaries of your broadcasting ability, and asked, 'How far do you want to reach?'

"I replied that I wanted to reach the entire world.

"'Well,' he said, 'that's the way you do it. By satellite.'

"He went on in detail about the influence of micro waves and the technical difficulty of finding anywhere in the area where a television message could be sent out to a satellite without interference from or to existing companies already in place, such as the giant utilities.

"Because of Clarence's detailed description of the problem of finding a proper area from which to beam our message skyward, I had yet one more major problem to consider. Prime location. Yet here was this fellow, out of a

34

clear blue sky, if you will pardon the play on words, telling me that he thought he knew of such a rare treasure, such a precious location, which was located not hundreds of miles away, but practically in our own back yard. And, he felt compelled by the Lord, to tell me about it. Awesome!"

Chapter 6

Could it really be? Apparently it could. In the vernacular of a winning sports franchise, the Shelton team was "on a roll." In lightning-like succession following his personal divine revelation, several incidents gave great confidence to Danny Shelton in regard to the pursuit of his mission.

First, a charismatic pastor had literally given him what then seemed like a small fortune in the form of television equipment. Following that, a Baptist working as an engineer at a Pentecostal television station had approached him with unsolicited information that, if true and accurate, could present a technological advantage of enormous proportions.

Sandwiched between all of this was injected a wonderful, warm attentive reaction from family, friends and everyone else Danny talked to about his dream project. Linda was unreservedly supportive.

In fact, the couple was married only ten days after Danny's vision urging him to build a TV station— a major event in their lives which will be covered in a later chapter. Most encouraging though, was Danny's true impression that God was showing Himself to really be a part of what was unfolding at such an accelerated pace.

Shelton was very excited, he saw these inspiring incidents as God working; using people everywhere to get the Three Angels message out to all the world.

Even when confronted with the first negative comments, from a pastor in a California church, Danny would not be subdued. The California trip had been planned for some time and therefore Danny and Linda's personal

"Three Angels" project had to be temporarily put on hold. Or, so they thought. Actually, their mission was never again to be impeded or neutralized by any trips, setbacks, self-doubts or, at times, seemingly impossible obstacles.

The grand design, which Danny was now convinced was set into motion by a Higher Power, was ever expanding back then, as it continues to today. In view of the events about to take place over the next few months, in retrospect, any thinking person would surely be inclined to agree with that proposition.

There were still great needs. Beyond donated equipment, free professional engineering advice and encouragement, as well as an optimistic outlook from everyone involved; critical monetary support was needed and would soon arrive.

As was becoming the "norm," the money came from a most unexpected source. Danny now had the start of fulfilling his global broadcasting dream in the form of special equipment. He also had gained the interest and help of an engineer who knew his way around a television studio. However, major barriers remained such as the big one, land! Land, a site... a "home" for 3ABN.

This was a major complication because of a specific requirement. Real estate humor allows that there are three main aspects to consider when appraising property value, "Location, location and location." That old cliché could well have found definition in Danny's situation. He could have acquired hundreds of acres that would have been useless in developing his project. That is because, as Clarence had made clear, there are only a precious few spots where you could be legally authorized by the FCC to beam C band signals to satellite, and they are "as rare as hens' teeth." There are now other frequencies such as KU band and a number of other systems available.

First of all, finding such a spot would involve an intense search.

As was the case most often in those early days the Shelton coffers were not low at that point. They were totally depleted. But the captain plunged his ship ahead in these rough financial seas encouraged by faith alone, and perhaps a smidgen of stubbornness not uncommon to his clan.

As he planned his California trip these problems weighed heavy on the young gospel singer. In the following account, Shelton reveals first hand the next poignant developments in the fast-growing legend:

Looking for a home for 3ABN

In Danny's words: "We had to travel to the West Coast. The trip had been planned for several weeks and the new project, as precious as it was, had to be put on a back burner. Or so we thought. We had been invited to perform at several churches in Southern California. This trip took place in December of nineteen-eighty-four.

"At one church, after singing at the service, and since it was always on my mind anyway, I began telling people in the congregation the absorbing story about what had transpired recently. I had not been asked to speak on the subject so this commentary was strictly impromptu. I just couldn't hold it in, it was such a moving personal experience.

"I told the story in simple, basic terms just as it had happened. The people seemed to be responding to this message too, paying close attention. Maybe too much so because eventually the local pastor went to the back of the church and began signaling me with a traditional finger drawn left-to-right across the throat. Even a rank amateur in television knows that this means 'cut,' or end your performance, or specifically 'you are out of time, wrap it up.' That is, I assumed that after hearing me sing he didn't want me to actually cut my throat. Practicing for the first time what would later be referred to on the 3ABN TV set as responding to the director's instructions, I broke off my story, excused myself and joined the pastor at the back of the church. I thought that maybe it was simply the time to take up a collection. I was wrong about that.

"He was very agitated and it quickly became apparent why he was in such a state of mind. He told me in no uncertain terms that he felt very uncomfortable about me appearing before his congregation and telling them about wanting to build a television station that would reach the entire world.

"Apparently he thought it was preposterous. He said he knew of my background (which I had also told the congregation) and he didn't understand why I would undertake such an involved project. He asked me how much money this project was going to cost. I told him I didn't know.

"'Well,' he said, 'is it going to cost a million dollars?' Again, I told him I had no idea. 'Will it cost five million dollars?' I repeated that I didn't know, but added that frankly, it didn't matter.

"I'd just as soon see God do a five million-dollar miracle as a one million-dollar miracle." I said.

"This seemed to frustrate him, but pointedly he said, 'I don't want any of my people giving money to something that's never going to happen!' Next, he asked me to finish my songs and make no further mention of the project.

"That kind of surprised me. Here, I sincerely believed that this was God's work, but it never had occurred to me that other people might think that what I was doing was off the wall, or especially less than sincere. I knew what had happened to me. I had lived it. I couldn't hold it inside me if I tried. But how was I to overcome this kind of misgiving? I had encountered non-believers all my life but I was taken aback by this man's attitude. It wasn't any self-doubt on my part, or lack of belief in the worthiness of the plan. His plan. But later on I did run across one other incident of this kind.

"It was at a Christian media broadcasters' meeting in California. Several hundred people were in attendance and individuals were getting up and taking turns telling about their plans and their various projects. Their ambitions ranged from putting together a five-minute radio spot, to the most extensive, maybe doing a thirty-minute show. A veteran, well-known TV minister was hosting the event. When I got up I said simply that I was going to build a television station that was going to reach the entire world. He was amused by this and couldn't hold back a little laugh.

"'Oh, really.' he said, drawing a twitter of laughter from the audience. He asked if I was an engineer and I told him no. He wanted to know how many hours a week I wanted to be on the air and did a double take when I answered twenty-four-hours a day , seven days a week. He played it for laughs commenting that I, knowing nothing at all about television, intended to build a network that would air twenty-four-seven?

"He too, finally came up with the inevitable question, 'What will this all cost?' I told him I didn't know, but that it was not my worry, that's for God to take care of.

"'Are you wealthy? How much money do you have so far?' he countered.

"I told him the truth, 'No, I'm not rich and I really don't have any money at all yet.'

"He thought about this and then told me that within the church, there was only so much money. It was like a pie. He held up his hands in a circle to make an imaginary pie.

'There are only so many slices to this pie,' he said. 'Then if a new ministry like yours comes along and takes a slice of that pie, it denies someone else some of it. Then, what if you don't finish your station?'

"He then asked if I had a prospectus on this project.

"That threw me because, quite honestly, at that time, I didn't even know what a prospectus was! Based on that ignorance, I figured I must not have one so I honestly replied that, 'No, I don't guess I do.'

"'You don't guess so?' he replied, therefore working

another giggle from the audience.

"Finally, he got right down to it. He said he wouldn't support the project. First of all, he didn't think it would happen because it was an awesome undertaking, bigger than I could ever imagine. He was afraid that people would start giving money to a project that seemed doomed before it started.

"'You must realize that each new ministry that begins makes the slice of the pie for the rest of us that much thinner,' he said.

"I responded that I understood that, but if they would look in life's refrigerator they would find that God has more than one pie.

"I said, 'You are fighting over one pie. But God owns everything, and if He says, 'Go ye unto all the world...' then surely there must be more pies, so you need not fight over one small pie.' Even after we became a worldwide network, this prominent Christian minister would not recognize or support us.

"These episodes, the attitude of the pastor and the Christian broadcaster, represented yet one more barrier to overcome. I couldn't understand their cynicism and it worried me. It also marked a time of self-evaluation. I asked myself how I was going to convey my total enthusiasm to people without sounding radical? It was certainly food for thought. But I wasn't about to falter or compromise my faith in any way. There is only one direction for God's work and that is forward!

"As it turned out the skeptical pastor was wrong—because the message I related in California actually did impress some of the people present in those congregations. They were to weigh in later with financial help to the project. Time and again this has occurred. People seem only mildly interested and calmly listen to the 3ABN story only to overwhelm us later with their incredible generosity. That help from California is a part of the story I will tell later in this book. Meanwhile, at the time, I was anxious to get back home and work on the plan that had now become so important to Linda, and me.

"We couldn't just buy a piece of ground anywhere. It had to meet the critical parameter of proper broadcasting location. Location, technical qualification, and the right price were needed. Tie all that together and throw in the incidental factor that the land must also be for sale and you would possess the complexity of the problem. What were the chances of tying all that together?

"Clarence had told us that we needed to be in the general vicinity of Thompsonville, Illinois, and that was yet another problem because there wasn't a lot of land for sale in that section of Franklin County. That was because the area was quilted with farms, often family owned for several generations, whose owners don't want to break up their property. In fact, I knew of one possibility and had approached the owner, but typically, he definitely didn't want to sell.

"On the following Wednesday, Linda and I attended a prayer meeting together. There were only a handful of people attending, ten or fifteen at the most. However, this small congregation included one lady named Fonda Summers, whom I met for the first time that evening. A pleasant lady, she belonged to the Christian Church but on a whim was interested in visiting our little Seventh-day Adventist prayer meeting that night. Somehow she chose that particular night to attend.

"Little did I know, at the time, that she would eventually play an integral part in the 3ABN story. At the meeting, I was asked to come up and share the miracles that had taken place, which I did. We finished off with a prayer.

"The next night, while we were planning our trip to the West Coast, my mother called me, and said, 'Danny, doesn't the Lord work in mysterious ways?'

"Amen that! I have always believed that, but what I

didn't realize was that mom had mentioned this heavenly trait for a specific reason. Then mother asked me if I remembered meeting Fonda Summers at the prayer meeting. I replied that I had just met her for the first time that night and, yes, I remembered her.

"'She's a nice lady,' I said.

"'Well, she called me last night,' mother continued. 'Fonda said that after she got home she couldn't get it off her mind what you had said about your hopes to build a television station to reach the world. She was so impressed that when she prayed that night, she told the Lord that she wanted to help but she asked Him what she could possibly do? She said I have no money, I don't have anything.

"'She said God then asked her what she had in her hand. Much like God had asked Moses that same question so many years before. She replied in her prayer that it's true she had no money but that she did have about eight acres of property. Then that is what you have in your hand was the answer that impressed her. She said she could give some of that land for the TV station's location.'

"The call from my mother was exciting. But I explained to her that as gracious and generous as the offer was land just anywhere might not fulfill our very specific need. It had to conform to the narrow geographic locations where broadcasting was technically feasible. A location where it wouldn't interfere with established airwaves.

"I told her that Clarence had indicated that it would have to be about eight miles east and six miles north of West Frankfort.

"A thrill ran through me when she replied, 'That's where it is, in the Thompsonville area!'

"It almost gave me goose bumps when I heard that because I remembered what Clarence had told me earlier about the potential for that area. I told mom that it sounded like God talking and asked her for the woman's telephone number. I just knew that this was God at work.

"When I called Fonda she said that she could not give away her six acres in the front of her property but there were two acres toward the back that she could donate for the Lord's work. And specifically to this project that she felt compelled to help with.

"'It's out of the way,' she said, "And you'd have to build a road back to it, but if it will help accomplish your dream, it is yours,'

"Later, after we had begun broadcasting, Fonda told my mother a touching story. She said that they had owned that property for about forty years. At one time she and her husband had discussed selling the land but somehow the Lord has impressed her to keep it. She said that several years prior to giving us the land she had had a dream in which she envisioned the south end of her property (the donated portion) fenced in with a big gate.

"'My husband would open the gate and the most beautiful fatted cattle came from all directions,' she said. 'They were perfect in every way. I knew that dream was somehow of the Lord, but I couldn't relate it until now. Now that your signal is going out and people are coming to know the Lord, from all walks of life, I understand. There are beautiful people who are coming here that I meet and it makes me realize that this is what the dream was all about. That those two acres of ground were to be used for His glory.'

"I knew the acquisition of this property at this particular moment was no coincidence. This had to be the making of another miracle.

"Clarence was still working for the same TV station but had also joined our team by helping us as a part-time technical adviser. He gave me the name of a search company, an organization in Virginia, that could run the proper testing to verify any given location for uninterrupted broadcasting. The company is one of only a few in America that do such work.

"When I called them, the executive I reached was polite and listened to my story about our humble two little acres in southern Illinois from where we wanted to launch a television network to reach the entire world.

"He listened patiently and chuckled and he said it would probably be a waste of money to hire his services. The fee would not be just pocket change either. It would cost about six-thousand dollars to pay him to come out to check only one such location.

"He added, 'It probably won't work, and then you'll have to pay us all over again to come out and check your next location. Why don't we come there and check the entire area and then give you the very limited number of locations, if any, from where broadcasting is possible. Then you can try to buy that particular property?'

"I finally convinced him that we believed this land was meant to be the right location. Everything else had come together so well thus far I wasn't about to start doubting His plan. We wanted his company to go ahead and make the survey and told him as much.

"'Well, it's your money' he said.

"'We'll do it.' I responded.

"I didn't burden him with the small details involved, such as we didn't have the six-thousand dollar fee. That was a veritable fortune to us. But up until now God had lived up to the promise that He would provide the needs, and I believed He would continue to do so.

"The study was conducted. We had to suffer through a long wait during the technical evaluation process but after about eight months I received the final report from Comsearch. It was about thirty pages written in Greek, or so the technical jargon appeared to me.

"I immediately showed it to Clarence and he admitted that his interpretive ability was also limited, but it looked to him like it meant that our location was actually viable for broadcasting. We were both thrilled.

"To be certain though, I called Comsearch and asked specifically what the lengthy report meant.

"The same executive I had talked to previously, laughed and said, 'You have to be one of the luckiest persons I've ever seen. To pick out two acres at random and have them be the only location in such a wide geographical area that is free of interference is astounding.'

"Why wasn't I surprised? Linda and I were aglow in God's accomplishments thus far, and this new gift was very special— this land, this sacred ground! We realized that there was still a big mountain to climb and much work to do. The task, at times, seemed overwhelming, but praise the Lord…3ABN now had a home!"

Another significant event took place during this time period, one that reflected Danny's compassion for people. It also more or less reinforced the proposition that God truly works in mysterious ways, His wonders to perform. Danny was visited with another consequential dream.

There is a western philosophy that suggests that even bad notes are important to a symphony. They have worth simply because the composer first writes the bad notes and then erases them in favor of new notes, to improve the music. They are, in effect, stepping-stones to purity.

In the following passage, Danny describes his revealing dream experience:

"Shortly after we set out to build the station, my thoughts dwelled on the compelling message to 'counteract the counterfeit.' So, when I would watch TV evangelists like Swaggert and Bakker, I felt like they were counterfeits. I couldn't even stand to watch them at any length. I would just turn them off. And I would get up in churches and say that we intended to build a station that would counteract people like them. This was even before they fell from their lofty positions. I went to several congregations and made those statements without reservation. I assured all that our station would not be like that, that we wanted a different kind of network.

"I never gave any second thoughts to this approach of speaking out, simply because I felt that, that was what we were supposed to do. But within a few weeks after we were impressed to build 3ABN, one night I had a revealing dream.

"In this dream I was standing in this huge apple orchard. The branches of the trees were very low and every one was filled with huge, ripe apples. Every tree was so heavily laden that you didn't even need a ladder. You could just stand on the ground and reach apples from every direction, as far as the eye could see. There was no one there with me, but I was talking to God.

"I asked Him, 'Lord, what am I doing here in this apple orchard? I've never seen such apples. And why are these trees all full with such beautiful, perfect red apples?' It was like the Lord said to me that, 'these red apples represent people who have come to know Me through the 'Jim and Tammy Bakkers' and the 'Jimmy Swaggerts' and many others like them that you, Danny, feel are false prophets. My Word does not return unto me void.'

"My take on this, the way I interpreted it was that I could hire an atheist actor to appear on a set, on the air, and do nothing but read the Bible, and some people would be drawn to God. It is not the messenger that is significant, it is the message. So, my interpretation of what the Lord revealed to me in the dream was, that even though there may be many preachers and evangelists who are either not living their lives consistent with Christian principles, or they simply may be just 'plain wrong,' in their theology, God can still bless, in spite of them, when they speak from His word. After all, I have seen the evidences of people who have been delivered from drugs, alcohol, tobacco, from watching some of these evangelists on some of these Christian stations.

"The Lord impressed me that these people who had

accepted Him as Lord and Saviour of their lives, and had gained victory over many areas of sin in their lives, were now like ripe red apples ready to be 'plucked' with the truths presented in the Three Angels Messages, of Rev.: Ch. 14.

"Step one of God's plan for their lives had been accomplished, step two, of God's plan was now they were ready to hear 'The rest of the story,' as Paul Harvey would say.

"God showed me my battle wasn't against my fellow man but against the powers of darkness, a spiritual battle against Satan himself."

Chapter 7

Home! It was only a barren piece of land, but to the 3ABN Family it was blessed acreage, hallowed ground. All that was to follow; all the lives that were to be positively affected around the world, the ongoing infection of the Three Angels message, all eventually emanated spiritually from this small plot of southern Illinois real estate.

The incredible saga of how this land was acquired and its consequential strategic value from a standpoint of broadcasting location, is the stuff that legends are made of. Nevertheless here it was, now a reality.

As 3ABN grew by leaps and bounds and the ministry spread from its infancy in southern Illinois to encompass the entire globe, the building erected on this original site would eventually not contain enough room for the explosion made by the organization. That first home was subsequently converted to house 3ABN Radio when the current new sprawling complex was built "just over the hill," in another location a few miles away.

But that first home still holds special memories for the first "3ABNers." They consider it the inspirational centerpiece of all the many buildings now laid out across a several square mile area.

The acquisition of the home-base property moved the project into high gear. The "someday, somewhere" aspect of the progress was eliminated forever. The "here and now" phase was firmly established. Linda Shelton often calls God that Great Gentleman and she knew His greatness was decidedly descending on this project.

On a day-to-day basis, though, myriad challenges arose

and it often seemed like those challenges were unending. They were certainly daunting and intimidating and appeared one after the other in fast order.

One of those challenges popped up almost immediately after the home location was established. It was an "Oops!" type problem noticed by Clarence and it involved the need for substantial electrical power, much more than was generally thought available in that area.

It had simply been a miscalculation on the amount of electricity that would be needed, a human error. But that didn't lessen the dilemma if the power was not available. Another stumbling block, which had been more predictable, was the labor force to actually begin raising the building. Of course, as to the latter, construction was a trade the Sheltons knew well.

Inevitably there was always the big question: Where would the money for materials come from? The Sheltons learned early in their ministry, "Where God guides – He provides." Expenses were mounting now, at an accelerating pace.

One significant money factor during the first year of the life of 3ABN was that the Sheltons did not accept a salary. This was reflected negatively each week in curtailing the grocery shopping for a family of five. The music studio at their home (described elsewhere in the book) was relatively busy during this period, bringing in a few dollars, and the couple traveled to churches a couple of times a month singing and sharing the sprouting 3ABN story. The family lived sparingly on free will offerings from the concerts and from the business in the recording studio. But they look back on them as very happy years.

The Sheltons would address this quandary in their prayers, but they generally had confidence that after taking the project this far, God wasn't about to bail out now. As the growth accelerated though, watching for needed funding to keep work alive often became an exercise in great expectation.

Linda said that one thing that very much sticks in her mind about the early days is that she would awaken in the middle of the night and find Danny kneeling in prayer at the side of the bed.

"He was undoubtedly getting his marching orders from God," she said.

As things progressed, each day seemed to bring new surprises. Unfortunately, most of them were problematical.

Despite these challenges, morale ran high among the members of the 3ABN family because they believed in what they were doing. Whenever a problem popped up, an encouraging turn of events would keep the overall spirits high. The family was developing a strong faith that their needs would be provided for as was promised to Danny from the beginning, and thus far, they had not been disappointed.

Dreaming about it, talking about it, especially entering the early stages of trying to do it, made for high drama. The tiny initial group that was involved held unending discussions rife with great faith and enthusiasm.

In the next passage Danny describes how some of those early obstacles were overcome. His personal observations also give insight as to how the constant, and often unexpected and unpredictable interjections of help served to recharge his emotional batteries, and reinforce his original convictions. It really did seem like every time a problem arose, help was forthcoming.

Building a 3ABN Center.

In Danny's words:

"Clarence called me at about nine p.m. one evening. He was in an agitated state over what he considered to be a grievous error on his part. It involved electrical power, or more accurately, the lack of availability of an adequate power source to supply our needs.

"Apologetically, and somewhat frantically, Clarence explained a factor he had overlooked.

"'Hey, I'm really concerned,' Clarence said, 'I've been looking into this a little closer, and it occurred to me that we'd have to have three-phase power when you put in an uplink system.'

"I asked him why it wouldn't be there and available to us. He explained that since the site was in such a remote area, with no coal mines or major industry around, there would have been no reason whatsoever for a utility company to have that much power brought into and set up there. He felt that the cost would have been prohibitive for them, along with a lack of need to do so. That made sense, and at once signaled a real problem.

"His specific concern was the financial consequence of that situation. Namely, that the site of our proposed building was well over a mile away from the main highway power lines— the nearest source of needed electricity, and that 3ABN would have to pay for at least four cables stretched along that distance, together with poles and hook ups. It could cost a veritable fortune. He was so concerned about this that he introduced the possibility of scrapping the whole project.

"'I'm nervous about this,' he said. 'Maybe the power company had a reason to bring three-phase off the main highway, but I doubt it, since it's all residential or farmland. If they did, we wouldn't have to go all the way to the highway and that would save a lot of money. I'm going to go out and check it right now.'

"Clarence, I'll go with you. Don't be too concerned, either God has already provided the needed power (three phase) or He already has someone picked out with enough money to pay for the project. Off we went in my van.

"Armed with a large flashlight we began what could have been a futile hunt on the main highway and then drove

54

slowly toward our site while checking at intervals along the way. It was not encouraging.

"At each stop we found inadequate (for our needs) single-phase power. Finally, after a mile of gloomy flashlight searching we reached our own road and turned toward our property.

"But Clarence suddenly let out a gasp. 'I don't believe this,' he said. 'There is three-phase power right here, but that doesn't make any sense. Why in the world would the power company install that here, in such an out-of-the-way location?'

"I had no answer to his question. I was just elated because this would be a real boost to our efforts, a tremendous cost reduction.

"The next day we traced the line more closely. It came off the main highway (Illinois Thirty-Four) down to our road, and looped around for no apparent reason, and went back through the woods returning to the main highway. It was truly baffling.

"I called the utility company and asked them if we could hook up and purchase power from them. The spokesman was delighted to make the sale and get a new customer.

"But when I asked the obvious question about the logic of establishing the multi-phase power to that remote location, he replied, 'I don't know why it's there. According to our records, this was done over thirty-five years ago. You know how it is. Back then somebody said hook it up and somebody did. Maybe somebody was going to build something big there at one time, or sink a coal mine, and eventually changed their mind. Frankly, it doesn't make a lot of sense. Just be glad it's there.'

"Glad it's there? Like in praise the Lord glad. I said a quick prayer, a sort of a wink and a whispered 'thank you!'

"Not looking a gift horse in the mouth, we hooked up for under two-thousand dollars to a power source that had been placed at that location over three decades earlier for no apparent reason. I'm simple enough to believe that this was no accident. It was God counting his resources way in advance in order to later supply the needs for one of His incredible designs. Clearly, this was yet another boost for the project, not to mention making Clarence feel a whole lot better.

"We now had our property and had survived the 'electrifying' experience of finding three-phase power. All we had to do now was get it to our property, which was just a field with tall weeds, and no access for the equipment that would have to be brought into play as the building went up.

"We rented the heavy equipment and began work on the new road. Meanwhile, I had continued making appearances and singing in churches on the weekends, mostly. Wherever I appeared I would tell my story with increasing enthusiasm. As a result of this, money would come trickling in. The form this took was in itself a moving part of the process. Those wonderful people would give five dollars and ten dollars, and occasionally we'd be blessed with a one-hundred dollar donation. By the time the bill came in from Comsearch, the company that had checked out our location to establish that we could broadcast from that site, God had supplied the six-thousand dollars we needed to pay it.

"But we never had a cash reserve. This was typical. Often we could afford to buy only five gallons of diesel fuel at a time and there was never a bank account per se. This did have one positive effect on all of us. It was basic training for being careful with the money.

"Even today, we don't have a long-term bank account in the broadest sense of the word. Money comes in and it is designated for specific projects, that being the Lord's work throughout the world. At that time though, and even sometimes today, it was a day-to-day dependance upon God to supply the needs. But I look back on it lovingly as a time of great fulfillment and great accomplishment by

Him. God kept the checkbook back then. And He still keeps it.

"As we had the fuel available for the heavy equipment, we began forging the road. It was designed to be about one-thousand, four-hundred feet long, twenty-five feet wide. There were many factors to consider, some of them ominous. We were very concerned about the upcoming rainy season. It can be devastating in southern Illinois. Wet weather could have hindered our work until spring. This was an incentive to move ahead quickly because without the road, working on the building was out of the question.

"So we got the roadbed laid out and we were ready to lay rock. I called the rock company employee and told him what we needed and he computed that it would take six-thousand dollars to deliver the amount of rock needed. It might as well have been sixty-thousand dollars. It was a staggering figure. On the other hand we couldn't just stop at that point. We had vowed that we were going to go forward.

"We couldn't borrow the money, (we had determined from the start we would not borrow money long-term and don't to this day), nor could we leave the roadbed in the condition it was in, at the mercy of the weather. And if winter set in before we had the building shell up it would be a major setback. The rock company spokesman said they had an opening the following Tuesday and could deliver the rock then. It was decision time.

"I had to make a commitment for money that we didn't have. So I made it based on everything that had happened up to that point. I made it based on my belief that God would provide.

"I told the man on the telephone, 'Deliver the rock.'

"After the bold 'rock' decision I had to go and tell Linda what I had done. I needn't have worried. She understood and also exuded confidence that God would bless and provide. By this time we were very encouraged because we had seen walls torn down, barriers removed and financial mountains scaled. This was a pretty immediate need, so we prayed together right then and there.

"As the rock delivery date drew closer I couldn't help but be even more concerned. These thoughts weighed heavy on my mind on the Friday before delivery when I went to the mailbox and found only two letters addressed to 3ABN (we were now formally using the name). Only two letters. That was not overly encouraging considering the amount needed. But I anxiously opened them on the spot.

"The first was from a lady in Chicago. The *Lake Union Herald,* a church-owned magazine, had printed a little article about 3ABN; about our dream, and what we were doing. There was a check enclosed in the envelope and the lady wrote an accompanying letter saying that she had read the article and that the Lord had impressed her to send us two-thousand dollars. You can imagine the positive impact this had on me!

"We had been getting donations of between five dollars to one-hundred dollars, but here was a Godsend— and from someone who had never seen us or visited us! Obviously, I was moved.

"Then I opened the second letter and it was from a member of the congregation of a church in Southern California where we had sung a few weeks earlier. There was a check in that envelope too, and also a note saying simply, 'The Lord has impressed me to send you this check.' The check was for four-thousand dollars!

"You don't have to be a math major to figure that one out!

"On Monday, the man from the rock company called and said they were set to deliver, did we have the money?

"'Of course we have it,' I told him. 'Bring it on.' God can make a road, when He wants to.

"Another faith-strengthening experience came when we actually began the building. With the road finished there was nothing to hold us back. I sat at home at night and began sketching plans, drawing on my experience as a contractor. I began by drawing a forty-foot by seventy-foot building on a blueprint. It looked confining so I went to a fifty-foot by ninety-foot alternate plan.

"When you're only working with ink and paper, expansion is easy. I thought we might even go for something bigger.

"When the big day arrived we finally went out to the site. We put a tape down and I began walking. The tape was one-hundred and fifty-feet long. I walked part way and stopped and asked my brother how that distance looked? He said that looked pretty good.

"So, I decided to walk a little further and stopped again to ask, 'How does this look?' My brother again agreed that that distance looked fine too.

"Finally, I just walked until I ran out of tape. I let it all out and once more asked him how that looked.

"'That looks even better,' he replied, so I marked it. And that's the way the size of the first 3ABN building was determined.

"We had measured sixty-feet for the width. This was to be a two-story building, which meant the dimensions, would be a total of about sixteen-thousand-feet. We just stood there for a while looking at what we had done. At the stakes in the ground. It certainly didn't look like a television network building. It was a bit intimidating. The task that lay ahead was enormous. But our hearts swelled with the love for that burden, and we vowed to stay the course. For Him."

Chapter 8

Until now, faith alone had fueled the project and the fuel tank had registered full. That faith had always been the backbone of the movement and it was always sufficient to motivate everyone involved. Their belief in what they were doing hadn't diminished one iota. But a subtle difference now pervaded the atmosphere of the project. It was a confidence in not just faith, but a reinforcing marketable skill when it came to what it was going to take to complete the next phase, the construction of the building itself.

As the Sheltons stood on the site of the future home of 3ABN, in July of nineteen eighty-five, Danny was suddenly thrust into an arena he knew well, construction! It was his area of expertise and that fact filled him with renewed vigor. In previous years the Shelton Construction Company had left its footprints throughout southern Illinois in the shape of the buildings and homes they had built.

Be that as it may, there was the ever-present offsetting question. Where would the money to build this studio come from?

Theoretically, it was virtually impossible for the fledgling network builders to have come as far as they had. The "from-there-to-here" of it all boggled the mind.

Had it been a fictional story, the reader would have been skeptical of the viability of the central plot. The glaring improbability was that no money had been borrowed and here they were with the property secured, a new road built, and plans prepared to begin construction of the studio. What had taken place to date awed them.

Incredulously, they were literally ready to pour the foundation of a structure borne of a divine dream. What with all their needs, thus far at least, God had provided for. But the degree of difficulty of continuing the burgeoning project was increasing tenfold at each new challenge.

The newest phase of the task at hand, and by far the most crucial to date, was actually building and outfitting the television station. All they had was prayer and a willingness to labor vigorously. Would that be enough?

There was an underlying confidence afoot. "We were never fearful about the future needs," Linda Shelton said. "Our mindset was that we would go forward as God provided. If God stopped providing, we would see that as a signal to stop."

By any stretch of the imagination they did not envision a grand temple or ostentatious structure on an exalted scale. They only sought to build a simple, functional building, a home base from where they could send out the message of the Three Angels to all the world. A roof over their heads would suffice. As it turned out, they didn't have to wait long to receive an answer to their question about help for a means to continue. And once again that help arrived in storybook fashion.

When God sends in the cavalry to save the day— sometimes even old western movie fans wouldn't recognize the heroes as such.

In the following paragraphs Danny Shelton explains the events that took place at this critical crossroad in the evolution of 3ABN.

In Danny Shelton's own words: "After we staked out the property, in dimensions much larger than we had originally planned, we realized that it would be a huge building. We also painfully realized that we didn't have much money in the bank (two-hundred dollars), but we were equally aware that God can read bank statements too. So, we moved forward.

"It was Sunday; we quit about noon and headed home. We had done our part. Now, we were waiting for God to do his.

"The moment I walked in the door Linda said, 'Honey, some people named Marvin and Rosella McColpin, from Chattanooga, Tennessee, called. They are coming up north on a missionary trip. They have heard about what we are doing here. In fact, they have already sent us a small check. Since they were traveling this way anyway they would like to drop by and see how we are progressing. They will probably arrive in the next few days.'

"I told her that was great, and that I would call them. We were always thrilled when someone expressed interest in 3ABN. Sure enough, they did come to see us.

"We began by grading the area and things continued on a very positive note. We had previously met a man in Minnesota, who is an Adventist. We had talked to him about what we were doing and he was extremely interested and supportive. He deals in sheet metal and said he would sell as much of that building material to us as we needed, and give it to us at his cost. This was a significant offer from a financial standpoint and the timing couldn't have been better.

"All we really wanted to do was get the shell up at this point. We were going to build it as a pole barn construction, which is common to the area. We were also racing the weather to raise the shell and the roof before winter, so we could continue to work inside during the inevitable bad weather. We began construction in the fall of nineteen-eighty-five.

"Meanwhile, we had used our meager two-hundred dollars in the bank to rent a backhoe, which was much cheaper than hiring the work done, and were digging a footing three feet wide and three foot deep. I had given our visitors directions to the job site and when the McColpins arrived in the area they came straight out to observe the work.

"Like most people, watching construction labor fascinated them. They observed what we were doing until we took a break and they joined us for a chat. They were really curious and inquired as to specifically what was happening. I explained that we were digging the footing. That it was the initial foundation, the first step. They didn't mince any words in the following conversation.

"They bluntly asked how much money we had set aside to accomplish the construction of this building. I told them point blank that we had exhausted our remaining funds to rent the heavy equipment.

"They were somewhat taken aback by this answer. They figured out that we had no money for concrete and asked a very logical question, 'Why are you digging the holes if you can't afford any concrete to fill them in?'

"I tried to explain that we trusted that God would, and has provided, and I had spent the last two-hundred dollars because if I did not use the money He had already provided, why would He be inclined to provide us any more? We decided to use up the resources we had and wait, and pray. So, we plunged forward in our mission. I couldn't tell whether my logic had moved them one way or another. I just told the truth.

"The McColpins did seem interested in what we were doing and stayed with us for several days, and then stayed with members of our family. They were the first in a long line of strangers who stayed with us in our home during the period of construction of 3ABN. Linda claims that she sure learned hospitality to guests during that period.

"Later, we had the opportunity to stay at their home in Tennessee. They were charming people and so frugal that they would freeze leftover popcorn. They served us some. It is a precious memory.

"The McColpins were simple folk and it was obvious

from their dress and vehicle, and everything else about them that they did not have much money. But we loved them for themselves and their expressed interest in our project. Their presence was most welcome and boosted our morale.

"We finished our trenching work quickly and I didn't think much of it when they politely inquired as to how much money we would need for the next phase of the project, to lay the foundation and put up the building shell. We estimated that phase would cost about fifty-thousand dollars, and so informed them.

"We were getting into the big league phase of construction now and we all acknowledged that this was a tremendous amount of money. This staggering amount overwhelmed them too, but they said toward the end of the week that they would like to talk to my family and me privately. They wanted to know if they could come back to our home for a short visit. I assumed that they wanted to say a prayer with us so that divine guidance might prevail and I told them that they were most welcome in our home any time. I did not realize how providential that welcome was until that night.

"Without any fanfare they gave us a check for twenty-five-thousand dollars. The next morning, they gave us another check for an additional twenty-five-thousand dollars!

"Now, these are people we had previously never met in our lives. They told us that they had changed their original plans to travel further north and instead they were going straight back home. They instructed us to hold the checks because they would not clear at that time. They, in fact, were returning home to make arrangements to put the money in the bank.

"That made sense because we were reasonably sure they would not have that much money in a checking account anyway, so they were probably going to transfer the cash from a savings account. Even at that we were stunned by what was taking place. We had welcomed these people as friends, asking nothing of them nor expecting anything.

"This unanticipated major event was to become an even more absorbing story. Do you know what they did? I did not even know about this myself at the time of the occurrence because they modestly did not mention it. In fact, I didn't find out about it until several months later.

"They told me that at the time of their generous commitment they did not even have the money. However, convinced that this project was of God, they actually borrowed the fifty-thousand dollars! Incredibly, as collateral, they mortgaged their home to, as they put it, 'Get this TV station going.

"One thing that might have convinced the couple to help was the fact that Marvin had been aware of the incident mentioned in a previous chapter when we discovered that the mandatory three-phase power was unexplainably discovered near our building location. He had heard other similar accounts during their visit. He, like us, and many other people then and now, apparently interpreted this ongoing phenomenon as divine destiny.

"We were told later that miraculously in the eyes of many, the McColpin's business enterprise made enough money in the next six months to pay off that loan. Throughout the history of 3ABN, and continuing today, there are people like this all around the world who help this ministry in a generous fashion. This network is their story too."

Off to Montana
"Armed with the Godsend from the McColpins, we moved forward with the planning. With the contribution of the new money we were able to get the shell and roof up, a giant step forward. Even in its skeletal stage the structure was inspiring to see. But, as it had been repeatedly from the inception of the project, the next phase loomed large and

carried with it a big price tag. Linda and I discussed pouring the concrete floor to the building and we estimated it would cost approximately ten-thousand dollars.

"Soon we got a telephone call from San Diego, from a man named Dale McBride. Like so many other people he was interested in our work. He had heard about us from Gary Rusk, a man I had worked for in construction, in Michigan during the late nineteen-seventies. Dale asked why we didn't go to the next ASI meeting. I did not even know what ASI was so he explained that it stood for Adventist Service and Industries, and they held an annual meeting where they considered various worthy projects to which they might give financial aid. It was held in Big Sky, Montana.

"I replied that we couldn't afford the cost of travel or lodging. He said that there were places to stay that would only cost about sixty-five dollars a night and that we should go there for the entire length of the meetings – Wednesday through Saturday night. He explained about being a friend of Gary who had told him about our project. Dale insisted that the story needed to be told in this particular forum. I told him it was simple. We would pray about it and if God wanted us to attend the meeting He would see that we received the money needed. If He didn't, we just wouldn't go.

"I told Linda about the call and we did pray, right then and there, for guidance in this matter. No sooner than we had finished praying the phone rang again. It was Dale calling again. Apparently he had been giving the matter a lot of thought too.

"He told us, 'You have prayed for an answer, haven't you?' I said yes, as a matter of fact we had.

"He responded, 'Let me be the answer to your prayer. I'll sponsor you,' he said. 'I'll buy your plane ticket, pay for your food while you are there and handle the cost of the hotel.'

"We were very moved by this generous offer from a total stranger. By the same token, we were beginning to understand that the ranks of 'strangers' were thinning and the 3ABN Family was growing by leaps and bounds. So, in August of nineteen-eighty-five, Linda and I were off to the ASI meeting in Big Sky, Montana."

One other incident during this general time period took place very quietly but turned out to be a milestone event in the history of 3ABN. It was in the early stages of the building process and Danny and Linda were at home one evening. It was about nine p.m. when a knock at the door announced a visitor. It was Melanie Walker and her husband, a local singer and acquaintance of the Sheltons.

At the time, Danny had a radio program through which he was helping people. The Walkers had a tape of a song.

"'This is a song that we heard and my husband and I were going to sing it. But it reminded me of you and for some reason the Lord told us to bring you this tape," Melanie said. "We thought somehow you might have a need for it."

Danny and Linda played the song called, *Mending Broken People.* Immediately, the couple was deeply moved by the words of the song and felt like it expressed perfectly what they wanted to do through 3ABN and with their lives. Linda says, "At one time Dan and I both felt that we had reached the bottom of the barrel. We were broken people. But we found healing through Christ and through each other. This same healing we wanted to offer to the multitudes through the saving messages of God's Word. We knew when we heard it this was the theme of what 3ABN was all about... mending broken people."

And so it was to be. A passionate theme song was born.

Chapter 9

Where did the trip to Montana fit into the overall picture? Why were all of these things seemingly happening in some pattern? How did 3ABN get its name? These questions and more are answered in this chapter.

The events that surrounded the early days of the formation of 3ABN might seem extraordinary to many people, but there is really a simple explanation, as Danny reveals herein. The Sheltons and others involved were beginning to embrace the project with a love and confidence which was growing stronger each day. But there were others too that were taking note of what was developing in a tiny town in southern Illinois.

Case in point: The call from California, from Dale McBride touched the Sheltons deeply. Here was a man that they had never met, who had found them through a mutual friend, and he had enough confidence in what they were attempting to do to pay their travel expenses to Montana, as well as provide their lodging and living expenses.

By now, the entire group was busy with the actual construction of the building and Danny wasn't sure if he and Linda should really take time off to make the trip. They had spent all the money they had accumulated in construction costs. The pressing need at that time was the ten-thousand dollars needed to pour a concrete floor.

As Danny had from the start, though, he interpreted this generous offer (to have expenses paid for the trip) as a significant sign and decided to follow it. Not knowing what to expect, but buoyed by faith and the unfolding drama, Danny and Linda, along with Rosella McColpin, headed west.

Somehow the name "Big Sky" seemed apropos for a trip in the service of 3ABN, given the nature of the network's eventual use of satellite systems and airwaves. The Sheltons inquisitively approached the ASI conference (which they were to become more familiar with in later years) as mere spectators, only to discover that the reputation and knowledge of their endeavor had preceded them.

Danny and Linda were the first to admit that when some unique circumstances fell into place for them, and they were thrust into center-stage as their project came to the forefront, that God was still in charge. Here, Danny explains the impact that the trip had on 3ABN's future.

Big Sky Country
In Danny's words:
"We were really impressed when we arrived at the meeting. Until we arrived, we didn't even know what ASI was. Hundreds of people were there representing many lay ministries, as well as a number of Adventists who, if impressed, sometimes offered financial assistance to what they deemed worthy projects.

"We had a cheerleader of sorts in Rosella McColpin, who had come with us. She could not contain her enthusiasm and told everyone who would listen about what we were doing. We were also sharing a booth with her, where we were selling our recorded music.

"Therefore, we had several people approach us and ask when we were going to tell our story about the new station.

"'Are you going to tell it here at ASI?' they wanted to know, and their interest was genuine.

"One evening I was in the hallway talking to a man who'd asked that very question; if we would give a presentation. Another man standing nearby, who happened to be an officer of ASI, turned and apologized for eavesdropping but stated that he too had heard people discussing the

70

fledgling network.

"'However,' he explained, 'even though people have expressed an interest in hearing from you, we have to plan these programs a year in advance. One of the reasons for this rule, is that at one meeting, ASI had allowed a person to speak spontaneously. He collected thirty-three-thousand dollars in donations and no one has heard from him since. Therefore,' he added apologetically, 'we couldn't put you on the program at this time.'

"I thanked him for his comments and explained that he need not worry. We had not attended the meeting to speak, but that a new friend had asked us to be there and we just wanted to watch the proceedings, meet new people and enjoy the meeting. I told him we were there for whatever God wanted us to experience.

"Suddenly the totally unexpected occurred. Linda, who at that time was normally very quiet and shy, spoke up.

"She quietly told the man, whom we had just met, 'You know, if the Lord really wants my husband to speak, he will speak.'

"I was very surprised. But she had seen door after door open and she believes absolutely in what we are doing. If the man was offended by her comment, he didn't show it, but said that since he was on the program committee he could guarantee that this year there was no room on the speaking roster. Again, I assured him that this was not a problem. I did not blame him, especially since they had been burned by a deception the year before.

"We just relaxed and enjoyed the conference by attending all the meetings on Wednesday and Thursday. ASI is a fine organization and the programs were interesting.

"During the week people continued to ask us about our exciting project and we were happy to talk about it on a one-on-one level. As the end of the week drew near, it appeared that nothing concerning our network would come forward officially.

71

"That was all right too, because if God really wanted us to speak there, He would reveal that to us in His own good time. Apparently, that was not going to happen because activities were nearing an end. I couldn't help but wonder if my time might have been better spent back home, working on the construction of the studio building. But the beauty and serenity of the mountains moved us and we were not a bit sorry we had attended the meeting.

"As things wound down for the approach of Sabbath, (there would be one brief meeting on Saturday night and then adjournment) there remained only the Friday early morning meeting on the regular schedule. The only eventful change otherwise was in the weather. It had been beautiful autumn weather all week but on Friday morning it began to rain. And it rained and rained and rained.

"Although it wreaked havoc to outdoor activities, the storm was a magnificent sight to behold at seven-thousand-feet altitude. In the glassed-in restaurant, we were almost sitting at cloud level. As things turned out, the rain represented more than God's beautiful artwork. It would also play a significant role in the projected outcome of our trip and the visit to ASI. And it would especially affect 3ABN.

"We decided to attend the Friday morning meeting and went over to the assembly where there were several hundred people already gathered. In fact, the room was packed. I was listening to the current speaker when I noticed the president, Phil Winstead, and vice president of ASI, Henry Martin, both of whom I had met during the week, talking in an animated conversation.

"What really caught my attention was that they were looking, or so I thought, directly at me. They were also giving me the traditional "come here" gesture with their fingers. I was across the room, and figured they couldn't have been beckoning me specifically out of all the people present, and I wasn't about to make a fool of myself by mistakenly standing up or going over there. They persisted though, and finally I looked at them again and pointed a finger at my own chest and raised my eyebrows inquisitively. Yes, they shook their heads, you. I took the plunge, figuring that if I got there and it wasn't me they really wanted I could be cool and keeping on walking, like I knew what I was doing all along.

"I couldn't imagine what they wanted with me, but when I got over to them, Henry Martin, the vice president, a tremendous man who we have gotten to know very well since that meeting, wanted to talk to me. It seems that Linda's words had been foretelling after all.

"Henry described his dilemma, 'The only time we had not scheduled any speakers was on Friday afternoon. That is because we planned on taking advantage of the magnificent scenery by taking the people up to the ski lifts to generally enjoy the beautiful mountains. But, Danny, as you can see, it's pouring down rain. Now, I have several hundred people here with no plans for how to occupy their time. Would it be an imposition on you to talk at the meeting about your plans for building a new television station?'

"Is God in charge? Is Linda's faith strong? After assuring the men that I thought it would be no imposition at all I went back to my seat next to Linda in the morning meeting.

"Later, in the dining hall, I told her, 'see that cloud?' It seemed we could almost reach out and touch it. 'God is in that cloud. That is the cloud that leads by day. Everything, even the rain is at His disposal.' Dr. Walter Thompson (a surgeon and Adventist who plays a significant role at 3ABN) once told me that God is always counting his resources in advance, and He is not wanting. How true Walt's comment is. This phenomenal turn of events was a brilliant example of that 'resources' theory.

"There is a more important message in this incident and I can't stress it enough. God was not doing this for Linda, or for me, because of who we are. He is doing it in spite of who we are. Like He blesses you in spite of who and what you are. We have talked in this book about miracles, as we perceive them. I would say to you that if you don't feel the Holy Spirit alive and well in your life, and if you don't see God performing miracles every day, maybe you should ask Him for a new touch.

"When people read this book they should not glean from it what God is doing for Danny and Linda Shelton, or 3ABN. They should ask Him, 'what can I do for You? Maybe You can use me more effectively.' That is what the 3ABN story, and this book, is all about.

"Linda and I still ask these questions. We are not content where we are. We know that God can use us even more than He is now. We thank Him, but ask Him to continue to open new doors.

"I did speak at the meeting and ASI proved to be a precious experience for us. We met several wonderful people there who opened their hearts to God, through 3ABN, and they have since remained staunch supporters of the network. Among them are May Chung and Ellsworth McKee who still serve on our board of directors at the network.

"Another unforgettable incident occurred at that conference. As I've mentioned, we were sharing a booth with Dr. Kay Kuzma, who was generous enough to give us a little space there to display and sell cassette tapes of Melody and me. She had even drawn a little map of Illinois and placed a star in the southern part to let people know exactly where we lived.

"I was a few feet away from the booth talking to someone and Linda came running over to me very urgently tugging at my sleeve and saying she needed to talk to me. I said I'd be right there in a minute, but she insisted she needed my attention right then and there. That was unusual for her to act in such a manner so I excused myself and broke away.

"She pointed to a couple that had just purchased two of

our tapes. They sold for about eight dollars each, but the man had given her a check and told her to just keep the change for the TV station project.

"I told her that was great, but why the urgency to interrupt my conversation?

"'But Dan,' she said. 'The check is for ten-thousand dollars!'

"She asked me, 'What do you think?'

"I suggested that maybe we had been selling our tapes too cheap, but she ignored my attempt at humor because the couple was walking away with no further comment. He had just handed Linda the check and walked away.

"I caught up with him and tapped him on the shoulder to thank him. His name is Bill Bower, he's from Florida, and he told me that he had heard about our project and was impressed to help.

"Thanks to his generosity, I telephoned my brother that night and told him to go ahead and proceed in pouring the concrete floor because we now had the money.

"Soon we were back home ready to take on the next challenge. We were happy beyond words that this broadcasting network was taking shape. A good example is found in how we later acquired the first satellite dish.

"We had checked it out and it had a price tag of approximately three-hundred-fifty-thousand dollars, a staggering amount! We approached it as we had everything else to date, with a belief that God would provide. Even when one man said he would give us ten-thousand dollars if we could raise the rest of the money. I was eager to start broadcasting as soon as the station was built.

"Only weeks after the Lord impressed me to build the station, the Lord gave me the name of the TV station in a dream. Nothing really came to me but it was heavy in my thoughts when one night the problem was abruptly solved. God provided the answer.

"I had a dream, and in my sleep I looked out and saw a

dark universe, a big void with stars, and maybe planets around. Suddenly, I heard a noise like a gushing wind. All of a sudden one of those little insignificant stars began to come toward me. It came closer and closer traveling at a tremendous speed. As it approached me I saw three angels circling this globe, and it was planet Earth. The angels were blowing trumpets. I was impressed that God was answering my question and, from that nocturnal inspiration, we officially became the Three Angels Broadcasting Network! It also gave us a meaningful logo.

"It is interesting to note that neither Linda nor I, at that point, had a clear understanding of what the Three Angels' messages are.

"Now, what about the satellite dish? Could God really provide over three-hundred-fifty-thousand dollars for one piece of equipment? Of course He could. More importantly, would He? Armed with and emboldened by the ten-thousand dollars, the man had donated toward the purchase of the satellite dish, I called a firm in Atlanta and talked to someone named Sue, who was the head of the finance department. I told her we wanted to order a satellite dish some thirty-feet in diameter, an uplink system.

"Logically, she responded by asking how we intended to pay for this system. Confidently, I told her that we had all of ten-thousand dollars in hand.

"There was a long pause and then Sue replied, 'Well, Mr. Shelton, the usual advance payment before we can begin building this system would be seventy-thousand dollars. We also require another one-hundred-sixty-thousand dollars on delivery. The balance of one-hundred-twenty-thousand dollars would be required when installation is completed.'

"I digested this and then explained that we really wanted to move along with the project and that we had ten-thousand dollars cash and we would send it right away. God would provide the rest, I assured her.

"Apparently, God was not on her list of acceptable co-signers so she made a counter-proposal: 'Can you get a letter of credit for this amount?' she asked.

"Her request, of course, didn't surprise me. I had already prayed and told God, if it is Your Will that we are to build this much-needed system now, we will need help. I must say that when I talk to these people it would be utterly ridiculous for a company of that stature to allow a fledgling organization like ours, with no established credit (because our policy was to not borrow money), virtually one-hundred-percent advance credit. So, I added in my prayer, You need to help me convince her to accept the meager down payment for them to proceed to build the satellite dish.

"Sue pointed out that if we did not have the letter of credit, and would not or could not borrow the money, there just wasn't anything she could do for us. 'Nothing personal,' she added. I told her that was all right and that I understood.

"A few days later, the company's district sales representative, who lives in Indiana, called me. He had visited our station as we were building it, aware that we would need to have his product in order to go on the air. Obviously, it would be a big sale for him. Therefore, he was aware of the whole story of how we had developed to this point because I had related it to him during his visit. He was apologetic and explained that the company really did want to provide the satellite uplink system, but they just couldn't bend the credit policy that much. I reassured him that it was okay, apparently it was just not in God's timing right now.

"Not satisfied with the dubious status of the potential sale he said, 'Why don't you give Sue another call? Tell her about the 3ABN story. I have already told her a little bit about it.'

"I took his advice and called back and talked to Sue again. After hearing about the project from its very beginning, she thought it over and made a decision.

"'Danny,' she said. 'I don't know what I'm going to do to you if this doesn't work out. I'll be in big trouble. But if you send me the ten-thousand dollars, I'll go ahead with your order and we will start building the satellite for you.'

"I promised her that when the equipment was ready, God would supply the needs.

"Shortly after that order confirmation I made a trip to St. Louis to talk about 3ABN. I spoke to people there and elsewhere brimming with confidence in the project. I explained that the Lord had not brought us this far only to let us fail now. And those people responded. They began to give money for this specific purpose. One person gave seventy-thousand dollars, a tremendous amount and enough to make the first payment.

"Sue nervously kept me posted in advance when each payment was due.

"Finally, when the satellite dish was actually installed, the money, which had seemed virtually unobtainable early on, was there. No longer did we speak in vague terms of the future and what we hoped would be. We were finally a television station.

"It was simple. As the needs began to grow, so did God's help."

Chapter 10

It was simple, Danny said. As the need grew, so did God's help. Simple? It seems the word profound would be more applicable. What a total faith such an attitude requires. Who are these remarkable young people, Danny and Linda Shelton? These two believers who have taken on such an incredible responsibility and challenge, never doubting that God would provide all the needs to carry out their work? What kind of childhood, education and special training does it take to tackle such an extraordinary task?

Were they rich kids, or from powerful families that opened all doors for them ensuring success from day one? Did they know from the time that they were children that this calling was to be their destiny? And, as 3ABN reaches out to every corner of the planet has their original basic simple faith in God changed at all? No, no, and yet again no are the answers to those questions.

Perhaps it was always in some preordained plan for these two to come together from so far apart, to meet and to become embroiled in this limitless theological adventure. Was it actually a divine project that has changed the lives of so many people worldwide? That explanation would seem most logical considering all that has come about. The occurrences supporting that theory from the start are appealing. Danny Shelton's story is one of pulling himself up from abject poverty to respond to an ultimate and unexpected challenge.

Danny's father is the late Tommy Shelton, who was born in Arkansas, but moved in the nineteen-twenties to the tiny community of Orient, Illinois. The community is located in the middle of coal country and when he moved there, that industry was thriving throughout the area. He had been raised in a family that included thirteen brothers and sisters. Tommy was a truck driver by trade but he was also a talented musician and singer, and had a Country and Western band that played in area taverns and nightclubs. In fact, for a few years, the Sheltons (mom and dad) had a radio program called the "Melody Kings," featuring Country and Western style music.

Music, always an enormous influence in Danny's life, also played a role in naming his daughter, Melody. When she was an infant, he prayed that Melody would be given the gift of a good singing voice so she could dedicate that talent, as he had, to God's work. God most assuredly came through for her and she has overcome a great personal tragedy, the loss of her mother, to indeed fulfill the wishes of her dad's prayer.

A few miles over the hill from Orient was the bustling town of West Frankfort, Illinois, a virtual teeming metropolis compared to tiny Orient, and boasting of a population of some eighteen-thousand people at that time.

One of the places to go in West Frankfort was a popular eating establishment known as Manis Café. For a time, Manis also served as a bus depot. Truck drivers frequented the eatery and it didn't take long for Tommy Shelton to take note of a pretty waitress named Goldie Rice, a native of West Frankfort. They soon discovered that they had something in common, music. Goldie was a piano player and inevitably romance bloomed.

After they were married, Goldie joined her husband's musical group for a while but soon determined that the tavern circuit was not for her and she quit participating. After religion became a dominating part of their lives, Tommy's playing music in taverns became a bone of contention. He had never smoked or drank and had looked unfavorably on bad examples of people led to excess in both. But playing music, using his talent, was a source of income that was sorely needed by the new family during otherwise hard times. Later, after Tommy's conversion, he quit the tavern scene.

However, he was still in demand, so nightclub or bar owners would drop by the house and attempt to get him to perform at their places of business. Looking around at the impoverished conditions, they would use a compelling argument that the family could certainly use the money to pay for the barest necessities of life. And they were correct, the family most assuredly could have. But every time Tommy would avoid the temptation and turn them away saying, "We'll make do, somehow."

Danny remembers a story his mother told him concerning her turning to religion as the foundation of her life.

"Back about nineteen-forty-nine, my father had a country band called the 'Melody Kings.' My mother didn't really want them playing in the nightclubs, even though at that time neither one of them claimed to be Christians, per se. But she didn't like the atmosphere. They didn't smoke or drink and she didn't want him involved in that. However, he didn't quit the scene due to the fact that he was earning money. Unable to dissuade him, she decided to travel with him, playing the piano for the group.

"Meanwhile, back at the old corral, as they say, my aunt and uncle, Mildred and Olen Shelton, began to give my mother Bible studies. My mother had gone to church. She had been raised at Antioch Methodist Church, near West Frankfort, but hadn't been to church in many years.

"When she finally accepted the Lord she began to study what she thought was truth taught by the Seventh-day Adventists. But she was reluctant to accept it because if she did, and her husband did too, that would mean no income since they would certainly have to give up their lifestyle of playing music in taverns. Neither had an education above eighth grade and therefore she was understandably concerned about their financial welfare.

"She put off making that decision to serve the Lord. Then something terrible began to happen. Her arms and her legs began to draw up and became discolored causing her to lose the use of her withering limbs. They didn't know what it was but many people in that era had undiagnosed polio. They called in a local doctor who came out to the house to examine her. The doctor took Tommy into another room and told him they had to take his wife to Barnes Hospital, in St. Louis, because she had polio in an advanced stage.

"When Tommy asked how long she would be gone, the doctor ominously indicated that, 'She might not come back.'

"My mother heard them talking in the other room and she managed to roll off the bed to get into a kneeling position where she prayed most fervently. If the Lord would heal her, she vowed she would never set foot in another tavern and would dedicate all her talent to gospel and religious music, and she would raise her family to do the same.

"Having heard her, Tommy helped her back into bed and she asked him to call Olen and the Adventist pastor. When they arrived, they anointed her with oil and they prayed for her. Mom said that she immediately felt better and her color began to return. She could actually feel the healing process. So much so that an ambulance that had been scheduled to pick her up that afternoon was canceled.

"Later, when Tommy called the doctor to report she was feeling better and was even up and about. The doctor's response was, 'no way.'

"He came back to the house to verify his original diagnosis and end that nonsense. When Doc arrived, he was amazed at her unexplainable (to him) improved condition.

"'I don't know what happened,' the perplexed physician

82

said. 'I know polio when I see it. All I can say is there must be a higher power than us doctors.'

"True to her word, my mother never walked into another tavern to sing that kind of music again. Consequently, she raised all of us in that atmosphere too, going to church every week. About four years after that, my father also became an Adventist Christian, which ended his country music career."

Tommy also had a "shattering" experience, which accelerated his acceptance of the new faith. The couple and their fledgling family moved to Chicago, seeking conditions to make a better living. Although they only lived there a few months before fleeing back to their beloved southern Illinois, an incident at that time greatly effected their thinking.

They had moved into an upstairs apartment in the low-rent district. Tommy had been studying the Bible, largely at the urging of Goldie, and he understood the implications of the Sabbath, and that he shouldn't be going out work on God's Day. But he didn't want to tell his employer that he wouldn't work on the Sabbath, because they certainly needed the money. Goldie countered that if they honored the Sabbath, God would provide for them.

"Somehow we would make it," she told him. "Even if you weren't working."

No sale. Tommy said he didn't have that much faith. The not-quite-yet-converted doubter then proceeded to walk out the door. As he started down the stairs, he fell down the steps, shattering his ankle. Had there been a huge neon light blinking on and off with the legend, "Tommy, it's the Sabbath," it couldn't have impressed him more. He was laid up for six to eight weeks and couldn't get out to work. Amazingly, as Goldie had predicted, they got along just fine during that period. This impressed and encouraged Tommy that there was a better way of life, in the Lord. He began attending church regularly and gave up the music. At least, as it pertained to playing in taverns.

Later on, as a footnote to the great Chicago tumble, almost as in punctuation to falling down the stairs, another incident further reinforced Tommy's faith. With a newfound contentment in his church, he settled into a regular routine that included faithful attendance with the family in tow.

One Saturday, he decided to play hooky. A truck, an imperative tool to his making a living, had broken down. He needed it on Monday and that meant he had to get it running over the weekend. He had been doing well, he explained to his wife, and God would understand that this vehicle repair should take priority over church.

Apparently God was inclined to disagree with that game plan. Fending off the complaints from Goldie as he sent the family off to church, Tommy plunged into the task at hand. The reports on exactly what went wrong were rather vague afterwards, and he never gave specific details on what happened. But what is known is the truck "blew up," due to a repair effort mishap. What is for sure is that Tommy once again found a profound respect for the Sabbath, which he honored the rest of his life.

If they thought they had troubles though, the Sheltons were about to learn that sometimes life's complications could increase manyfold. When it rained it poured for the Sheltons during the early years. It seemed as though their faith was constantly being challenged.

Tragedy struck the energetic Tommy at the young age of thirty-six, when he was stricken with a heart attack. He was no longer able to continue as a truck driver because of the heavy loading and unloading demands that go with the territory, but he made good use of his truck nonetheless by becoming a scavenger. Taking the children in tow from the time they were toddlers (everybody worked, always) Shelton would find abandoned cars, strip them and take the scrap to St. Louis, about one-hundred miles to the north. There he would sell the metal. Another sought after item for recycling was glass. Therefore the family also rooted out glass items to smash and transport to the River City. The group would search for glass jars and bottles along highways and in junkyards. A large rock was placed in the bed of the truck and the glass was smashed against the rock to shatter it and thereby make the load more compacted. The latter activity proved to play a significant negative role in Danny Shelton's life.

While throwing bottles and breaking them a shard of glass flew up and hit Danny's eye. That accident at the age of three caused a scar to form over the pupil rendering him legally blind in the right eye. Danny has overcome the handicap so well that most people, even close friends, are unaware of the problem. Especially when he participated in sports, which he still does on occasion.

There were also times when the family's struggle to survive economically could prove awkward for young Danny and his siblings. For a short period of time Tommy operated a septic tank (emptying) truck quaintly nicknamed by local folks as a "honey-dipper." It was a vehicle that provided a critical service in rural America. But the societal benefits of the service didn't diminish Danny's embarrassment when performing the work of removing sewage at the homes of classmates, after school was out. Years later, on a Mothers' Day show on 3ABN, Goldie would recall that during those years she and Tommy, Sr. never had the luxury of pulling the truck into a service station and saying, "fill it (the gas tank) up." It was always a matter of buying a gallon or two of fuel at a time. Making things do.

On another occasion, Danny, who was a pretty fair amateur athlete in his youth, made the grade school basketball team. It was especially rewarding because he was the only fifth grader to make the "first five" of the sixth grade team. A scheduled team photo proved to be a potential disaster for Danny.

The Joiner School (West Frankfort, Illinois) players were going to pose for a team photograph. The problem was the other players all had white tennis shoes and Danny's hand-me-downs were black. As shabby as Danny's shoes were, the cost of a new pair put them out of reach of the Shelton's sparse budget. Danny was panic stricken but Goldie devised a plan that would save the day. With a flash of fashion ingenuity, mom took white paint and converted the "tennies" into footwear that would have made the then world champions, the Boston Celtics, proud.

All went well at the photo session but by half-time of the following game such derring-do turned calamitous. It seems a small trail of white paint had mysteriously appeared from one end of the gym floor to the other, while Danny sat inconspicuously at the end of the bench, a picture of innocence.

A similar experience befell his sister, Tammy, when she was in the fifth grade. She had the honor to be featured in a music festival and needed a nice outfit. She explained to Goldie about the white satin shoes that she wanted with just a little heel to make her look all grown up. Her mom came home with a gaudy pair of slippers of purple and pink, and with pointed toes.

When Tammy wailed about the impropriety of the style it was explained to her that they had been in the "dollar bin" which added to their attractiveness. She decided on a radical course of action. This one time, Tammy tearfully took her case to plead before her older brothers. More often than not, they harassed and teased her.

Years later she recalled that, "after they fell down laughing at the new shoes" Danny and Tommy mercifully chipped in and bought her more appropriate footwear.

Years later, Tammy Shelton Chance was to get her "evens" for the childhood teasing, when she was at a family reunion show aired by 3ABN on the first day of two-thousand-two. "Danny was a tattletale when we were little," Tammy told an international audience.

"When I would do something bad he would hold it over me and threaten to tell our parents if I didn't do his chores for him like make the beds or take out the garbage."

Looking back, Danny never tries to hide any part of the poverty of his youth. In large measure, that is because he feels he had a rich family life which he attributes to the values held by his mom and dad, that were handed down.

"We lived in what was called the poor section of a town that was itself economically depressed and below the national level for average income," he says, when discussing his youth. "And we had a lot of company, families like our own. As kids our dad let us play sports. We could take time out to participate on baseball teams and such. But he taught us also that idleness was the Devil's workshop. So our time had to serve a purpose. He would never let us wander the streets. To this day I have never entered teen-town. We could not join the other kids when they loitered around sitting on Main Street. We all had jobs or chores. Always."

Danny's singing voice came into play in high school when he was cast in musicals like "*Oklahoma,*" and other popular shows of the day. Other than work, music and sports, in either order, dominated his time. In junior high school he chose the most difficult field event, pole-vaulting. Southern Illinois, like neighboring Indiana, is known as basketball country, but Danny was not involved in that sport at the high school level. He could shoot and hustle with the best of them, but the key games were usually scheduled on Friday nights, and he couldn't, or wouldn't, profane the Sabbath.

On arriving at high school, fans who had seen him play so well in the lower grades were anticipating cheering him on as he sparked the "Redbirds." Not a chance.

His older brothers had already traversed that trail and it was well known that playing on Friday night, the premier games, was restricted for the Sheltons. Therefore the coaches avoided this potential conflict by simply cutting Danny in the first round of tryouts, even though he obviously outplayed several of the "keepers." Respecting his ability, sometimes the coaches would use him in team practice sessions to play defense against the "A" team to hone their skills.

Danny would still play pickup games when and where he could and his love of basketball is reflected to this day. This led to a memorable moment.

On one occasion during the early construction of the Russian Cultural Center, Russian workers heard a commotion, dropped their tools, and gathered in awe to watch Danny playing one-on-one basketball with David Lee, a former All-American guard from Southern Illinois University (nineteen-sixty-five through nineteen-sixty-nine). After graduating from SIU, as a high school basketball coach, Lee won the Illinois State championship (nineteen-eighty-four). A friend of 3ABN, Lee had traveled to Russia to observe the progress of the construction of the center.

During a work break, Danny and David had thrown up a crude, makeshift backboard and rim in a massive garage where the bounce of the ball sent echoes off the far walls. 3ABN had provided the equipment for the Russian workers to use at their leisure.

It was a treat for the locals to see Americans (still a rarity shortly after the fall of Communism) going all out like they were playing in the NBA finals. Just for the record, if you check the archives, Lee won that game.

Danny had three older brothers and a younger sister. Did they get along as kids? He answers succinctly, "No!"

Tommy is the oldest sibling but he was the studious one. He grew up fast. His love of the piano set him aside from most kids his age and he became a professional at age eleven, going on tour with an adult gospel quartet, to raise money for the family. Kenny is nearly four years older and

88

Ronnie is three years Dan's senior. Both Ron and Kenny were good athletes. The younger three boys were active as youths, with an emphasis on sports. They put up a hoop in the yard and a bar between two trees to accommodate Dan's skills at gymnastics. That skill, and the older boys' tendency to exploit it to the fullest, would sometimes lead to trouble on West Warden Street.

On one occasion their mom received a call from Nellie Smith, a panicked neighbor, telling her to hurry out to the back yard, that the boys had tied a rope around three-year-old Danny, and had him swinging about thirty-feet above the ground. Mom got the gleefully smiling high-flyer down safely and read the kids the riot act, thus probably nipping a future circus act in the bud.

Being the little one, Danny had to learn to hold his own when it came to backyard scuffles. But they had to be private clashes on the brotherly field of honor because their dad would not allow any fighting. If one of the kids hit a sibling, he could be assured that he'd get a spanking. Or, as Tommy, Sr. called it, a "whoopin."

Tommy told them that the parents were in charge of the family and if there was punishment to be given out, they would administer it. These little sibling rivalries were more than offset by binding family ties. If an outsider picked on one Shelton, they took on the lot.

Also dominating their spare time was music. All of the kids played instruments and sang, and even after they were grown they would continue to perform together at family gatherings, mostly at the urging of mom.

The defining influence on them though, was their father's discipline. It was firm but fair as Danny recalls, but most of all, it was consistent. It was dependable.

The kids could go out and play in the yard, but if they fought or argued, he would give them work to do. It made for overall domestic tranquillity. The kids could have dozens of friends in their yard. They even organized little track meets. But they could not go wandering off to play elsewhere unless their parents knew exactly where they were and what they were doing.

"My dad's philosophy was that we, as a family, could make living together easy, or we could make it hard," Danny said. "He told us that the Lord put him there, in charge, that He gave the kids to him so apparently He had confidence in him doing the right job. He told us kids that he was the oldest, and he was the boss. He told us he would tell us to do something just once, and he expected it to be done. If it wasn't done, a 'whoopin' would soon follow. But he would never whip us when he was angry. He would wait until he settled down.

"Sometimes, you would think he forgot about the punishment because some time would go by without it happening. But he had a memory like an elephant. He never forgot. A day or two later, just when you began feeling cocky about it, like you had beaten the system, he'd call you in for your comeuppance. That has helped me more than anything else in life has. Having parents who were consistent. If he'd have disciplined me once for something I did wrong and then let it pass the next time, there would have been no stability. No life lesson learned."

Danny remembered one example of the long arm of the (family) law reaching out, when he found out that there was no statute of limitation to avoid a good whoopin. Despite ominous looks from his parents, he and a cousin had been giggling and acting up in church, a Class A Felony in the court of Tommy Shelton. As the service ended, Danny began thinking about his lack of discretion and the stern looks from his father.

He had to come up with a deft maneuver to circumvent his just due, so he suddenly developed a taste for his Aunt Mildred's cooking. He asked his mom if it would be okay to go home with his cousin Dennis, for dinner. She already had twelve mouths to feed anyway so one more wouldn't make any difference.

"Go ahead," Goldie said, "we'll come out this evening and pick you up."

That evening there was nothing mentioned about Danny's less-than-reverent behavior in church that morning but he decided not to take any chances. He asked permission to stay overnight and work for his uncle's tire business the next day. When permission was granted, the jubilant youth yelled a silent "Yeah!" and gave his cousin a high-five figuring he had for sure beaten the odds, and outfoxed the stern patriarch.

Sunday saw Danny working hard, a small price to pay for amnesty, albeit even if said relief came through a bad parental memory. Sunday night his parents came back to pick Danny up. They played a little music, socialized and had an enjoyable time. On the way home his dad amiably asked Danny about his time at his uncle's place. Did you have fun? Did you work hard? Did you ride the horses? These inquiries all got an enthusiastic positive response. Danny was overjoyed. He had pulled if off, he thought. That is, until they arrived home.

As they were getting out of the car his father said, "By the way, don't forget to come and see me before you go to bed. You have a good whoopin' coming!"

"My dad was the most consistent person I have ever met," Danny said. "He was always jovial, even though he had great health problems. He made me feel so secure I didn't realize that we were among the poorest people around because our home was a home full of love. They didn't just send us to church, they took us. My father and mother lived everything they taught.

"Emotionally they were happy and healthy even though they were very poor. They had a good marriage. I never heard them argue. I'm sure they did, but the kids were never aware of it because they did it privately.

"One other thing was very important to me. When we

would talk about a sports idol, and rave about their accomplishments, dad would have none of it. He explained that that particular individual is just like everyone else. Anything that anyone else can do, you can do. God gave you a good brain, so use it. This gave me confidence and taught me perseverance. It taught me to not give up easily."

One other experience helped to shape Danny's character and makeup and he remembers vividly to this day. His skill as a baseball player as a young boy afforded him the luxury of "playing up." This meant he was in demand to be accepted to play in a higher league, with older boys. When Danny was seven, they promoted him up to the eight-nine-ten-year-old level. It was clearly a prestigious position for a youngster and heady stuff. Who wouldn't be tempted to get a little cocky?

One of his coaches, Robert Whitt, who ran Whitt Memorial Company near West Frankfort, was the manager of a little league baseball team. Despite his being two years younger than the other boys were, Danny was asked to join that team. Danny remembers well how he strutted around once he donned the "big league" uniform, and still tells the story.

"Bob Whitt was a wonderful man, with a heart of gold. He had kids of his own the same age as our family so we had contact. He was aware of our financial condition and didn't want to embarrass us by outright buying things we couldn't afford, but he would miraculously "find" ball gloves and shoes lying around and bring them by our house to give to us kids.

"Because I was short anyways, the fans would compliment my play as a pitcher or outfielder. It began to go to my head and I showed it. During one time at bat I hit a homer and trotted around the bases making 'look at me' gestures and hot-dogging it. Coach Whitt never said a word," Danny recalls.

Coach Whitt never said a word, but the next practice

session he called all of the players aside for a conference. He told them they had to make a decision about a player on the team, and whether the team should keep him, or let him go. "We have a player that must be dealt with."

Danny trotted over to the dugout with the rest of the players wondering who was on the hot seat, and what the poor wretch had done to deserve potential banishment.

When the coach began to discuss one of the team members "showboating" a pang of fear struck Danny like a bolt of lightning. He knew it was himself who was on trial before his peers and all that he held dear was suddenly on the line. He was numb. His throat was dry and he felt like bawling out for them to please give him another chance. He didn't get that chance to speak though because the coach called for a show of hands of players who wanted to give little "Mr. Ego" another chance.

The dearest thing in life to him, outside his family, was at stake. It seemed like an eternity, but one by one the teammates raised their hands to vote for mercy, for redemption, for another life!

"I have never forgotten that lesson," Danny tells people today. "Never again did I consider myself more important than anybody else, nor brag about anything that I might have accomplished. At once I learned humility and the power and beauty of forgiveness. Coach taught me that there is a higher calling than just winning, that fair play and sportsmanship should always be our fundamental goals. And that we should never feel superior to anyone, nor more important."

Grade-wise Danny did better than average in school. He carded mostly A and B scores in grade school. An occasional "C" would get his dad's attention pretty quickly and he'd work a little harder on that subject. He would not study in the normal sense of the word. Rarely did he take a book home and he would "crash" for tests and do well. He did not take after his older brother, Tommy, who was a straight-A student all the way to the eighth grade. In the eighth grade Tommy got the only "F" grade of his entire schooling, along with a spanking. His principal reluctantly applied that corporal punishment because Tommy absolutely refused to accept the science class curriculum explanation, as it pertained to the theory of Evolution.

Tommy, Jr. said on his test, "The text book says...." But then, he added that he believed the Bible version. On the test he put down the textbook answer, but also jotted down chapter and verse describing Creation. But the teacher was having none of it, so he took the failing grade and the paddle in defense of his religious beliefs. Tommy and formal academics parted prior to high school when music, as a profession, kicked in.

But if Danny was not an academician the measure of his oldest brother, that fact was offset many years later when he was conspicuously honored by his high school.

Summer Time Was "Pickin' Time"

The work ethic Danny alludes to started early in his youth. Come summer, Danny's family, including Uncle Olen Shelton and all of his children, and Grandma and Grandpa Shelton, would load up the vehicles and head to northern Indiana to pick tomatoes.

The caravan was vintage *"Grapes of Wrath,"* but with all due respect to John Steinbeck; it led to the type of hard work and honest labor that shaped Danny's character and helped him meet later challenges.

The work (picking) assignments would be issued according to each Shelton's size and age. This was done to establish how many hampers of the fruit they were expected and required to pick each day. The little ones picked one row, the older Sheltons two rows.

This way the fruit pickers would cover a large field finishing at approximately the same time. These excursions into Amish territory lasted until Danny was about ten years old.

The family lived in a meager Amish house rented by the tomato cannery, for their temporary habitat. The houses had make-do strung up lights, but no running water or bathrooms.

Local Indiana preachers were always happy during picking time because their church attendance took a dramatic upswing when the Sheltons would march in en masse and fill the first several rows.

In the fields, it was a family affair and competition was keen when they went at it. Danny and his cousin Dennis are about the same age and they would battle tooth and nail— especially at the urging challenges of their respective dads.

On one occasion, Dennis was tired after rising at dawn and he lay down in between the rows to "rest his eyes for a second." When his family found him and shook him awake, he discovered that Danny had thumped him and won the day, big time. He chastised Dan for not waking him, but Danny was not above grabbing an easy victory when it came his way. Naturally, when the families get together today and tell war stories about tomato pickin', Danny chooses this particular account as his favorite.

Of course, when such nostalgic tales are exchanged at reunions, the renowned Aunt Ruby's feat dominates. She picked three-hundred-twenty hampers of tomatoes in one day, crawling at the end, and clawing at the ripened fruit; arms stained green from the vines, all the way up to her shoulders, as legend has it. She was going for, and beat, a record held by a man. However, the story has never been authenticated, or picked up by ESPN Sports.

All of the picking money went directly to the family coffers, but once in awhile the youngsters would get a little reward for their gallant work.

"On Friday, we would go into the local stores and we might get a little fifty-cent pocket knife or a little dollar flashlight," Danny remembers.

"We didn't know any better and we were happy with that labor contract.

"About us kids, they used to say that we were as happy as if we had good sense."

It wasn't until years later that the older brothers would get a few bucks for their picking prowess, no small reward when money was scant.

The "tomato time" was a cheerful period for the smaller kids because it made them about six weeks late starting school. If such tardiness caused school officials chagrin at the time it was obviously forgotten when, over thirty years later, Danny Shelton was ceremoniously inducted into the exclusive and prestigious Frankfort Community High School's Special Achievement Society.

There are only a few members in this august group and, modestly, Danny seemed almost embarrassed about the whole thing when he was inducted. For days prior to the ceremony, he was unaware of what was afoot and had he known, he probably would have avoided it altogether.

On the evening of his induction, before a large crowd of townspeople, Danny told a friend that he didn't understand what all the fuss was about. Or why he was being honored.

"It (3ABN) is all God's doing," he said, "not mine." Nonetheless, to this day anyone visiting the FCHS Library can view a plaque with Danny's photograph and the following tribute:

> The story of FCHS alumnus Danny Shelton's success is remarkable. He was raised in well-below-average economic conditions. 'Poor' would describe them. However, he now presides over and hosts a daily program with his wife, Linda, on a television network that he raised up from a cornfield in Thompsonville, Illinois.
>
> Three Angels Broadcasting Network airs twenty-four-hours-per-day, seven-days-a-week. He has also built television studios in Russia and Romania. The signal that origi-

nates from the 3ABN Production Center, in Thompsonville, covers all of North America, parts of Central America, many islands, Europe and North Africa. It is estimated that 3ABN currently covers three-quarters of the globe and plans are being made to expand coverage to encompass the entire globe in the near future. This international expansion compliments a huge network of over one-hundred stations in the United States.

Although religion is the cornerstone of 3ABN's broadcasting, it would be a misnomer to use the word television 'ministry' to describe the (sole) content of the broadcasts. The station's programming is untypical in the sense that the words 'television ministry' mostly conjure up images of the more standard 'beg-a-thons' where money is king. Above all else, 3ABN is dignified in its format. More importantly, the programming also delivers good health advice, cooking and clean living messages. It is a wholesome overall schedule. For example, shows on organic gardening, home schooling, and children's' activities spice the schedule. These are regular programs along with preaching prophecy and poignant testimonies.

Specifically, as far as local achievement is concerned, 3ABN's signal shows '3ABN, West Frankfort, Illinois' to the world (flashed on the screen regularly, twenty-four-hours-a-day). Likewise, mail comes here from around the globe, as well as international visitors (once, the president of a foreign country)...all of whom take back with them a part of West Frankfort.

Mr. Shelton has shared his success locally in many ways. He has contributed both money and equipment for the use of (school) District one-hundred-sixty-eight, specifically through anti-drug use messages and programs. He has arranged for financing national TV coverage for our young people's sporting events. He has also made generous cash donations to local projects he deems worthwhile for the community. Most recently, he has been working with our community council to promote West Frankfort worldwide.

Danny Shelton is recognized internationally. However, he is modest in dress, demeanor and attitude. In fact, large segments of this area's population are unaware that the multi-million dollar, internationally known entity of which he is president, is located in their midst."

Danny Shelton, inducted May 9, 1998

If that presentation, made in his old high school gymnasium, was one of the higher points in Danny's life, it certainly did not change him. His humble background has shaped his life to this day.

During the hardship period of time for the Sheltons every family member worked at any form of labor they could find to chip in money to provide the barest necessities of life such as food, clothing and rent. Said food was not of the catered, gourmet variety. Often ingenuity was set afoot when Goldie had to put together a meal.

"For breakfast," Danny said, "we would make icing sandwiches."

This meal is conspicuous in its absence from most cookbooks, but Danny ate enough of them that he remembers the ingredients to this day.

"You start out with flour and sugar. Milk is called for but we had to substitute water. Add to this food coloring to make different colors of icing (variety is the spice of life) and then put it on two pieces of bread. That's probably why I'm not six-foot tall today.

"When I went to Central (junior high) School, my friends used to get fifty-cents to a dollar for lunch. I usually got a nickel. You couldn't buy anything at Mike's Restaurant, the popular hangout of the day, that only costs five cents. So when my friends would ask me to join them for lunch, I would beg off with some important business that I had to take care of. I'd tell them I would meet them later at Ben Franklin, where they would go to buy candy after they had their hamburgers and fries. There I would buy hot peanuts as if that was just to top off a non-existent lunch. Also, the school would provide milk.

"White milk was a penny and the treat of treats, chocolate milk, was two cents. We never got to taste the latter. Our parents would point out that that was a penny a day extra, compounded by four kids multiplied by five days a week... a virtual fortune. The dietary aspect of the kids' lives boiled down to pure economics."

The family now included Danny's older brothers

Tommy, Kenny and Ron, and younger sister, Tammy, who replaced Danny as the "baby of the family" when Danny was eight-years-old. Since there were no pension plans in those days and their father never paid into Social Security, it was always a struggle to survive.

As previously mentioned, when young Tommy was eleven-years-old he was playing piano for a gospel group and bringing home money to buy food. Tommy, Jr. had become fascinated with the piano at about age three when he would toddle up and reach over his head to the keyboard. Startling his mom and dad, he would actually play discernible sounds.

Danny says of his older brother, "When we were out playing ball and having fun, Tommy would be home teaching himself to play the piano, and practicing. He was smarter than us."

Later, Tommy would share his musical talent by cutting a commercial tape on the basics of how to play the piano. It sold briskly.

Danny and his mother would paint houses in the summer and do house cleaning, and Danny would mow lawns. Coal was king during this period and hauling the black gold to homes and maintaining furnaces provided an opportunity for the burgeoning young Adventist to pick up additional coins.

This common goal, survival, inevitably brought the family closer together. Later, their collective talents led them to play group music, mostly for the church. After they became Christians, when Sabbath rolled around all other activities ceased from sundown Friday, until sundown Saturday evening.

Sabbath was (and is) sacred to them and even later on, when the Shelton Construction Company sponsored a softball team, the dugout would be half-empty when the team played a rare game on a Saturday. That would only occur when an unpredictable tournament schedule placed them in a weekend game.

One former classmate of Danny's relates an amusing story about playing basketball against Sheltons when they were kids.

"Every Sunday morning we would leave for church early and play a pick-up game against them," he remembers. "We would stay as long as we could and then have to run to get to church on time. We cut it thin nearly missing the service sometimes. We were always thinking they would have to leave too, because they talked about going to church all the time. It became a challenge to stay longer but they always outlasted us. It wasn't until a few years later that we realized their Sabbath was on a Saturday, accounting for their endurance over us on the Sunday basketball court."

Danny survived these economically depressed years and went on to attend Frankfort Community High School. A former teacher describes him as "Not the best student and not the worst." A former classmate said he recalls Danny as a nice guy and a "straight arrow", a guy who was always courteous and never smoked or used foul language.

Along with having a natural adeptness at softball and basketball, he was also a skilled gymnast. Even before television made this an internationally popular sport, often the coach would have Danny show intricate gymnastic moves to the cheerleaders to add to their routines. After high school, Danny considered becoming an anesthesiologist and studied first to become a Licensed Practical Nurse.

At that time, while working as an orderly at the United Mine Workers of America Hospital, in West Frankfort, Danny met a man who had a great impact on his life, Dr. Richard O. Fox, now a retired surgeon and published author. Fox allowed the impressionable youth to observe surgical procedures in the operating room and during these sessions, Danny was again impressed with anesthesiology. Fox also told the future 3ABN president that he could do or be anything he wanted to and that he must shrug off the oppression of poverty and make something of himself.

Danny has never forgotten that mentoring confidence and to this day continues a valued friendship with the good doctor.

Another defining factor in Danny's life came during the summers of his years at high school. That's when he learned carpentry while working for his uncle, Vernon Johns. To be more accurate, Danny had been helping his uncle for years, on Sundays and other times away from school. But his construction skills began to flourish during his later teens.

The pace was accelerated when, at age eighteen, he met his first wife, Kay. They were married when he was nineteen. He had increased responsibilities, and had to make a dependable living. Carpentry in an impoverished area (the coal mines were going down by then, ergo the overall economy) assured the young family a steady wage coming in.

Shelton attacked the job in the carpentry and construction trade much like he would the challenge of 3ABN later on. Namely, with total faith. He approached his brother, Kenny, about leaving his good job in the mines and forming the Shelton Construction Company.

With typical "Sheltonese" confidence they plunged in. The young men built Kenny's house and used it as a model to gain other contracts. That enterprise lasted until nineteen-seventy-five.

Danny moved to Berrien Springs, Michigan, where he managed a local lumberyard. Thinking of home, Danny and his family moved back to West Frankfort in nineteen-seventy-nine, where his life would take a sudden dramatic and traumatic change.

"We can't find your wife."
During this time Danny, his wife, Kay, who people said

101

sang like an angel, and their daughter, Melody, had been singing in churches around the nation. It was after one such trip that the most devastating incident in Danny's life occurred.

On June thirtieth, nineteen-eighty-two, the trio had just returned from an exhausting trip through several states in the mid-west. They were enjoying a well-earned family day around the house and were taking delight in the summer sunshine.

Kay had taken the family poodle to town to be clipped and was leaving to pick up the pet. Melody went along. Danny was puttering around in the back yard working. It was at noontime. He heard a dull thump and a car horn that was stuck, but paid no particular attention to it. It was, however, one of the most critical moments of his life.

A neighbor came to get Danny.

"There has been an accident," the friend said gently. "you had better come with me, Dan."

As it turned out, Kay had only gotten two blocks from the house on her ill-fated journey. It was reported to Danny that a young fellow who had only recently received his driver's license did not yield the right of way at an intersection and had hit the Shelton vehicle broadside.

When Danny arrived on the scene, someone told him that they had found Melody. She had gone through the windshield and had a broken arm, but apparently would survive. The man added, "We can't find your wife!"

But Danny did. It is a scene branded in his memory forever. The van had spun around and slid into a ditch. Kay, who was killed instantly, was under the vehicle, face down.

"I touched her, and softly called her name, but I knew at once she was dead," Shelton said later. Rekindled once again was the age-old painful awareness of the fragility of life.

Melody was rushed to the hospital and treated by the

102

above-mentioned Dr. Richard Fox, for whom Danny had worked as an orderly several years previously. The girl's arm was placed in a cast and her bumps and bruises were attended to. And then they went home to what had suddenly become a lesser house.

That night the eleven-year-old suffered a sleepless and painful time, running a fever and undoubtedly replaying the accident in her mind.

Danny sat up all night with her gently telling her not to be mad at God because the Bible says, in John 10:10, that "The thief talking about the devil comes not, but for to steal, kill and to destroy; but Jesus says I have come to give you life and to give you life more abundantly."

As the restless hours dragged on, Danny read the Twenty-Third Psalm, "The Lord is my shepherd, I shall not want..." and reassuring scripture such as 1st Peter 5:7, "Casting all your cares on Him, for He cares for you."

Huddled together in a cocoon of God's love, father and daughter sought initially only to survive that night of utter tragedy as they talked about Satan being responsible for sin, death and disease. Somehow, they made it to the dawn of a new day and what would be the start of a new life.

As morning embraced them, Danny said to his daughter, "The sun is coming up Melody, we will need someone to sing for your mother's funeral. Who should we get?"

Setting pain aside, the courageous little girl replied, "Well, Daddy, after what we talked about all night, I think I should sing. I know Mamma would want me to sing and I think Jesus wants me to sing. And if the devil is responsible for all of this, then we're not going to quit singing and let him win. We are going to continue singing."

And so they did continue to sing. As a trio they had made commitments in advance. Churches that had scheduled them to sing offered understanding if they decided to cancel, but were delighted when the Sheltons did show up, singing as a duet.

Also at this time, Danny was beginning to get involved with recording in Nashville, Tennessee, and doing more radio work. He devoted most of his time to his daughter and their singing. Other labors, such as carpentry, dwindled away to make time for this new dedication.

As Danny put it, "I didn't go back to driving nails. I wanted to stay with Melody as much as I could. I wanted us to make it together." And so they did, making a living solely with their music, until Danny was impressed with a remarkable dream; a mission, a calling.

To counteract the counterfeit.

In retrospect, Danny has no bad feelings about what most people would consider an impoverished youth.

As he describes it: "When one looks back at the details of growing up in the nineteen-fifties and early nineteen-sixties in the Shelton household, you might at first feel sorrow for my family and me. But because of the love my parents showed for God and us children, I wouldn't trade my past experiences for anything in the world. I only write or talk about some of the seeming disadvantages of growing up amidst poverty in order to encourage someone who might now be where I once was, to have hope.

"I want people to know that no matter what their background is, they can become anything God wants them to be. When Jesus says 'Go, Ye...' He was talking to all of us.

"I look back at my childhood with fondness. I remember only a household where love and laughter abounded. It reminds me of an old song which declared, 'The love of God is greater by far than tongue or pen can ever tell. It goes beyond the highest star and reaches to the lowest hell.'

"There is no substitute that can fill the empty soul, like the love of God shown through the human family."

With such a marvelous, loving attitude borne of family life, it is proper that today Danny embraces a "family" that

104

counts in the hundreds of thousands, around the world. The real and vibrant, constant and ever-growing 3ABN Family.

Chapter 11

Linda Shelton's background was completely differ ent than her husband Danny's. One of the most defining moments in her life came at age twenty-two, shortly after the birth of her daughter, Alyssa. It had been a difficult and complex delivery during which she began hemorrhaging profusely when an artery ruptured.

In a tense flurry of activity she was rushed into surgery where she received three pints of blood. The young mother survived the ordeal and was on the road to complete recovery, or so she thought, but yet another critical test lay ahead.

About two weeks after that trauma, Linda had been back home for only a few days when the hemorrhaging again erupted. She was rushed to the hospital Emergency Room where they did what they could to stem the bleeding and yet again sent her directly into surgery. The loss of blood was taking its toll and three more pints were administered. This time when she awoke her embattled body ached all over.

She remembers, "Every muscle in my whole body hurt, even my tongue."

But a personal phenomenon also occurred at that "defining" moment. It was a change that was to continue to shape her life to this day. She was awash with a great truth.

"They thought I was going to die. I thought I was going to die, but God gave me another chance," she says of that personal discovery.

Though pale and shaken to the core of her physical being, Linda was deliriously happy. Transformed emotionally, she was fervently seeing the world through new eyes in the aftermath of her duel with and victory over the Grim

Reaper.

"If I would have died at that moment, my life would have been meaningless both to God and mankind," she pondered.

Ablaze with this realization, she made a solemn vow in her heart that she was going to live for God, seek out truth and was somehow going to make a positive difference in this world. Although she didn't know it at that blissful moment in her life, that faith was to be severely tested more than once, and she would have to sacrifice much to maintain it.

However, with this fresh outlook, she was ready to face life anew and follow a steady, confident path. It is a trail that has been carved out by a strong reaffirmation of faith. Somewhere out there, she knew unequivocally, there was a calling, a way for her to serve, and she meant to find it.

At this point I invoke the most overused and possibly hackneyed expression in the word arsenal of any writer, "the rest is history." But if ever that cliché was applicable, it is here.

Early Years

Wisconsin, the Badger State. Racine Wisconsin, to be specific. There began the journey that led Linda Shelton on the circuitous path to 3ABN and the great faith that now sustains her. The miles from one to the other are measured in less than five hundred geographically. But the lifestyles are worlds apart. And the road was often bumpy along the way.

She and Danny now pray daily, potentially into hundreds of thousands of homes, both on television and through radio broadcasts. But her childhood prayers were mostly those familiar to ongoing generations of little ones.

A five-year-old Linda and her seven-year-old sister, Cheri, would both say prayers from their tiny twin beds as darkness descended over Racine each night. Cheri usually won the race to slumber land and Linda was left awake with her own musings.

She opened a direct line of communication with God, informing Him regularly about the most important issues of the day. They included such items as Chatty Cathy Dolls, an Easy Bake Oven and, oh yes, finding a good husband.

Later she recalled thinking, "If God really loves us so much, he surely wants to hear from us more than with just the, 'Now I lay me down to sleep…' prayer. It was when I arrived at this conclusion that I began talking to the God of the Universe, on my own… without instructions from an adult."

This line of communication seemed to work for Linda, because most of those simple childish prayers were answered.

Linda's upbringing early on was idyllic and happy. Racine is a lovely city in a pastoral setting, which borders the shores of Lake Michigan. To this day, her thoughts of home conjure up wonderful memories of tobogganing with her family on cold winter nights, corn roasts and block parties with neighbors. To this day also, when Linda closes her eyes, she can ponder these childhood memories which reflect family, a warm home and, those two magic words "safe haven."

Although no one suspected it at the time, later in life Linda was to be instrumental in returning some of her love for the city of Racine, in the form of an impacting ministry there from 3ABN. Her personal involvement, especially her music, was also to play a touching, vital role in the life of her father. She was raised in a home where her parents were not poor, by any standard, but not rich either.

There was always food on the table, clean clothes to wear, and in contrast to Danny's upbringing, indoor bathroom plumbing facilities.

Linda's father was a hard working chemical engineer.

Although he worked hard five days a week, he was always available and ready to do dishes and help with the chores around the house when he was at home.

He had a gruff German temper when the kids misbehaved, but often showed that he was a kid at heart when he would follow the children outside and plunge into the bustle of one of their many games. When the kids chose up sides for baseball, kickball or kick the can, he was among those available.

In the following passage, Linda tells a story which mirrors the serenity of that phase of her life. It includes a special closeness with her father and appreciation for her mother's input into her life. And a Christmas present that was to play a lasting role in the familial scheme of things:

In Linda Shelton's own words: "You hear some advertisers talk about gifts that 'keep on giving.' In actuality, there are few meaningful gifts that really reflect such continuity, but I recall one that so impressed me and my sister and brother.

"When we were very young, as children are given to do, we would awaken at the crack of dawn and rush into the living room to reconnoiter what exciting gifts might be sprawled under the tree. On one such Christmas morning we were halted abruptly by an intimidating dark looming shadow in the corner. We convinced each other that discretion is the better part of valor and scurried back to bed, the better to investigate it with more courage after the morning sunlight made the room more children friendly.

"When we cautiously tiptoed back to the room in full daylight we were delighted to discover that the monster-like shape was actually a toboggan (sled). For many years thereafter my dad, Wayne, would take us to a park where they had a big toboggan slide and steep hills and we enjoyed many good times together in this pursuit.

"Let me tell you something about my dad. He was a

person who detested clutter so much that as children we were very much aware of the fact that if we didn't keep our treasured toys tucked away in a drawer or closet, they were in harms way. Their destiny was the trash heap if dad found them lying around. But one of the things he kept clean and polished at all times was that toboggan. Even after we owned it for many years it looked brand new. It was a family treasure that was to become an heirloom.

"When I was older and had children of my own, one day dad asked me if I wanted that toboggan and of course I said yes. As a result of this gift, Alyssa and Nathan were also able to enjoy it while they were growing up. Since there are no gigantic hills in southern Illinois, they would connect it to a four-wheeler and pull it around in the snow. They loved it too and their happy laughter still rings in my heart.

"A few years ago my dad passed away which was a terrible loss. One winter day I pulled the car into the garage and spotted the toboggan. I have to confess it was all dirty and scratched with paint chipping away. It needed some elbow grease pretty desperately. Then I remembered how dad used to take care of it and I realized I just had to take some time to clean it up.

"It was a labor of love and as I began scrubbing, the old fond memories came flooding back of the wonderful time we all had on this sled. I began to wonder how this snow vehicle had survived all these years after my brother, sister and I had left home, scattering to different states. I pondered why dad had kept it all that time when his policy was to toss everything out that was not in use.

"At that moment it struck me. Dad only kept the things that meant the absolute most to him, and my tears began to flow. My thoughts turned to our Heavenly Father who has shown me that God keeps the things that mean the absolute most to Him, too. Inspiration tells us that Jesus will present His hands with the marks of his crucifixion, the marks of cruelty He will ever bear. Every print of the nails will tell the story of man's wonderful redemption and the dear price by which it was purchased.

"This was my 'toboggan experience.' It is priceless to me and will live with me always.

"But then, I was always 'daddy's girl.' I remember waiting and watching by the window nearly every evening for dad's car to pull up into the driveway. Then I would run outside to be the first to greet him. I loved the feel of my tiny hand in his big, strong hand, the smell of his after-shave and his leather coat. And I loved to just hear him say, 'Hi, Toots.'

"Mom was definitely the nineteen-sixties mom. In those days, mom stayed home with the kids, had coffee breaks with her friends and would spend a lot of time hanging laundry on the clotheslines. I still very much appreciate the fact that I wasn't raised in daycare or by a baby-sitter. Thanks, Mom!

"She was multitalented and she pursued her love of dance. She was also active in some women's groups and in politics. When we kids were older she went to work for a few years while remaining active in the Racine Dance Theater. Later she had her own dance studio where she gave lessons.

"I'm sure mom's interest in dance transferred into my genes. I began formal dance training when I was ten-years-old and continued this study through my college years. The Racine Dance Theater also became a big part of my life and provided some of my fondest memories. The RDT was composed of a dance troupe that included age thirteen and older. The group would perform all different types of dances including ballet, tap, folk, modern, and Broadway musicals, all before Racine audiences. They even participated in parades.

"I developed some really close friendships during these years with my dance partners and I learned a lot. Dance taught me a lot about discipline, as well as the great theatrical tradition that 'The show must go on.' In later years, when 3ABN emerged, my experience in those shows from my youth would be helpful in my responsibility to develop and produce shows of a very different nature.

"Along with the dance, I had a very early urgent need to create music. Neither of my parents pursued music other than listening to the radio or singing in the church choir. But at a young age I began asking for a piano. Soon my asking turned into begging. And then my begging turned into tears. None of these tactics worked and finally my parents told me to stop 'hounding' them about the issue.

"One day, and I'll never forget this day as long as I live, I came home from spending the night at a girlfriend's house. This friend's father had just taken us to the bank where he worked to show us a strange new phenomenon called a 'computer.' This huge monstrosity took up an entire room, made a lot of noise and didn't really impress me at all until he punched a request for it to print pictures. The pictures were black and white and not much better than what you would find in a coloring book. But they were life-sized...at least my 'life size' at that time. That impressed me, and he even let us keep the pictures.

"Upon arriving home I walked into our upstairs 'flat' living room. Therein my mom and dad, sister and brother were all seated in the living room and looking at me expectantly. But I was so excited about my adventure at the bank that I didn't even notice their concentrated attention and I rattled on about my little drama at the bank while holding up my picture in a 'show and tell' fashion.

"I was talking a mile-a-minute and suddenly realized that something was amiss. So I glanced over to a corner of the room and spotted an object that seemed out of place. It was a small synthesizer! Instantly I stopped talking in mid-sentence. My jaw dropped and tears started rolling down my cheeks. I stood mute for several minutes, but inwardly I was the happiest girl in the world on that day. Thus I started my piano lessons at age ten, but I could already play 'my own' tunes before the first lessons began.

"Unfortunately, my early piano teachers strongly discouraged playing the piano 'by ear.' They insisted it would be a stumbling block to my progress in learning the piano. So I obediently stopped experimenting with the instrument on my own. My lessons were standard with the addition of a lot of classical music and hymns.

"By the time I was fourteen, I was bored with such unchallenging exercises. I wanted to quit, and pressed my parents to let me do so. This request wasn't received well by them because by that time we had a regular piano and they really enjoyed listening to it being played.

"To discourage me from quitting, mom found a new piano teacher, and said, 'Just give her a try and then we'll make a decision on you quitting or not.'

"Much to my surprise, Betty Hansen turned out to be an incredible blessing. She made me fall in love with music all over again. Betty arranged and printed songs that the teens were listening to on the radio, and she made them available to all of her students. She encouraged going beyond the music that was printed on the page and being creative, employing improvisation. And even when I didn't play a song as well as Liberace, she would always make me feel like I did.

"She was a musical cheerleader, a teacher and a friend. Today, I'm still not a Liberace, but I am a songwriter because of Betty Hansen.

"I began writing songs when I was seventeen. Songs that reflected my background of classical, pop music and hymns, a unique combination. A dear friend of mine, Cara Norovich, loved to sing. Often I would gather a little band together which included my brother, Dave, on the drums, a few of his friends on guitar and bass, myself on the piano and Cara as lead vocal.

"Then I would take my prized reel-to-reel tape recorder,

which I received as a high-school graduation present, and record to my heart's content. Nothing in the entire world was so heavenly as making music with my friends. Recently I talked to Ellen, one of my dearest friends from high school. She said to me, 'I still catch myself singing those songs you wrote when we were in school.' And then she proceeded to sing some of them to me. The lyrics included, 'Why do I feel this way, what have you got to say of a heart that's no longer mine?'

"Although it was a painful experience to be reminded of some of my first songs, I was flattered that after some 25 years she remembered them. I was quick to say, 'Ellen, I'm sending you my new CD of songs so you'll forget those awful excuses for songs.'

"Whenever I ponder a lifetime of music I am drawn back to the advice fervently given to me by my maternal grandmother when I was a teenager. 'Linda, don't ever stop doing your music. Don't ever stop.' I have often thoughtfully reflected upon these words because through the years, and through my music, the most significant doors of my life have been opened, including meeting my husband, Dan.

"When contemplating my music I find it is amazing how a song will capture a particular moment or a special feeling, much like a frame of film in a camera will freeze a moment in time. Although I don't have a complete record of the songs I have penned over the years, little snatches of melody and rhymes remind me of how I felt and where my mind was during certain periods of my life.

"The first song I wrote was to the Lord and was entitled, 'You Came As Starlight' (which I still have a copy of). I then went through a period of 'pop' and love songs. Shortly after I had turned twenty-one, I wrote a song called, 'Where Do I Belong?'

"Although I do not remember much of it, I do recall the earnestness and the heartfelt cry from my heart to find my niche in life. It was a song about not wanting to go through

115

the motions of life, but to find my calling and especially to make a difference. To make a positive impact on the world before my brief period called 'life' was over.

"I am convinced God heard this plea from my heart because in just a couple of years afterward my life was pointed in a direction where I could indeed make a difference. Not just in my hometown, not just in my state, or country, but throughout the world! And, most importantly, I knew it wasn't my own choices that were guiding 'my ship.' It was undeniably God. And He didn't just change my direction in life. He changed ME!"

Childhood Church

Linda Shelton was baptized (sprinkled as a baby, as she put it) which was the tradition of the Lutheran Church and, at age thirteen, went through a series of church teachings in order to be "confirmed." The latter process was a reaffirmation of the baptismal vows.

The church itself reminded the young girl of a massive, beautiful cathedral with Gothic rounded ceilings several stories high and intricately painted. Huge pictures of Christ adorned the walls. There were strong pillars and a large altar that stretched nearly to the ceiling. These ornate trappings, combined with booming organ music, gave Linda's young mind the impression of a magnificent and solemn God.

She looked with respect upon a pastor attired in flowing robes who each Sunday proclaimed, "I, as called, ordained servant of the Lord Jesus Christ, forgive you your sins in the name of the Father, the Son and the Holy Ghost."

In Linda's searching mind, surely not everything was so concise. She pondered much about religion and the implications of what she was taught.

She remembered during one confirmation class when a fellow student told the pastor that the Bible isn't always easy to read. How could one be confident that they were rendering a proper interpretation?

The pastor delved into the simplistic to answer his student. He opined that salvation is simple. "The Bible says 'Believe in the Lord, Jesus Christ, and thou shall be saved,' he explained.

He voiced his conviction that believing is the most important part and it matters not if you don't understand the rest of the particulars. He also said that Bible study was not necessary for salvation. You only need read it if you're curious to know more about it. Linda noticed that the same attitude was evidenced at her church because there was no Sunday school, and no one brought a Bible to church services at that time.

Some of these things were perplexing to Linda, but her first real encounter with Jesus was at age fifteen. The Lutheran high school she was attending was having a special retreat and excitement ran high as she helped distribute literature about the services throughout the neighborhood. That night, several young people came forward to share their personal testimony. One especially moving story came from a young girl who had been involved in prostitution, but found victory through Christ.

A sweet presence filled the auditorium that night. It was palpable and Linda was caught up in its thrall. It was something she had never experienced previously and she wept with joy, as did many others who were attending. "That night I just knelt by my bed for the first time and just cried and prayed, and prayed and cried," she vividly remembers. "God was no longer Someone thousands of light years away from me in heaven. He was real. He was close and somehow I knew He really cared." And, "From that night on, my perception of God was changed forever."

Still, there was no premonition as to what was to come later, such as religious activities of global significance through 3ABN, and even a higher calling. In fact, life was stereotypical during her teens. Her earthly joys consisted of love for her constant companion, a white toy poodle named "Toodles," a circle of girl friends, dance and music lessons and utilizing those emerging skills by participating in the Racine Dance Theater.

There also prevailed a tomboy spirit, which was actually antithetical to her shy, lady-like demeanor that is so well known by her TV admirers today. For instance, she took pride in beating her brother, Dave, (who was a year younger) at various sports.

Linda's affection for her poodle, "Toodles" was indicative of her lifelong love of animals. Over the years, much to her parents' dismay, she had pet butterflies, caterpillars, grasshoppers, goldfish, gerbils, rabbits and assorted and sundry other diminutive critters. Her parents only allowed this wee menagerie as a compromise that there would be no larger creatures furtively prowling about the house.

But at age twelve "Toodles" was given to the family for a Christmas present. Toodles lived to a ripe old age and even made the move to southern Illinois later on. However, a black labrador turned out instead to be a "black sheep" of the family by digging holes in the walls and, on one ignoble occasion, devouring Linda's graduation cake, which became fair game after it had been left invitingly on the kitchen table.

The Sheltons' modern day pet, "Fluffy," entered the year two-thousand-two at age twelve, hale, hearty... and somewhat famous in the bargain. Fluffy was a stray pup that got lucky. Melody brought her to the house with the age-old imploration, "Can we keep him?"

To expedite the adoption, Danny swore it would be his dog and he would faithfully take care of her. Sure he would.

"That lasted about two days," Linda said. "Then she suddenly became my dog."

Although not formally under contract, Fluffy makes regular appearances on 3ABN and is recognized on several continents. That's because she has the run of the set and she has grown used to the theme music that begins the program.

It seems that to her that theme song means that Danny and Linda will be together and she wanders in to sit with them and sometimes even rewards the TV viewers with a smile. The Sheltons ignore the old show business adage that "kids and dogs will always steal the show."

Fluffy does pretty well for herself too, she gets fan mail and an occasional doggie treat from canine-loving viewers.

Although her childhood pets enhanced her early life, Linda's self-described "little cocoon of shelter and safety" was to be shattered abruptly at age eighteen, when her parents were divorced. Things fell apart quickly after that.

Linda's sister Cheri was living and working in Illinois at the time, and her mom moved to California. Linda was placed in an impossible situation at that time, thrust emotionally between a rock and a hard place.

Perhaps not understanding the full impact of the trauma she was inflicting on Linda, her mother told her in advance of her secret plans to leave home and move to the West Coast. Linda carried that terrible burden for a few weeks, torn between love and loyalty to both parents, and it scarred her permanently. The "secret" was so debilitating emotionally that Linda could not concentrate and dropped her college classes. This disturbed her father who, of course, didn't have a clue as to the real reason she dropped out.

When the end of her parents' marriage came, it was jarringly abrupt. Shortly after Linda's dad left for work one morning, a moving van appeared. The furniture was loaded and, along with Linda's mom, headed off to California. Along with it went half of Linda's heart.

Linda had been under the strain of this no-win situation for weeks and now had to face the final trauma alone, since her siblings were now gone. When her father came home from work to an empty house and a goodbye note there was only shock and stress in the aftermath. It lasted for weeks and through it all. Linda had the impression that her dad strongly held it against her that she had not confided that awful secret (that her mom was leaving) with him. Linda felt he interpreted her muteness on the subject as betrayal.

Unable to cope with her father's emotional state during the separation, Linda went to live with her grandparents for a year.

"At age eighteen, my security blanket had been jerked away and I had to grow up fast," Linda said. In a total about-face in lifestyle she went to work as a waitress...on the midnight shift! Her faith was bent, sorely tested, but never broken.

"I thought that everything solid in my life had been plucked up by the roots. I felt so incredibly numb in these circumstances that church attendance and much of my prayer life just slipped by the wayside," she remembers. "But in retrospect, when I look back at those years now, I realize that it was He who actually carried me through the ordeal."

The adjustment brought on by the parental divorce was difficult during that initial phase. Eventually, Linda's mother invited her to come out to the Golden State to live with her. Linda was happy about the move. She and her mom got together and lived in Westwood, a suburb of Los Angeles. Linda got a job with a "temp" agency working primarily in law offices.

But things were different than they were in their past life in Racine. Perhaps it was the fast pace of life in the City of Angels, which was so different from that of Racine. Linda began thinking of returning to the Midwest and her dad helped finalize the decision when he told her, "Honey, it's time to come home."

A New Life
As such family affairs are wont to change, things looked better a year later when her dad met a charming lady named

Mitzi, and the two were married. Her mother remarried too. Linda decided to return to college, namely the University of Wisconsin, at Milwaukee.

Joyously, her close circle of friends from high school was among the student body at the university, a fact that eased reentry into school life. She was an inter-arts major while also taking daily ballet classes. She also took creative writing and art classes and those latter skills that proved so vital to her today while sharing the stewardship of 3ABN. She has employed that knowledge specifically in such areas as set design, writing (print and song) and carving innovative new trails in religious radio broadcasting. Also, producing the daily "3ABN Presents" program and developing formats for new programming on the network. Collectively, she is the bottom-line producer for the network's three studios.

Enter romance! With a lovely young woman away from home and essentially fending for herself, the law of romantic inevitability soon came into play. A friend introduced her to a young man from West Frankfort, Illinois, a small former coal-mining town some four-hundred miles south of the college campus. Enamored of her, the geographical distance or any variance in social background did not deter the enthusiastic new beau, from showering Linda with flowers, letters and phone calls.

She hadn't dated much in her young life and was smitten by this sudden onslaught of attention. It was something new to the impressionable young coed and, coupled with the emotional vulnerability brought about by her then precarious family life, things evolved in a predictable manner.

Her heart which, as she put it, "was still under reconstruction," was won over by the long-distance persistence of the Prairie State suitor. After about a year of letters, calls and a long distance relationship, they were engaged to be married.

Youth, innocence and inexperience denied Linda a romantic road map to follow or to generally chart the potential pitfalls of any marriage. Then too, for all practical purposes, she was alone in the world and had no confidants to advise her on a matter of the heart of this magnitude.

Swept off her feet by the persistent southern Illinois swain, who rescued her during her emotional shipwreck, she was wed at age twenty-one. He was then nineteen-years-old. In fact, this period of Linda's life can be written in a "twenties" format. She was married at age twenty-one, had her daughter, Alyssa, at twenty-two, her son, Nathan, at twenty-three, was separated at twenty-four, and divorced at twenty-five. To round out that numerical scenario, she married Danny at twenty-seven.

After the difficulty accompanying the birth of Alyssa, the medical trauma described at the beginning of this chapter, more specialized care was called for. Therefore eleven months later, when the couple's son, Nathan, was born, Linda was considered a high-risk pregnancy. It was decided in advance that for the delivery she should travel to Racine, her hometown, where the medical facilities were much larger and specialists were available.

The birthing went without complications but the blessed event necessitated an unexpected six-week separation for the couple, an alienation that proved to be portentous. Things seemed to change after that.

The early years of their marriage were pleasant, happy ones. They had inherited a house and her husband was a hard worker and was a good provider. Things went well. But choice of religion, as it has with thousands of couples, proved to be divisive.

At first the couple did attend the SDA church together, and her husband was in attendance when Linda was baptized. Linda thinks that it was pressure from her husband's family members that ultimately changed his opinion about attending the SDA church. In fairness, it is pertinent to note that West Frankfort had a very small Adventist membership, thus there were misconceptions about just who the Adventists were and what they believed. In this void of knowledge, some people even believed they were a cult.

"From my perspective," Linda states, "the doctrines I learned from the Bible and the SDA Church were the answer to my quest to find where God wanted me to be. These doctrines presented God in such a light that I was drawn to Him like never before. I had peace in my heart that I had never previously experienced.

"When my family heard about the problems regarding my choice of church, they said, 'Well, just go to church on Sunday!' Although I tried to explain, they just didn't understand.

"But I knew I couldn't go back to where I had been before. God had come alive in my heart and it was because of the perspective found in the doctrines of the SDA Church."

Thus, it eventuated that her husband wanted Linda to leave the Seventh-day Adventists, and pressured her to do so. When given an ultimatum by her husband to leave the church, Linda could not, and their union was doomed to failure.

She certainly wasn't the first person to suffer greatly for religion. But it must have seemed like the weight of the world on the shoulders of a young woman hundreds of miles away from home in an argumentative family environment and under great stress. A situation compounded by having two babies, and bills to pay.

A doorbell rings

Life went on. Linda's transition from her early Lutheran upbringing to SDA came about during this general time period in her life, while she was still married and Nathan was two years old. One morning Linda was working around the house when she heard the doorbell ring. She had no way of knowing that this sound was a harbinger of wondrous things that would change the course of her life. Linda herself relates this very personal story eloquently:

"I was the happy mother of three-year-old Alyssa and two-year-old Nathan when I heard the doorbell ring one day. At the door was an acquaintance of mine, Debbie, the wife of my husband's stepbrother. I barely knew her. She was selling some beautiful religious books. Seeing these books reminded me of a book my loving great-grandmother had given me a few years earlier entitled, *'Your Bible and You.'* At the time she presented it to me, she said, 'Linda, I want you to have this book. It's a beautiful, wonderful book and I think out of all my relatives, you will appreciate it the most.'

"I had no idea until later that it was a Seventh-day Adventist book, I had never even heard the name Seventh-day Adventist until that day.

"That morning I had just returned from a fast food restaurant in town where I had purchased a breakfast containing eggs, biscuit and pork sausage. I had been preparing to have breakfast when the doorbell rang.

"Debbie showed me the books and I was impressed enough to purchase a set for my children. After those details were worked out we talked about other things and the conversation turned to the topic of clean and unclean foods. That launched us into a discussion about the health aspect of clean and unclean meats. My pork sausage sandwich specifically came under scrutiny.

"I rationalized it by saying, 'Don't you remember the vision that Peter had when God said he could eat anything?'

"She unhesitatingly got out her Bible and showed me the conclusion of the chapter, which proved to me that the text was talking about bringing the gospel to the Gentiles. We became so wrapped up in our discussion that she invited me to come to her next prayer meeting and I accepted the offer. In fact, I began attending church with her regularly and we became good friends.

"After she left, and still considering our conversation, somehow I just couldn't bring myself to eat that pork sausage that was still lying in the kitchen. I knew then that I had to further investigate these ideas. My diet, and, in turn, my entire life, were about to change dramatically."

Investigating, probing, studying… pondering truth has always been an integral part of Linda Shelton's philosophical makeup. When she was sixteen years old she began coming to the conclusion that her church just did not have all the answers about God that she so fervently sought. Something was missing, and an incident at that time marred her perception of the church.

She was attending a wedding where a minister was too drunk to say the prayer at the reception. Thus began a search for alternative enlightenment.

Linda began visiting other churches always trying to keep an open mind. Through the years this included Methodist, Nazarene, Baptist, non-denominational and even Mormon institutions. This quest often became an exercise in frustration.

"After each visit I would pray and ask God if this was the right one," Linda recalls of this emotional roller coaster of the highs of anticipation and the lows of disappointments. Searching and seeking, and not finding.

"Yet each time I felt God was lovingly urging me to continue my search and I was content to do so."

It was in this frame of mind and with an open heart that Linda attended that prayer meeting at the Seventh-day Adventist Church along with her new friend, Debbie, who had sold her the children's books.

Debbie had been raised in the church but had left it for several years. She had been back in the church for only a year when she befriended Linda. Linda calls her a "walking Bible." Through that Bible scholarship Debbie taught Linda things she had never heard before, even though Linda had been raised going to church regularly and attending Christian schools.

What an explosive testimony it would be here to relate bells ringing and sky rocketry announcing a thrilling conversion! But alas, it was not so. At least it didn't happen with such storybook immediacy.

"It (that first prayer meeting) was no different than many others I had optimistically attended," Linda says when telling about the prelude to accepting to the Seventh-day Adventist religious philosophy.

"That night I said my prayers and went to bed as usual. My husband was working a late shift, so I was alone. I had reached a state of the twilight of sleep when suddenly a high voltage electrical force filled the room. Fully awake now I sat up in bed, wondering about the buzz in my ears and the sheer intensity about the presence in the room.

"This strange phenomenon lasted about ten seconds and just as abruptly it was gone. I thought, 'God, what is it?'

"I lay back down, now wide-awake and filled with awe and wondering. Suddenly, the thought struck me, 'What did I do different today?'

"That was easy to determine. The only thing I had done differently was in attending the Seventh-day Adventist prayer meeting. I had not been particularly impressed and had left with the intention of not going back. Then the thought struck me— was this exhilarating experience actually God urging me onto the right course? After all, there are no set rules for locating a path to Him. The premonition was so strong that it made me determined to go back to the church the following Sabbath. Why not give it a chance?"

Why not indeed? The die was cast. It was a divine wind under Linda's sails that set her on course from which she has never deviated. And that resolve has made her positive strength and influence at 3ABN inestimable.

In the following paragraphs, Linda describes the process of that glorious transition:

"I learned the profound truth of the seventh-day Sabbath which changed my entire concept of God Himself. Up to that point in my life I had had a blurred vision of my perception of God and a teeter-totter opinion of Him.

"I was raised in a very formal church with a large pipe organ, tall ornate painted ceilings, with a pastor who came out with long flowing robes and walked slowly and distinctly as if he were marching in a long processional. He would climb several steps up to his pulpit and with a booming voice that echoed through the cold church, proclaim his message. Somehow this painted picture of God seemed to me as being this regal being who was to be revered, but one that remained aloof from His people.

"In addition I was taught, from my earliest childhood, that God loved me. But if I didn't accept Him and go to church, I would be damned and roast in the eternal fires of hell. When I thought about the love of God I would 'teeter.' But then when I thought about the eternal fires of hell, I would 'totter.'

"I guess I was brainwashed because although this kind of theology made absolutely no sense at all and was pretty scary, I accepted it. Perhaps because everyone else appeared to be convinced that this was correct. But now that I look back, the jury was still out as far as my opinion of God was concerned. And while the jury was out, I still prayed that God would lead me to the church where He wanted me to be

"I still read my Bible searching for that unknown 'something,' but I kept my conception of God at arm's length because my unstable conception of Him could not and had not fully gained my absolute trust.

"The Sunday mornings I remember went like this: My dad would call out, 'Time to get ready for church.'

"In my younger years, a family of five had to share one bathroom, so it was a real challenge for all of us to be ready on time. As a result, there were many times when a lot of fussing went on before we finally ended up in the car. Although by that point our family would barely be on speaking terms as a result of our mad scramble to get ready.

"We all smiled and greeted our friends and fellow church members and found our places in the pew. Church normally started on time and ended on time and in one hour we'd be on our way home. Often Sunday afternoons consisted of dad watching the football games and mom going shopping. This frequent experience again underscored in my mind the picture of a God that only required for us to weekly 'pay our dues.'

"Debbie showed me in the scriptures the fourth commandment, 'Remember the Sabbath Day to keep it holy.' Six days shall you labor and do all your work, but the seventh day is the Sabbath of the Lord your God and in it you shall not do any work, wherefore the Lord blessed the Sabbath and hallowed it (Exodus 20:8—11).

"Although I'd read these words before, through the spin of the teaching of others, I now just read the words for what they said.

"First of all God said 'remember.' He didn't say 'remember' in front of any other commandment so this one for some reason must be particularly important. Then it said to stop doing work on the Sabbath. Why? I discovered that God cherished my relationship with Himself so much that He set a standing 'date' every week so there would be no way that our relationship could evaporate! In addition, He blessed this 24-hour period and made it holy, completely different and separate from any other day, because He loved me and because He loved you! And because He wanted to fill our empty dark lives with JOY!' In your presence is fullness of joy; at your right there are pleasures forevermore (Psalm 16:11)'

"Wow! This was better than I could have hoped God would be. The darkness and confusion in my mind about God began to disappear and I was hungry for more. In fact, all I wanted to do was study the Bible. And when I did, my understanding of the words was radically different to what it was previously. I discovered it was as if I had never read the Bible before. I was beginning to truly fall in love with Jesus. The more I discovered about Him and His love for me assured me that I had to know still more.

"Debbie was so patient and understanding. I called her several times a day with this question or that one, and no matter what she was doing she would stop, get her Bible, and answer my questions, not with her own opinion but with a 'thus said the Lord.'

"I was happy. . . no I was exuberantly ecstatic with all I was learning! God really was fair and just and good, and worthy of my absolute trust. And my absolute service, too.

"Although my spiritual self knew this was real, I still had questions. If this was truth, why were so many people out there doing the wrong thing? I made an appointment with my pastor then to ask him some very direct questions.

"Debbie and I went at the appointed time to meet with him and the questions began; like why does the Bible say to remember the seventh day but this church remembers the first day? I was shocked when the pastor didn't pick up his Bible to refute the claim to worship on the seventh day. He lamely smiled, and said that since Jesus rose on the first day of the week it had become the tradition of the church to worship on Sunday instead.

"I pressed him with, 'But where is it in the Bible?' It took him about 10 minutes to say the change wasn't in the Bible. There were more questions and more resultant answers that were clearly based on opinion and not the Bible. I left that church office that day knowing that God had answered my prayer. He had clearly shown me where He wanted me to be.

"When I came to this realization it was obvious that I was at a crossroads. I knew which way God wanted me to go, but by then I also realized there would be a price to pay. There would be no more parties with my friends, because there was no more room for alcohol and frivolous fun times with my new walk with God.

"In addition, I already sensed that my friends and family were going to perceive me as weird. I was already somewhat of a misfit being a new transplant from out of state, but this would really draw some lines in the sand. For the period of a couple of weeks I wrestled with God about this decision. During this period I had several unmistakable answers to prayer and also a dream wherein I was baptized. In the dream it was a heavenly experience and I awoke feeling the presence of God around me. I knew then what I had to do.

"I called Debbie on Monday and my baptism was scheduled for that Wednesday evening in February of 1982. I didn't want to delay it allowing the devil to create in my mind more excuses why I shouldn't move forward with my decision to follow Jesus all the way. At that point I had no idea the price I would have to pay for this step in faith. But still yet I never had any regrets and I never looked back.

"It is said that confession is good for the soul, but hard on the reputation. I have to confess that one of the reasons that a Wednesday night baptism sounded so good was because much of the congregation wouldn't be there. I come from a long line of 'behind the scenes' folk.

"My parents strongly disliked public speaking. My grandmother didn't attend church because crowds made her too nervous. During high school and college if I discovered the class I was taking required my making a speech, I dropped the class. When I was finally out of school I remember heaving a sigh of relief with the thought that I would never have to worry about public speaking ever again. The Lord must have chuckled when he heard me thinking that!

"The one thing that distressed me about my new church home was that every Wednesday night when prayer meeting was coming to a close, those assembled would break up into small groups of four or five people where all would be expected to say a short prayer.

"Well, this was absolutely out of the question for me. I was raised in a church where it was taught that women were to keep silent in the church. Actually, that was one belief that I wanted to hang on to as tight as I could. It became my habit in those days that as prayer meeting was coming to a close I would exit stage left as quickly as possible, using the restroom as an excuse.

"This happened for many weeks until I heard the Holy Spirit tenderly speak to my spirit. 'I died on the cross for you. Couldn't you whisper a prayer for me?'

"I tried to convince myself that it wasn't important to do this, but finally I knew that this was indeed God speaking, and I had to obey.

"So one evening instead of 'exiting stage left,' I stayed. I was sweating, my mouth felt like sandpaper and my knees shook. But when I knelt to pray I finally did choke out a prayer without fainting. My words didn't come out right and my voice shook, but I left that night feeling like I had conquered the world, and I thanked God.

"Once I crossed that seemingly impossible hurdle, I realized that God had more in mind. My study of the Word of God started to lay a conviction on my heart. It was a conviction that grew and grew until finally I had to do something about it. That conviction was to 'pick up my cross and follow Him,' and to stop being a bench warmer. I wanted to do something to honor God and be a blessing. Shortly after I was baptized I gave my song-writing talent to the Lord and I decided that the songs I wrote from then on would be for God and for God only.

"I started writing a few songs and felt that God was impressing me to share them. The only thing harder than praying in public to me was playing the piano in public or singing in public. Now there was impossibility!

"Yet finally the conviction was so heavy one Friday night that I said, 'Lord, if you impress someone to ask me to do something in church, I will do it.'

"I think I kind of chuckled to myself because I knew this was impossible because no one at church even knew I played the piano or wrote songs. The very next day at church, Goldie Shelton, Dan's mom, (who was nearly a stranger to me at the time) came up to me and said, 'We'd like you to participate in our services. Don't you play the piano or some other instrument?'

"My jaw dropped. I couldn't answer for what seemed to be a full minute. In fact, I never did really respond at that point. I just went home with a big knot in my stomach. After a couple of weeks of reading the Bible and praying, I finally had the nerve to confess to Goldie that I did play the piano and, yes, I would play one of my songs if someone would sing it for me.

"Goldie's daughter-in-law, Cathy, was recruited and I discovered that she was just as scared to sing as I was to play the piano. I discovered the old adage 'misery loves company' was a true statement. The dreaded moment finally arrived when 'we' were the special music on that Sabbath morning.

"Although I wrote the song, the sweat pouring out of my hands made my fingers slide to some unusual notes. I hoped and prayed no one noticed my leg on the pedal of the piano shaking like I was driving over some railroad tracks. But somehow and someway I survived the dreaded moment. And it warmed my heart every time I knew I had been obedient to what I knew God had impressed me to do. As time passed, the challenges grew.

"Would I read a poem in front of the congregation? Would I teach the children's Sabbath school class? Each time, I felt in my own strength I could not and my flesh squeamishly crawled at the thought of another scary challenge. But much of the time my love for Jesus prompted my lips to form the word 'yes.' Truly, God comes to us many times in the form of people who ask, 'Will you...could you...would you, please?'

"It has taken a lot of years, but here is what I have learned, 'God says My grace is sufficient for you, for my strength is made perfect in weakness.' Then Paul responds, 'Most Gladly therefore will I rather glory in my infirmities that the power of Christ may rest upon me.' For many years I saw my fear and trembling and weakness as a curse. But now I see it as a blessing. My fear is the vital link to my dependence on God. My trembling is the vital realization that my flesh is weak, but He is strong. My weakness is the vital evidence that if I'm available, God will use me! Nature demonstrates to us that the smallest, weakest things of His creation declare His glory. A tiny leaf has a distinct message of our Creator God. The myriad tiny wild flowers in a field speak volumes about our God. And a little helpless newborn baby profoundly communicates to the world what words could not begin to explain about God.

"Am I ready to be small, so God can be big? You bet! Don't get me wrong. The Lord still sends challenges my way, challenges that send chills running down my spine. But I remind myself, I walk by faith and not by feelings. The greatest blessings lie in ignoring the flesh, leaning hard on those everlasting arms and getting the job done."

A date with destiny

One question that is always asked by people who talk about 3ABN and probably contemplated by multitudes of viewers at home at one time or another is, "How did Danny and Linda first meet?"

It is of course germane to the story of the television station, and this book would be sadly lacking without describing that event. Discussing that happy episode brings a pause in her activity and a smile to Linda's face. It didn't involve the romantic movie version that shows two people running across a flowering meadow toward each other, arms outstretched, and with music playing softly in the background.

Toss all that out... except for the music. Anyone who watches 3ABN or knows the Sheltons could easily predict that music would somehow be involved in their first meeting. Linda remembers that first meeting well.

"Dan and his family traveled around the country and sang on weekends so they were not in church very often," Linda recalls. "Even when I saw them occasionally, I was not introduced to them. Dan's wife was asked to sing at my baptism but she couldn't make it. When she declined, Danny came and sang instead.

"Even then, amid all the activity, I didn't get to meet him and thank him. I may have said hello to him at a camp meeting in September of that year, three months after his wife had been killed in an automobile accident, but the first time I actually met him was in November. By that time I was separated from my husband with a divorce pending. I was searching for a way to support my children and hoped music might play a part.

"Dan's brother, Kenny, was my Sabbath School teacher and I happened to mention to him that I was a songwriter. He suggested that I get in touch with Mike Adkins, a very successful songwriter and singer from West Frankfort, Illinois, and show him my work. Mike was very kind but told me that he usually sings only his own songs. He advised me to take my songs and show them to Danny Shelton.

"I mentioned this to Kenny and he arranged for me to go to Danny's house and get him to evaluate my songs. I was extremely nervous about going to Dan's house. I was shy and nervous and, looking back, maybe experiencing a partial state of 'shell-shock' considering the events of the last few years.

"Nevertheless, I collected my courage and showed up as scheduled. I even took my guitar since I had recently written a song that I had worked out on that instrument. Even though I don't play it I can manage to pick out a few chords, enough to serve the intended purpose. I also brought along songs that I could play on the piano, on which I had 10 years of lessons.

"I was really nervous when he opened the door. First of all, he was virtually a stranger to me. Also, I was not a soloist and here I was about to be sharing my songs alone in front of such an accomplished singer. I began to wonder why in the world I had gotten myself into this situation. When he came to the door he was very nice, very friendly. After a little small talk came the moment of truth.

"'Why don't you play one of your songs?' he said. Even though we were alone I asked him if he would turn his back while I sang. This startled him somewhat and he asked why. I explained that I was not a soloist and it was tough for me to just sing to him face-to-face in that small room.

"He replied, 'I hate to do this to you, but if you are really going to be a singer, and a songwriter, you'll have to get used to this. You might as well break in with me.'

"That was it, I was finished. My throat tightened up and I knew I couldn't even speak, let alone sing. I was strangling and was about to use sign language to tell him to forget it that I was leaving immediately. At that very moment the doorbell rang and Danny excused himself to answer it. While he was talking to whoever was at the door I uttered an impassioned prayer.

"I pointed out to Him that He knew just how frightened I was and asked if He would help me get past this ordeal. By the time Danny came back into the room I had gathered my wits about me enough to plunge in, for better or for worse.

"I began my song and managed to get through the whole thing without passing out. When I finished he looked at me for a few seconds. I'm having anguished fantasies about him grabbing me and the guitar and throwing us out the door, but he simply said, 'Yes, that was good. Do you have another song for me?'

"A feeling of relief flooded over me. I'd survived the first song! Then I went over to an old friend, the piano. I'm much more comfortable at that instrument, and I played him another of my songs. When I finished that, he was very genuine when he said that he really liked that song. By then I was relaxed and comfortable with him and we had a nice visit."

Linda's story is moving, but she leaves out a classic piece of Danny Shelton humor when she tells about that initial encounter when she asked him to turn his head while she sang. It's no surprise that the meeting of these two people involved their mutual lifelong enthusiasm for gospel music.

In Danny's own words he recalls that first get together also, with one humorous addition:

"One of my sister-in-laws came to me and told me that there was a young lady who recently began attending our church, and who had been writing some songs. Since I had been working with a song publishing company in Nashville, she wanted me to hear some of her songs. My sister-in-law added that the woman, in her early twenties, was almost painfully shy but really wanted to have her work evaluated.

"I said that was fine, and we made an appointment for Linda to drop by my house the next week. I had never met her before but had seen her on a few occasions. When she showed up she had her little guitar with her and we had a piano at the house.

"We got through the awkward introductions and I saw

she was scared to death and tried to get her to relax a little. When poised to play she asked me to turn around so she could render an audition. I asked her why the unusual request and she replied that she could never possibly play or perform if someone was watching her. I told her that here she was visiting my house, at her own request, for the first time, and I had never met her and therefore I could not turn my back on her. When she asked why, I said that for all I know she might be a mugger.

"This preposterous comment had the desired effect and evoked a nervous giggle, almost a full-fledged smile. Failing in establishing the 'no-peek' condition, Linda plunged forward nearly breathless with apprehension. It seemed by her disposition that her whole world was on the line, but her intensity and love of God, through her music, radiated through.

"Many people who are inexperienced song writers send me tapes of their music and it is rare to find the genuine article. But it was obvious that Linda had that wonderful quality exclusive to the gifted creators of music and words. I couldn't believe the talent that she has. She's very gifted musically. We became friends and collaborated on a few songs we took to Nashville and eventually we started traveling to churches to sing together. Our friendship blossomed and after a few years we were married."

Chronologically, that matrimonious event followed closely on the heels of the night that Danny had the vision, which was the precursor to the unfolding drama of 3ABN.

On Saturday, November seventeenth, nineteen-eighty-four, the couple was preparing for a drive to Farmington, Missouri, where they were going to sing. They packed the automobile and gathered the kids up and headed west, toward the mighty Mississippi River. It was very early morning and still dark out. After the usual buzz of idle conversation that goes with the excitement of starting a journey, a silence descended in the car as they ate up the miles.

A warning should be issued here to those readers who are romantics and foresee Danny whipping the car over to the shoulder of the road, leaping out, dropping to his knees, and begging for Linda's hand. It was a tad subtler.

Breaking a long silence, Danny calmly said, "Let's get married."

A bit startled, she replied, "What? When?"

He said right away, but she pointed out that there were a few legal details, not the least of which were getting blood tests and a license.

"Okay, as soon as possible then," the proposaler agreed.

Linda said yes, but to say there was no misgivings would be inaccurate. She loved Danny dearly, but she had been through a bad time in a previous marital commitment and had an understandable reservation. Marriage to each other was not a new idea to the couple. They had discussed marriage in general terms during their relationship.

But Danny, too, had been reluctant to press the matter of the heart, but only on an economic level. He was concerned about being able to support and provide for an expanded family. His early life had taught him the importance of financial stability.

As far as timing was concerned, he later revealed that during that drive the Lord had impressed him confidentially that, "You might as well marry her and get the honeymoon over with because I have a lot of work for you to do."

By the end of the trip the vows to wed were made. Years later, on a 3ABN broadcast, Danny described this trip and pointed out that it was practical to get married at that time; that it would be convenient because of the upcoming trip to California, which could double as a honeymoon.

Linda, on the set with him, cut in and protested that, "That's not very romantic to describe it that way."

138

Employing logic and always cool, Danny replied to her, and to a global audience, "It worked, didn't it?"

It did work. But Linda, due to previous life experiences, developed an eleventh hour uneasiness the night before the wedding. She phoned Danny to express her concern. He didn't get angry or upset. He just told her that foremost, he wanted her to be happy and safe. If she determined that this marriage wasn't right, so be it. But either way, he wanted her to know that she would always remain his best friend in life. This melted her heart and broke down all doubts. They made this lifetime marital pledge and have never looked back.

Dan's cousin, Marilyn Thomas, quickly planned the wedding, with most of the family present, and they had a small reception. They were married November twenty-fifth, nineteen-eighty-four, at Dan's brother Tommy's church, in Pershing, Illinois. Their dear friends, Hal and Mollie Steenson stood up with them with Hal performing the ceremony.

On a sad note, in the first week of June in nineteen-eighty-five, Linda went to the doctor with some "female problems." The physician basically played it down as "no big deal."

During the last week in July she began showing symptoms of poison oak on her arms. Linda had previously been through a severe bout with that rash infliction. Forewarned is forearmed. Linda sought medical help immediately.

"The only doctor I had was a gynecologist," she said. "So I went there. My regular doctor wasn't there, so when the substitute doctor looked at my chart, he asked me if I was still having the female problems. I told him that yes, I was. He replied that I was to go right down and have an ultra-sound to determine what was wrong. After the test, they didn't tell me what they had found, but I was surprised when they took me for a pregnancy test, which came out positive. I was then scheduled for emergency surgery the next morning, for tubal pregnancy. We thought this was a real miracle that the poison oak popped up when it did, because many women die when a pregnancy of this type ruptures and they hemorrhage. I was very near this stage.

"For the most part though, things went very well. Dan and I were happy as newlyweds and the children were happy too. Melody and Alyssa often played 'Barbies' together while Nathan was thrilled with a home that had a swimming pool and a playhouse. The early miracles began unfolding leaving us in total awe of how the Lord was leading. But in those early years I developed an inner turmoil that threw a wet blanket on an otherwise blissful time in our lives. Dan invited some of his family to participate in 3ABN early on and they had a lot of previous experience in such areas as construction, finance, organizing books, etc. Therefore, their job descriptions and responsibilities naturally evolved based on their individual skills.

"Dan's previous experience had been with singing and sharing during services, so the television work was a natural transition for him. Eventually it dawned on me that surely I must draw on my own experience if I were to discover where I was to fit in the ministry. Could I use my ballet, or my art lessons? What about my song writing? Where in the world did I fit in this ministry?

"As the weeks turned into months and the months evolved into the first year I still didn't have any answers. I hate to acknowledge it but yes, I began to have misgivings and wonder if God had made a mistake in choosing me for this job.

"I remember tearfully sharing with my husband how I felt. It seemed like each person involved had experience that contributed positively to his or her calling as it pertained to our work, but I didn't.

"I asked Dan, 'What am I supposed to do for 3ABN?'

"Dan couldn't hide the fact that he didn't really have an

immediate answer either, but he mustered up, 'Honey, you can write the thank you cards!'

"Well, let me tell you, that particular 'calling' didn't exactly sweep me off my feet. And besides, I had absolutely no clerical skills and had no idea where to begin. My typing prowess at that point was about three words per minute. But, I decided that if God wanted me to write thank you cards, I was going to write the best thank you cards that I could. So that's exactly what I did. I had many a tearful battle with 'my enemy' the typewriter, and file folders and receipts, but I was determined to do the best that I could, for Jesus. But I still prayed about my inner turmoil.

"I was indeed the proverbial 'duck out of water.' And these were feelings that I often struggled with in those early years. All the things with which I was comfortable had to be laid aside while I struggled with duties that made me hugely uncomfortable. We traveled from church to church singing and doing church services, but who would have guessed that I struggled with learning to sing that alto part and that inwardly I cringed at the thought of being in front of a crowd of people? At least with dancing I never had to say anything. I never had to get every note right while singing with a group.

"But if anyone ever looked over my shoulder at those services they would find that I wasn't just holding my Bible promise book, I was clinging to it. I read those promises and I prayed, and I obeyed despite my knees knocking and my mouth feeling like a cotton ball. And just about the time I felt that I had the congregation of people fooled someone would come up to me and say, 'Boy, you looked like you were scared to death up there.'

"Needless to say, it was intimidating singing with Dan and Melody, who were professionals. That's why my pleadings with the Lord were so heartfelt.

"I prayed, 'Lord, please help my voice! Please give me some vibrato! Lord, I beg you to help me to learn to pick up parts in songs as easily as they can. I need this gift to do my job better.'

"I practiced with tapes over and over again. I even took a few voice lessons and in two years I began to notice there was some vibrato in my voice! And praise God, I began 'hearing' parts when I listened to songs.

"One summer morning, while in a frustrated state of mind, I landed on a swing in our back yard. I was coming off an emotional battle with that despised foe, the type-writer, and it was in that state that I cried out to God, 'Lord, I just need to know. What is it? What is it I'm really supposed to be doing? It seems like every one else just naturally fits into their responsibilities. But where do I fit?'

"At that moment I flipped open my Bible and my eyes landed on one verse. It said, 'Thus speaketh the Lord God of Israel saying, Write thee all the words that I have spoken unto you in a book,' (Jeremiah 30.2).

"At that moment I knew that God was speaking not to Jeremiah, but to me. It was no accident, no coincidence, but it was the voice of God that grabbed my heart at that moment. I'd never written a book in my life and, truthfully, I had no desire to write a book. But at that moment my heart was flooded with peace and I was content to go back and write my thank you cards.

"As the months went by my painful strokes on the type-writer got a little faster and more accurate. And the number of thank you cards increased. Finally it reached the point where I could no longer manually handle the cards myself but we were not yet financially at the point where we could hire help.

"Thus my 'cards' evolved into a monthly newsletter. Initially, I made copies on our small copying machine and handled all the mailing myself. But eventually the numbers grew to where we had to take the newsletter to a local printer. Later, we were able to get a computer and I learned to handle the desktop publishing myself.

"Many times when it came time to do a newsletter I would sit in front of the keyboard with a total writer's block, blank about what to write. At those times I would pray, 'Lord, you know I can't do this but I know you can. So please do Your thing. I'm available to help!'

"Then the words would begin to flow so fast and furious that the pages would fill up and I'd have a lot left to say that would have to be saved for another time. God really taught me some important lessons through my writing. First of all, He taught me that when I can't do it, He can! He also showed me that we really can 'do all things through Christ, who strengthens us.' And he taught me that no matter what we give Him if we give Him our best He will bless it.

"Someone once said, 'God doesn't call the qualified, He qualifies the called.'

"That little newsletter has grown over the years from a couple of hundred per month to over one-hundred-fifty-thousand per month in two-thousand-two. And, what's more, I have developed a resolve which makes the larger writing assignments, like the scripts and magazines I write for 3ABN, seem like small tasks. And it is all because I said 'yes' to the call to do those thank you cards.

"In the offices of 3ABN there are a couple of very thick 'books.' These books contain newsletters that date back almost to the beginning when I first began writing them. God certainly knew what He was talking about!

"In the earlier years when our numbers were few, we all had to wear a variety of hats for 3ABN. I mainly wrote the newsletters, handled those 'cards,' answered mail, decorated sets, acted as the secretary to our board of directors and was in charge of scheduling for our studio. This meant I found guests for our 'Presents' program and I also developed formats for new programs for the network. Since there was so much to do, many times some things fell through the cracks.

"What mostly suffered in my responsibilities at such times was scheduling the studio. But I learned that God was the One who was really doing that scheduling. I knew that because over and over again, when a day would come up where there was no guest for a '3ABN Presents,' someone would walk through the door who, as it turned out, couldn't be a better choice as a guest. And wouldn't you know, they'd be more than happy to go in and put a little powder on and do a television program. And somehow it seemed that these impromptu shows would always make the best programs.

"When we began to do '3ABN Presents,' once again I was reminded that I was still a 'duck out of water.' Words did not flow out of my mouth easily like they did for my husband.

"When I shared this grief with Dan he would say, 'Honey, just give a try for fifty programs and by then you will find if it will get easier for you.'

"Fifty programs went by and it still wasn't easy. Then Dan told me, 'Honey, you just need to give it a better chance and wait for one-hundred programs to go by.'

"A hundred programs went by and it still wasn't easy. In fact, it was so 'not easy' that one summer I lost ten pounds from beating a path to the bathroom before the program began. That added to the fact that I was already 'skinny!' Finally we reached a point where we had done three-hundred-fifty programs and I was still very uncomfortable with those unrelenting staring cameras. Finally it was D-Day for me. I had reached my limit.

"I went to the Lord and said, 'God, I can't do it anymore. If you don't perform a miracle in me today, right now, I'm going to have to quit. I've given it my best shot and that hasn't been good enough. You have to take over.' Inwardly I threw up my hands in despair and gave up.

"The next day was a new day for me. Overnight God

144

had changed me. Immediately, I was given a peace about the programs and they became easy for me, even fun to do. I began to actually look forward to them and on camera words began to flow without reservation. Oh, I knew this wasn't me. It was God! And a few thousand programs later, God is still in control!

"No one ever taught us how to do it. But now, as I look back, it is nothing short of a miracle that we were able to develop twenty-four-hour-a-day programming when the resources in our church only offered a handful of programs. We had to throw typical and standard business practices out the window to make it work. And the bottom line was we found individuals, laymen, ministries and simply people who loved Jesus, and we put them on camera, free of charge.

"Very few people who felt they had 'something to say' had any money 'to say it with.' So we invited them to come in and promote their ministries on the air. We praise God that many ministries that are now represented on the network say that their ministries are really prospering because of the exposure given to them on 3ABN. And many new ministries were developed because of the responses from their exposure on 3ABN.

"In two-thousand-two, 3ABN/America had grown to three studios, a production truck that is on the road full time and a radio network that has three studios to record new programs. The operation and scheduling of these studios, as well as developing new programming still ultimately falls on my shoulders but I, in turn, place these responsibilities on some much bigger Shoulders. And yes, I can peacefully go to sleep every night knowing that those 'Everlasting Arms' are holding 3ABN. And I thank God every day for the great team of workers that He has called to 3ABN who represent the 'nuts and bolts' of making programming happen.

"But I have to go back to those 'Thank You' cards one more time. I've learned through my experience with those cards that when you accept God's small challenges, the big ones that land on your plate may seem large at the time, but they shrink quickly as new challenges come forth. When we are faithful with the seemingly small insignificant tasks, God gives us the ability to handle the larger challenges. And His ability can surely handle them.

"I often contemplate the road where God has taken me. It hasn't been an easy road but looking back I know it was the right road and the best journey for me. I was put in a place where I extraordinarily, desperately needed God. (And that's the best place to be!) And the larger the cavern of need grew in my heart, the more I discovered that God was faithful to fill it. Through it all I've learned to trust more and lean hard on those 'everlasting arms.' And God isn't finished with me yet! There are still challenges; there are still many new opportunities that make me 'shake in my boots.' But I'm aware now, I know that the faithful God of my past will take me through whatever I need, and to wherever I need to go."

Goodbye, Dad

One other very special story about Linda Shelton, specifically her music, is significant to this chapter of her life. For some time she, Danny, and Melody, had been traveling and singing together, and they performed as a trio on 3ABN in the early days. But once 3ABN was launched to satellite, unfortunately the song writing and singing had to be moved to a back burner to accommodate the demands of the ministry.

After ten years of marriage, one day Linda shared with Dan that the Lord had really impressed her that they should put some songs that they had written on a CD. He readily agreed and the massive work that goes into such a project began. Musicians were gathered at Nashville, songs selected and other imperatives, not the least of which was fitting it into their busy schedules. They finally got the album finished, much to the delight of their myriad fans and viewers of 3ABN. But this particular album, *"A Picture of His Love,"* has always been special to Linda for another reason too. That is the special effect that it had on one particular person. That person was her father.

"The Lord had impressed me to do this tape with Dan. We recorded it in August, and in November of that year we received the early test tape that was almost finished. I sent a copy of that unfinished tape to dad," Linda said.

"He was actually enthralled with the music. Nothing I had ever done in my life had made such an impact on him. Every time I telephoned in the following weeks he would tell me how that music and the words had touched his heart."

The following January, Linda's father died suddenly of a heart attack at age sixty-one. There was no question in anyone's mind that divine guidance had moved her to send him the early tape, even though it was unfinished. Those closest to him say that the music most assuredly had helped prepare him to sleep the sleep of death.

"There is no doubt in my mind that he was the most spiritual and closest to God that he had ever been in his life," Linda said.

Although a Lutheran believer, he was eased to his eternal rest by this 3ABN offering. So much so, that Linda's stepmother, knowing how much her husband loved the tape, gave a copy of the CD to everyone who attended the funeral. Had Danny and Linda not made the tape when they did, her dad would have never heard it.

This factor also had an influence on Linda's personal singing career. Over the years she and her father had held lively discussions about religion. He was of staunch German descent and Lutheran, and whenever Linda would approach subjects like the Sabbath, he just didn't want to hear it. But in the end, her music melted his heart and moved him closer to her and to God. In awe of this wonderment, Linda felt that if her work could do that, she should follow God's lead and move further in that musical direction.

Linda Shelton pointed out that, "this chapter would not be complete without extending my deepest appreciation to our children for their support of 3ABN, especially in the early years. Melody was thirteen when Dan and I married, and for two years she traveled and sang with us in the church services all over the United States to promote the sprouting ministry of 3ABN. She was a trouper! She then went to academy for the next couple of years."

"Alyssa and Nathan were only ages four and five when Dan and I married, but their lives changed quite dramatically with all of the travel and the many house guests we had as the ministry was growing. But they never complained and were happy children which made it so much easier to do what we had to do for 3ABN. Alyssa and Nathan also sang and participated in the church services in the early years, and many were drawn to support 3ABN when they saw us working together in ministry as a family. For a couple of years I homeschooled them at 3ABN and when they were finished with their school work, they helped in the mailroom and did little chores around 3ABN. And they were happy to do it because they felt this was what they could do for Jesus. Their happy, supportive attitudes were priceless in the early years and contributed greatly to the construction of a worldwide ministry.

"Thank you Melody, Alyssa and Nathan. . . truly 3ABN exists today because of your constributions."

Chapter 12

Late in the year two-thousand, 3ABN aired a program that heralded a significant milestone of sorts. In America there has always been a special aura surrounding the sixteenth birthday. An atmosphere of sweetness often accompanies it. For the Sheltons and the 3ABN family this particular airing was indeed a "sweet sixteen" celebration. Sixteen years of "Mending Broken People."

For the Sheltons it was incredible to think that sixteen years had passed since the initial vision visited upon Danny in the middle of that long-ago night. A visitation that changed his life and those of many others. They couldn't begin to count the ensuing miracles and there was no doubt in their minds that 3ABN was not a ministry that was made with human hands. Rather it had been and continues to be fashioned by a God of all-consuming love.

The "sixteenth program" was significant in one respect. It featured not a fanfare and seventy-six trombones and hallelujah chorus; rather, the Sheltons giving a quiet and dignified recounting of the rich history of 3ABN, intertwined with a nature walk depicting scenes of natural beauty.

Also in the opening segment was E.T. Everett gracing the piano, in accompaniment to the Sheltons' songs. E.T., and her husband, Dave, have been musically associated with the Sheltons on and off for about fifteen years. Their newest role is operating the magnificent new Sound Center located at the 3ABN Complex.

In a moving discussion Danny recalled how they began operation with just "a few of us." Linda agreed that they all wore many hats and told of how she would answer the mail, design sets (her forte), schedule programs and more. All, as Danny pointed out, "For four dollars per hour, and at first, no salary at all."

At the airing of that program, 3ABN was approaching a staff of one hundred workers.

Those early days included primitive operating conditions compared to the modern, sophisticated operation of today. During November, nineteen-eighty-six, 3ABN finally went on the air; the actual studios were not yet completed. While the finishing touches were being applied to the formal studios, there was a little building called the "remote shack," about ten-foot by sixteen-foot in dimension. Smaller than the average office, it had noisy transmitters inside and the crew put in tape machines to broadcast with. The uplink dish had already been installed.

On Thursdays, on a part time basis at first, they would fill the little shack with people and shoot a satellite signal of tapes of other ministries, such as George Vandeman and John Carter, which were sent to them.

"As soon as we'd go up in the air, we didn't even know if anybody was watching or not," Danny explains.

"We knew people would surf the channels and figured maybe they'd land on us by chance and watch for awhile. We decided to test this theory by making a free offer. We'd offer a little book, 'Steps To Christ,' free to anyone calling the number on the screen. We were stunned when the phone began to ring immediately.

"We could barely hear it ring because of the internal operating noise in the shack so we had to take the phone outside the shack to answer it. There we were, shivering in the brisk fall weather, taking calls and acting like a network.

"We were so amateurish that we stacked the tapes we were broadcasting on cardboard boxes while we weren't using them. Whatever ministry we were sending out, we would superimpose over it a little promotional tape we had made in Nashville. It proclaimed, 'You are watching 3ABN,'

150

and the telephone number.

"Here people were calling in thinking they were contacting a huge television network and we would pick the phone up and hand it out the door so someone could jot down the caller's address for us to send their free gift.

"We went two hours on Thursday in the beginning. Then we began going a little more time until April of nineteen-eighty-seven, when we started broadcasting eighteen-hours-per-day."

Linda pays great tribute to those early volunteer workers who helped make it all happen. Amazingly, to this day, many people still volunteer to work for 3ABN and provide tremendous support.

"The drive of our workers then was exemplary," Linda said. "We didn't have the finances to hire professional television people. Even Danny and I would not draw any salary until much later when the network was on its feet. So we sought out young people who had graduated from high school and had a lot of drive and ambition, and taught them the computers and the equipment. They would pick up on it quickly, as young people can do.

"As we began to grow they would become more quality conscious. They would watch other television shows and pick up on the lighting and camera angles. They would study the sets and backgrounds, and graphics, things the average viewer would not even be aware of. These are precious memories to Dan and me. They would stay until the early hours of the morning working on the lighting, the sets and graphics, using the information that they had picked up.

"They wanted to make our programs the best that they could be. It was inevitable that the quality of our programs increased because of the drive and energy that our workers had.

"One special aspect of all of this," Linda recalled, "is that many of these people who worked so hard, without being

151

driven by monetary compensation, were not even Adventists (nor are all the workers at 3ABN today). But they had a vision of what we were trying to accomplish and a desire to do God's work.

"I remember when we first got started and were so inexperienced that we had people come in and light our set, and when we did our programs, and our programs were an hour long, the lights would drive the temperatures on the set well over ninety degrees. By the time the program was over, we would be sweating profusely. That was just because we were inexperienced. But some of those first volunteers and workers, those early pioneers, are still with 3ABN today."

There was one other charming characteristic that Linda possessed during those early years of 3ABN. A shyness that made her going in front of the camera (on the air) unthinkable, in her own mind. "The Lord had given Dan a dream early on where he saw me in front of the cameras reading from what appeared to be some books as well as the Bible," said Linda. "This is the one part of the 3ABN story I couldn't accept. I knew I could never be comfortable in front of cameras and crowds."

This show stirred deep memories in Linda, which she revealed at that time, and for this book:

"Someone once said that other books are given for information, but the Bible is given for our transformation," Linda explains. "Let me tell you in a nutshell how God's Word has changed me personally. About sixteen years ago my husband felt impressed by the Lord to build a television station that would reach the world with the Three Angels Message of Revelation. I was really excited about that, but during the two years it took to get the building finished and get the big uplink dish installed I had great plans of doing a lot of wonderful things for 3ABN behind the scenes, because I was definitely a behind-the-scenes person.

"I enjoy decorating and touched on this skill in college

so I was involved in decorating the very first '3ABN Presents' set and I couldn't wait to learn to run a camera and all of those neat things that transpire behind the scenes. Even though I was very vocal to my husband about staying behind the scenes, he would just smile and say, 'Uh huh, sure honey.'

"Then the time finally came when we were going to begin videotaping programs. The set was finished, the cameras were ready and the moment of truth was at hand.

"Danny came up to me and said, 'Honey, I know you said you wanted to stay behind the scenes, but would you reconsider?' I told him absolutely not because I can't talk. I get too nervous. I explained further that it is just not my calling.

"He looked at me in that understanding way of his and said, 'Well, I just feel that with you sitting next to me that I can do my job better.'

"What could I say? He got me when he said that. You see, I knew even then that the Lord used my husband when he spoke and if just sitting there helped him do it better, maybe I could do that much to help to help him and Him. But I issued fair warning. . . don't you dare ask me to say anything.

"After the first dozen or so absolutely terrifying programs Dan asked me if I would consider reading just a Bible text on the program. The thought was horrifying to me and I told him there's no way I could do it, that I would surely choke to death right there on the set. But this time, the Holy Spirit stepped in and convinced me so I conceded. But made it clear that it would be a brief verse. I did so for a dozen programs and that extended to four dozen and then one hundred programs and a thousand.

"I began to determine that the Bible texts I had selected to be a blessing for the audience really blessed me, more than I could ever say. God carried me over and over again. For those among you who have been extremely shy and bashful like I was, you'll know what I mean when I say this. But I would read a text and maybe make a comment and reach a point where the breath was gone and I couldn't utter another word if I tried. I was fearful that there would be a glaring pause in the show and everybody would be staring at me. But it would always come to pass where Dan, or a guest, would pick up the thought and keep the conversation going so no one ever knew of my dreadful predicament.

"God literally carried me moment by moment through those early programs and I learned a great truth from all of this. Many times the gifts that seem so obvious to other people are in God's opinion just secondary gifts because He wants to take us out on a limb where it's just you and Him, and no one else. Because out there He can reveal to you that with Him, all things are possible.

"With me, under these on-the-air conditions, God's Word was a critical part of the heart surgery He did on me. That is because I spoke the Words until they took root in my heart. I went out on a limb with God and saw that He really meant what He said. And that's what He wants for all of us."

Linda arrived at this poignant attitude after a long soul-searching trek through the minefield of varying viewpoints of different religions. She was raised in the belief that miracles were and are a thing of the past.

"Being a part of 3ABN has strengthened my faith, broadened my scope and vision of God and given me a desire to work for Jesus for the rest of my life!" Linda said. "He is real, He's wonderful and He's worthy of our best efforts!"

Surrounding the sixteenth anniversary show, Danny and Linda traced the network's history down to a very basic level. They felt. . . and they unfailingly know to this day. . . that the Lord reveals to them some Bible principles, which He wanted to be a part of the basic structure of the ministry.

154

It was foundational at 3ABN, then and now. The Sheltons believe that by following those biblical standards it allows Him to bless the network abundantly, more than they could ask for or expect.

They gave an example of such chapter and verse in their *Catch the Vision* magazine:

"Now these are the commandments, the statutes and the judgments which the Lord, your God, commanded to teach you... Hear therefore, O Israel, and observe to do it, that it may be well with you and that you may increase mightily. . . . And you shall write them upon the posts of your house and on your gates." (Deut. 6:1, 3-9.)

The Sheltons knew that this meant in God's book there is no such thing as a "closet Christian." Despite advice to the contrary, they kept the faith. During the early days of 3ABN so-called professionals warned them that there was no way a network could air one-hundred percent Christian programming and survive.

"You had better mix it with light comedy shows like '*Leave it to Beaver,*' or '*I Love Lucy,*'" they were warned.

But Danny replied that, "God knows what He's talking about! There is not enough time left on this earth for simply entertaining the public."

They embraced the proposition that the message was pure. That even in the wee hours of the morning, someone out there is searching for God. Someone is searching for the truth, which would set him or her free. Therefore, they reasoned that partial truth (such as fragmented religious broadcasting) would offer only partial freedom. It became the policy, the unfettered belief, that 3ABN would resolutely follow the shining example of Jesus, to always stand tall for the straight message with, "lots of love mixed inside."

This was a defining moment in the history of 3ABN and that credo was as binding on the network's sixteenth birthday as it had been from its inception. And it remains so today.

Indisputably, there is one exceptional, unprecedented quality that makes 3ABN unique; they extend a bridge, a helping hand to other ministries by giving them priceless on-the-air exposure that they could never otherwise afford.

In an age of "beg-a-thon" television, when some networks preach wall-to-wall, "Go to those phones, send us money!" 3ABN will not only give center stage to other ministries, but will urge their own viewers to support them too, "When we give and bless others, God gives and blesses 3ABN."

An even more compelling example of this mission purpose, this operating procedure, is found in the Bible principle, "Give, and it shall be given to you, good measure, pressed down, and shaken together and running over shall men give into your bosom. For with the same measure that you mete withal it shall be measured to you again," (Luke 6:38).

Without question, that belief has opened the floodgates of Heaven to 3ABN. Through generous contributions and love gifts the network has thrived and in return has given back enormously, throughout the world. This writer has personally witnessed wondrous things both near and in far lands where a better way of life has been brought about by 3ABN, in turn, through the generosity of their viewers. Through letters and other communications received at the studio it is learned that inspired viewers also independently participate in such good work in a secondary manner, carrying 3ABN's philosophy through word and deed. This tenant not only keeps on working for 3ABN, but it grows inexorably bigger each day, like a circle of water expanding from a rock thrown into a pond. A poetic rock of ages, perhaps.

Danny explained how giving can open all good doors in life. "You can't out-give God," he said. "The network does not operate on standard business principles where you give a service and you get paid for it."

He related an example that took place during that time frame, of a production by citing a series by evangelists Kenneth Cox and Samuel Thomas, Jr. The satellite airtime cost for the series was completely sponsored by 3ABN.

Danny explained that he followed the Word. "God said and God led," he said.

Even though the expenses to grant camera time to other ministries are enormous, Shelton clarifies why he does it. "That's where faith comes in. We believe in using what God has given us to help others in ministry. Obviously, this is a principle where discretion and God's leading must be used, but we believe in promoting other worthy ministries so they can prosper and grow in their localities. Working for God is a family thing."

Yet one more Biblical reference was brought to the fore during the 16th birthday celebration. "For do I now persuade men, or God? Or do I seek to please men? For if I yet pleased men I should not be the servant of Christ," (Galatians 1:2).

"We at 3ABN have been blessed in that when God moves, we can move too," Danny said. "We don't have to struggle through ten committees and a lot of red tape to make something happen. Someone once said, 'committees take minutes but lose time.' "

Danny and Linda concluded their 16th anniversary celebration with a simple thought to their viewers, "Why are we all here as the family of God? We are here to demonstrate to the world that God's ways work. So we need to stand on the promises of God to have His promises work for us."

One very interesting story took place in two-thousand-one. I enter it in this particular place in the book simply because it is what we call in journalism a "stand alone" piece. And this is as good a place as anywhere to relate it. Danny shrugs it off as no big deal, but I think the story has great worth and certainly is worthy of the telling of it.

In fact, at my urging, Danny himself tells it in the following paragraphs:

"We had purchased a new riding lawnmower the previous fall. It is a right nice one, twenty-four-horsepower and a pretty green color. I have about three acres that I mow with it. There are some folks in our town that I have known over the years, but have never been close to them.

"Let it suffice to say that, because of our lifestyles, we live in different worlds. When I would drive past their house, I'd wave in a friendly manner and they would return the distant greeting in a like manner. One day, as I drove past their house, I was moved with a strong impression to go home and get my lawnmower and give it to my neighbor.

"I began to think about this. I thought that this was too weird. I have had many odd things happen over the years and for the most part always followed my instincts. Most often these things were explainable later on, and turned out very well. I'm not one of these guys who hear voices all the time. In fact, I'm leery of people who are guided totally by impressions. That's because sometimes people like that allow impressions to override the Bible and they do strange things in churches.

"But this feeling was odd, and indeed it was very strong. First of all, I knew he had a riding lawnmower because I had seen him working on it. Second of all, I needed mine. The tool was like new and we had just bought it the previous fall for about three-thousand dollars. If I did this strange thing, how would I explain it to Linda? I decided to forget about it.

"When I arrived home and pulled into my driveway, the impression came on, even stronger. Go get the lawnmower and take it to him was the clear message. Finally, I decided that I wasn't going to fight it. I was going to get the machine and take it to him. I went to the barn where it was housed and cranked it up. As I began driving out of my driveway

158

it was like the same voice said to clean it up before I delivered it. Wait a minute, I thought. It's bad enough giving it away, but I should clean it first?

"But, I got out water and soap and scrubbed it down pretty good, to where it looked like new. I started it again and headed down the road toward his house, feeling a little foolish as I proceeded.

"He was outside washing his car and his wife, who I rarely see, was standing there with him. Now that I was there I wasn't quite sure what to do. He looked even more confused than I did since we had never socialized and here I come calling, on a lawnmower.

"I asked him how he was doing and he replied that he was just fine.

"'What can I do for you?' he asked. As foolish as it must have sounded, I just blurted it out; that I had been impressed to bring the lawnmower here and make him a gift of it.

"He looked incredulous and said that I must be kidding. I went on to explain that I'm not the type of guy who goes around hearing things like this all the time, but this impression was very strong.

"Something happened that I would have expected the least from him. He is a rough-and-tumble type person and in my mind I could picture him tossing me and the mower off his property. But that didn't happen. In fact, I saw like tears come into his eyes.

"He said to me, 'You can't mean this.'

"His wife stepped forward and told me, 'You have no way of knowing this, but in the last few months he has quit drinking and we have really tried to change our lives around. What changed it is 3ABN. We started watching it at home. But since we've tried to become Christians several bad things have happened to us. So much that I asked him if we had really done the right thing. We agreed that if only we could be given a sign to know we were on the right path, it would help us along the way.

"'Then, just this morning, he was out mowing and the lawnmower engine blew up. It seemed almost like the last straw because we didn't have the money to fix it. I began to wonder if the Lord really did love us.' She pointed to the open barn, which didn't show from the road, and sure enough, he had the mower parts strewn around trying to repair it.

"He looked at me with tears in his eyes and said he couldn't believe this was happening. 'You couldn't have known about this' he said. 'It just happened a little while ago. You will never know what this means to us.'

"I felt good about the whole thing. I hadn't even known that they watched 3ABN, but if I had, it would have made no a difference. Later, I heard from other independent sources that their lives really had been changed."

As a journalist I pose the question to you, personally: Does 3ABN's message work to make life better for people?

I have spent several years of my life and eight trips to Europe and to other countries observing the Sheltons and their labor of love. No intelligent person could deny the long reach (global) their influence has and the positive impact they have made. And it is not just measured by the many converts they have made.

Religious beliefs are never questioned when people seek benefit from the network's projects. In fact, Danny likes to give all credit to his God, and the contributions of his viewers, and other supporters. Whatever the source, tens of thousands of people have better lives today because of this unique network. That, as we newsmen are wont to say, is in black and white, indelibly factual, and provable.

One of those examples of 3ABN's work allowed this author to experience one of the most tender and rewarding moments of my life.

The network has brought forth many people from around the world to be baptized. A few years ago, I sat on

160

the bank of a lake in Nizhny Novgorod, Russia. I was witnessing the baptism of over fifty Russians who had come into the fold through the magnificent 3ABN station that has been built there.

I was only at the lake to take photographs to compliment the series of newspaper articles I was writing at the time. I was working mechanically, in that dispassionate frame of mind reserved almost exclusively for journalists. We pompously label it objectivity.

Suddenly I took pause and was overwhelmed, overcome with emotion because of the spectacle unfolding before me, actually "seeing" it for the first time.

In foursomes the converted Russians entered the waist-deep water and walked confidently to their pastors to be totally submerged. Disregarding the frigid water they emerged from the lake with a beatific smile that radiated a new feeling, baring their very souls for the entire world to see.

Camera set aside and forgotten, it moved me deeply and unhinged a longing in me that was worse than the physical hunger of my poverty-stricken youth. What they had gained in that brief heartbeat of a moment was written on their faces more eloquently than any words offered by the greatest of bards.

I vowed then and there, that even if I couldn't personally know that inner glow, and I have not as of the time of this writing, at least I could narrate what I observed for those readers among you who might strive to comprehend it. And most especially, to benefit from it. Thus is borne my humble offering in this book.

Chapter 13

The sound of music. The phrase conjures pictures in the mind's eye of a beautiful lady running through a hillside of flowers, arms raised and gaily singing about the entire area being alive with the sound of music. Sound is the key word here and a better quality of it usually increases the enjoyment of music and lyrics for the listener. Music has played a dominant role in the lives of the Sheltons. It was a cornerstone in the life of Danny's family, even before he was born.

Those who play music or sing at any level know how important it is to have the proper equipment and acoustics. For many years the Sheltons and all other area musicians and singers had to go to "music centers" to record their songs. For the Midwest America, Nashville, Tennessee arguably offered the best recording studios. Both Danny and Linda have recorded many songs in such locations.

Although available to the artists this solution was also problematical because the cost was prohibitive. It could cost as much as two-thousand dollars a day to rent space and a like amount for professionals to handle the technical aspect of recording. "Cutting" an album could cost anywhere from fifteen-thousand dollars to thirty-thousand dollars. But the state-of-the-art equipment today is profound, albeit expensive.

Danny was always appreciative of the technical advantage of a recording studio, but to have one built in southern Illinois to accommodate artists seemed far-fetched— a distant dream at best. But as 3ABN expanded and grew, more and more artists began coming to the West Frankfort, Illinois, to perform at the studio. The television shows were handled adequately at that facility. Always, however, there was that increasing need for recording excellence. In true tradition of 3ABN that problem was going to be solved. With Danny it seems that necessity is often the mother of invention.

When asked why he built the sound studio he offers the simplest of answers, "I just didn't like seeing all that money sorely needed for other 3ABN projects, the Lord's work, going to those other places."

Thus was born what had previously been the dream of many aspiring musical ministries. The dream which eventuated into the completion of a million dollar plus sound studio that is now nestled in a beautiful setting just south of the main TV studio and within the large 3ABN complex. The epitome of professionalism in sound technology, the studio took a year to build and was finished in two-thousand-one.

Artists can record and make CDs from beginning to end and walk out with a copy of the finished product. With a master copy, the artist can have as many recordings made as they desire.

The building also includes residence for E.T. Everett and her husband, Dave, long-time friends of the Sheltons who live at the studio and operate it. Dave is a singer, and E.T., a world-class gospel pianist. They have performed in Russia for 3ABN too. There are also guest facilities at the studio and in nearby housing.

Now that the studio is up and running it would seem to provide an excellent source of additional income for 3ABN. But this is not to be.

"We have had quite a few ministries use the studio and we also have some thirty projects lined up," Danny said on the occasion of an early two-thousand-two interview. "But many of these ministries are struggling financially and the Lord has impressed me to not charge these folks to carry on their work. That's our way of taking what God has given us and channeling it to someone else. They in turn can go out and sell their tapes to help them carry on their work. We don't have anyone scheduled to bring a dime in. But the beauty of it is that the Lord has paid for this as we went along and we are simply sharing His blessing."

The groups that have used the studio thus far have commented on the brightness and openness of the facility and also a more compelling quality, a "spiritual atmosphere."

Bobby Bradley is well known in the music recording business, especially in Nashville, Tennessee. He has been involved in musical projects with Danny for about twenty years. Bobby helped design the building and oversees engineering operations.

The average insulated wall in the building is sixteen to twenty inches wide to accommodate the mandatory acoustics. There is also a layer of cloth in the walls with additional insulation blown in over that. The floors are "floating," or individually set under each room so no sound can escape under foot.

Bobby's uncle, the late Owen Bradley, is somewhat of a legend around Nashville. He worked with some of the biggest names in Country and Western, as well as Gospel music. He started out around Nashville as the popular big band leader of "The Owen Bradley Orchestra." At the same time, he worked for WSM on the Morning Show. Later, he became a producer and had many big hits.

"I started working for Owen in nineteen-seventy-one, at the original Bradley's Barn," Bobby said. "That was a landmark place, but it burned down October twentieth, nineteen-eighty. The following year I went to work at Doc's Place, also well known in music circles, in Hendersonville. A dentist and a musician, Dr. Billy Burks is an Adventist who has appeared on 3ABN. Danny Shelton brought in his daughter, Melody, to record an album shortly after her mother had been killed in an auto accident, and that's how I met the Sheltons.

"Melody's recording came out very well and apparently other people in southern Illinois were impressed with the sound because Danny began bringing other people down to record. After they began building 3ABN, the original building, they started to build a sound room and even had some of the equipment in place. I came up there once during that time, but the network was growing so fast that they needed the space and converted it into a video room."

Bradley definitely became interested in the current new sound studio and made himself available as an advisor to E.T. Everett as she supervised the construction and fitting. He has been involved ever since and is proud of what they have built.

"This place is sophisticated and state-of-the-art. All of the outboard gear is as good as you would find in any studio, in any city. Danny doesn't do anything halfway." Bradley said.

Anyone interested in 3ABN can call to set up a tour of the studio. Be sure to include the sound room, which is a separate building. As you enter the building you move to the "tracking room" where the musicians play.

A small glassed-in vocal booth allows the singer to be isolated from the sound of the musicians and blend in through earphones. A piano room is also segregated from the main music room, as is a percussion room.

The piano room houses a treasure— a magnificent nine-foot grand piano, valued at more than fifty-thousand dollars, which was donated to 3ABN by Ogden Music Company of Portland, Oregon.

All of these rooms are contiguous and in visual connection with each other but separated by glass so that the louder instruments do not "bleed" over into the other sections. The reason for this isolation is that, in this manner, every instrument can be registered on its own individual tape recorder. At the command of the engineer is the potential for over one-hundred individual tape recorders, on tracts of twenty-four per machine.

Because of this high technology the engineer can go in and work on improving the sound of an individual instrument without interfering with another artist's effort that is playing the same piece of music at the same time. It would be akin to removing a spark plug from a car while the engine is running and fixing it without disturbing the accomplishment of the rest of the parts.

No great Philharmonic orchestra conductor ever had more avenues of simultaneous robust sound at his command than the engineer sitting at "the board." The purity of each sound can then individually be mixed and honed to perfection and blended as one through the master production control area, an inner sanctum of music that is dubbed "Bobby's (Bradley) Room."

The final phases of the recording process is when the digital tape visits the Pro-Tool Room or, in slang, the "tool shop." Here, sounds are broken down to screen that shows sound wave that almost resembles science fiction. This is an editing sweep where each nuance of voice or music is evaluated.

Bad notes can be corrected as a technician, like 3ABN's Joe Carrell, a Carmi, Illinois native, watches colored sound waves move across a large screen. Sound travels in waves of positive and negative energy.

For example, if a singer inadvertently renders a little gasp of breath on high notes, using this technique the trained person can zoom in and capture each miscue and wipe it out. If a fly on the ceiling sneezed during a crescendo of an instrumental performance you'd never hear it on the final recording. Often a person can record and return home unaware that their "voice" is continuing to improve.

Linda Shelton was the first to record voice there. The music had already been pre-recorded in Nashville before the studio was finished, but she added the vocal part in the new building.

"It is absolutely awesome," she said while discussing the experience, "I was really excited. And I realized as I was singing that familiar 'Presence' reminding me I was standing on 'Holy Ground.'"

Meeting Danny was a significant event in the lives of David and E.T. Everett. They had been working as a quartet and the group needed to cut a tape for a competition they had entered. Another musician, who had played backup for Danny, told them that Shelton had built a sound room in his home (mentioned later in this chapter) and might be able to help them. They called and set up a meeting and taped.

They followed with great interest Danny's vision and subsequent drive to make 3ABN become a reality. They were on hand when the construction of the original building was skeletal and the only area completed was "The Green Room." Early on, the Everetts huddled there in prayer for the project, a memory vivid to E.T.

The Everetts had a group called "New Beginning Ministries," and they had taped for 3ABN. The association became more permanent when Tommy Shelton moved to Washington, DC to pastor. The Sheltons invited the Everetts along on weekend trips, when she played the piano. That expanded to her playing the piano on 3ABN also. Tommy Shelton and E.T. had in common that they both began playing the piano at age three. She went on to get a college degree in music.

E.T. was shocked one day when having a conversation with Danny and they were discussing sound and recording in general. This was during a trip to Oregon, where the group had been performing.

Afterward, at the hotel, Danny, without preface, said that if she would join the 3ABN staff and head up the project, they would build a proper sound studio.

She wasn't quite sure that she had heard him right until

Danny calmly repeated, "The Lord has impressed me that if you will come on board, we can build a sound studio."

She had no training whatsoever in this field and was startled, to say the least. She indicated this to him but once Danny sets his mind to an idea, no matter how preposterous it might sound to others, it will usually move forward. She decided to act on Danny's faith in her and agreed to take on the awesome task.

Unbelievably, she began at the very fundamental level of reading magazines, calling friends in the business and even referring to Internet sources on line.

Obviously E.T. also hired professionals to do some of the work— like an acoustical engineer, from Nashville. As the word spread, key guys like Joe Carroll and Bobby Bradley wanted to be a part of the project. From this humble start grew a studio which fulfilled a long-time dream for Danny Shelton, a music studio to be a "channel of blessing" to other ministries, as well as 3ABN artists.

The "other" recording studio.

An imperative addition to this chapter is a mention of the "other" sound studio; the facility that Linda referred to briefly in an earlier chapter.

Before 3ABN was even a dream, Danny was facing the same problem shared by all of the singers and musicians who performed in southern Illinois at that time. They didn't have a satisfactory place to record. After beating a path to Nashville for years, Danny had an inspiration that would alter that confining status quo. He explains it here:

"For years I had been taking people to Nashville, Tennessee to produce tapes and records for them," Danny said. "We would rent a studio, hire backup singers and contract an engineer. We would go down and do their tracks and do their vocals, we'd add all this together to make a complete album for them. Back then, we used albums rather than CDs like they have now.

"Many of the people who seemed to have talent and were interested and were into part-time gospel music could not afford to go to Nashville to get involved in this process. Even then, in the early nineteen-eighties, it was costing as much as ten-thousand dollars to do a project and some of these people were barely making ends meet.

"At the time, I had a radio program that aired from Ava, Illinois, and I would take them and do a radio program so the public in the area could hear their sound and, if they chose, could invite them to perform at their churches. I got to thinking about this and praying about this. There were a lot of talented people who couldn't afford to do this, but they were talents that should be heard. If the Lord was in it, there had to be a way they could go.

"To help these people, I was impressed to build my own recording studio, but I didn't have any money. What I did have was a little pole barn at my house. It had three sides filled in and one open because we used to stack and store lumber there when I was in construction. I told Linda about it and one day while we were discussing it I just walked out to that building with her.

"All that was in there was a leftover two by four. I remember picking it up and studying the walls and thinking, 'If this were closed in, it would have the makings of the kind of studio we need.'

"So I nailed it up. Observing this with great interest, she asked me why would I nail up just one piece of lumber. I told her that one of the things I have learned over the years is if you expect God to bless you, you need to use up what you already have first. I have done that, so now I've put him in a position to bless because as long as I have used all I have, it is now up to Him.

"Within three weeks of the time that I did this, we played the first recording we had on the air. I didn't have equipment and I especially needed a multi-track recorder. What I did have at the time was a Gibson, Les Paul guitar. It was

170

precious to me and I vowed I would never part with it.

"A guy came to see me and was admiring the instrument. He couldn't afford to buy it, but asked me if I would trade it. I told him absolutely not. He said that I didn't even know what he was going to offer and I told him it didn't make any difference, I'd never part with it, that this was the only thing I had of any value and I planned to play it for the rest of my life. Obviously disappointed he just shook his head and started to leave.

At the door he stopped and said, 'Too bad. But do you know anybody that needs what I was going to offer in trade, a multi-track recorder?'

"All of a sudden it hit me hard that that was exactly what I needed for the studio. I said to him, 'You've got to be kidding?'

"He said no, that was what he had wanted to trade for the Gibson. I assumed that this was the direction I was supposed to go. So, painful as it was, I traded my precious guitar for the multi-track recorder.

"I had a bedroom in the back of my house where I set up the multi-track recorder. The room was about ten-foot by twelve-foot, with a six-foot, six-inch ceiling. People would use the equipment and pay us a few hundred dollars for Tommy and I to do the music. With the money we made there we kept trading up for better equipment.

"We used it for about two years and before we went any farther and finished that studio, the 3ABN project began with the construction of the original TV building at Thompsonville.

"I still had high hopes for a recording studio and thought we might just build it there. I was even optimistic enough to mark off a space where that studio would eventually be built. We actually framed it up but never got to use it as such because we grew so fast and moved into the new complex, and that original building was converted to house storage at first, and now 3ABN Radio.

"Finally, after seventeen years, we got to build our recording sound studio here at the new place. We were blessed and it was worth waiting for."

Chapter 14

Afriend of mine, Bruce Fasol, a radio personality who also writes a newspaper column, always closes the latter with the amusing remark, "See you on the radio." Perhaps the old cliché is true that it is sometimes difficult to see the trees because of the forest. The technology for radio was always present at 3ABN but it was more or less overlooked in the shuffle.

Since the inception of the 3ABN television network broadcasting, there has always been present three technical audio channels that surround the video message that goes to satellite, but they were not used... until recently.

That is a very simple factor in terms of basic technology but profound in its implications for potentially using this tool as an information outlet. More significantly, at least from the standpoint of expense, these radio signals can be "piggybacked" (in layman's terms), in such a manner for little or no extra transponder cost! In turn, this is important because the Sheltons are crucially aware of squeezing every penny that is donated to the ministry for the exact purpose for which it is given. In other words, this potential, in terms that anyone can understand, is a real bargain.

For a long time during the ongoing beehive of activity at 3ABN twenty-four-hours per day seven-days-per-week, no one paid particular attention to this latent possibility. No one that is, except Linda.

Linda Shelton works with programming and program scheduling on the TV side and an idea kept gnawing at the back of her mind that much of this material could be as powerful as an audio tool as it was visually. Why should any restraint be put on God's Word? He had already provided the means. All 3ABN had to do was to further utilize those same tools. In addition Linda observed, "I noticed that television stations were quite expensive and people who lived in small towns didn't usually have the means to make such a large investment. However, low power FM stations can be installed for as little as twelve-thousand dollars which could reach an entire community. I had a real burden to make this inexpensive evangelistic option available."

Magnificent in its simplicity, the most awesome aspect of the plan was that these radio signals could go (and currently do) to the most remote places on the planet and even reach people where television is not available.

The programming plan would be threefold (as in angels). Material from other Adventist radio shows could be aired. Also, some of the audio portions from the 3ABN television network shows would fit just fine into a radio format. New and creative material developed in the 3ABN radio studios would round out a new medium.

Tried and true and truly new could well be their motto.

It was a piece of cake, right? Well, no, not actually.

Month after month, Linda would put the word in Danny's ear about this wondrous possibility which was pressed on her from the Lord. She didn't "bug" him, you understand— but she was persistent in telling him that he should launch the radio project.

Like any wise husband thus besieged, Danny chose not to ignore her once he realized how inspired she was. He finally told her outright, "The Lord isn't impressing me to do radio. If He is impressing you that way, you should go ahead and do it."

Wow! There it was. Just do it. Of course, it was a formidable task and Linda was pretty apprehensive about tackling it on her own, so she reverted to that which had sustained and guided her since childhood... prayer.

The following passage is how the mighty 3ABN radio

network came about, in Linda's own words:

"I was pretty nervous about stepping out on my own on such a massive project but I thought, if God is in this then He will open the doors. I went to our 3ABN family (the entire 3ABN staff at the TV station begins every morning with a mutual prayer session) and to our local church family and urged them to pray for direction in the radio project. We specifically asked that if we were supposed to move on this project, He should reveal that to us.

"Meanwhile, I put together a business proposal taking into consideration all the equipment needs and the costs to make radio happen at 3ABN. It was intimidating to learn that it would cost about three-hundred-seventy-five-thousand dollars to go into operation. I sent this information to different places and then sat back and waited to see what the Lord would do.

"The miracle wasn't long in coming. In less than two months one-hundred percent of the equipment expenses and costs for the project were committed to us! This was incredible because even throughout the history of 3ABN, it was always a rare occasion indeed when we would have total funding for a new project even before it started. Usually, we would go forward on faith alone and the money would come forth as we proceeded with the plan. Thus, when this happened, we knew it was the will of God.

"The miracle happened through the vessels of the Adventist Services and Industry (ASI) whose board was moved to give 3ABN two-hundred-fifty-thousand dollars. An individual board member put up the remaining one-hundred-twenty-five-thousand dollars.

"Reassured by that encouragement we went to work. A few months before the money was committed, the Lord impressed me to ask Theresa Boote to come to 3ABN to help develop the radio station. Her first contact with 3ABN was in 1987, when she had come to the studio with her family to be baptized.

"She and I had first talked about radio at an ASI meeting in August of nineteen-ninety-eight. I approached her at the dinner and told her what I had in mind for her. Her first reaction to the suggestion that she should be involved in organizing and running a radio station was that it was ludicrous, and she dismissed it with a 'no way.'

"She said to me, 'Oh, Linda! You know I would do anything to help you. But this is just not me.'

"I told her to at least go home and pray about it.

"Looking back, I can understand her reluctance. I suppose it was quite scary to her at the time. But I was convinced that Theresa was meant to play a key role in God's new adventure through our network, in part because she had visited 3ABN to be baptized after watching our programs at her home in Canada. Also Theresa was a vivacious Christian, enthusiastic, a hard worker, an organizer and a woman of faith.

"We were thrilled to learn that she was converted to become a Seventh-day Adventist Christian after watching 3ABN. We knew her to be a devout Christian and that she had strong organizational abilities. She had been a teacher in the past and when I was praying for guidance as to who should head up this part of the ministry, her name just kept popping up.

"History has proven this choice to be correct because she has been a real blessing. She was the one who initially made the phone calls and contacted consultants to come in and help us organize and put the radio package together. But as to her joining 3ABN, the issue was in doubt early on.

"When I first talked to her she was hesitant. For one thing, we didn't have any money for the project at that time. She kind of used that as a reason to hold off and told me to call her when finances were available. When suddenly those finances were in place I called her to tell about the blessing.

"I heard her exclaim to her husband, 'Frank, they have

The Early Years

❶ Linda (center) in the early years with siblings Cheri and Dave. ❷ Linda and Cheri. ❸ Linda, Cheri and Dave. ❹ Linda, Dave and Cheri with Mom and Dad.

The Early Years

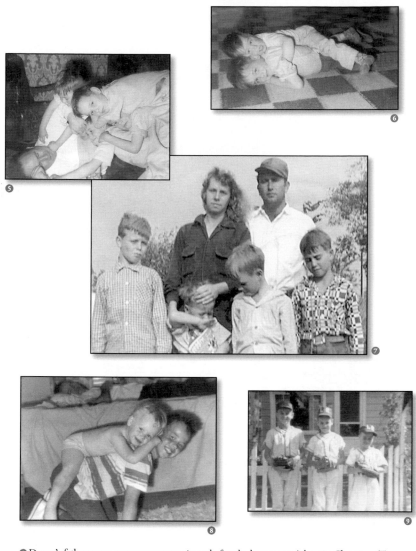

❶ Danny's father was a country-western singer before he became an Adventist Christian. (Tommy Sr. is second from left.) ❷ Danny's parents, Goldie and Tommy Shelton. ❸ Summertime was tomato picking time. ❹ Danny's family picked tomatoes for the Amish in his early years. ❺ Dad (Tommy Shelton Sr.) wrestling with Tommy Jr., Ronny, Kenny and Danny. ❻ Danny wrestles brother Ronny. ❼ This is an early photo of Danny's family, he's the shy one. ❽ Danny with his sister, Tammy. ❾ Danny, far right, enjoyed many sports while growing up.

The Family Years

❶ Danny and Linda on their wedding day, November 25, 1984. ❷ April 1990 family photo
❸ Melody recording in Nashville, TN at age 11.   ❹ One of Danny's favorite hobbies is horses.
❺ Horse's were a big part of the Shelton family's liesure time.   ❻ Alyssa and Nathan with
"famous" Fluffy.   ❼ Alyssa and Nathan, with their grandparents Wayne and Mitzi Lenz.
❽ Danny and Linda receive honorary bachelors degrees from Union College in Lincoln, Nebraska.
❾ Linda Shelton's family, including Mom, sister Cheri, brother Dave, and their families.

5

6

7

8

9

Building 3ABN

❶ This was the "shack" that housed the first satellite equipment and 3ABN's first master control. ❷ 3ABN's first satellite dish under construction. ❸ The first Uplink Center under construction for 3ABN. ❹ Danny and Kenny with Marvin and Rosella McColpin. ❺ 3ABN's first satellite dish. ❻ 3ABN's first "primitive" master control. ❼ 3ABN's Uplink Center today, it is also the birthplace of 3ABN. ❽ Clarence Larsen was 3ABN's first engineer. ❾ The first 3ABN Presents set. ❿ The second 3ABN Presents set. ⓫ Our current 3ABN Presents studio. ⓬ God's amazing technology to bring the saving message to the multitudes. ⓭ 3ABN Call Center, where calls and mail orders are processed. ⓮ There is always a flurry of activity in the mailroom of the 3ABN Call Center. ⓯ 3ABN's worldwide headquarters and Production Center. ⓰ The 3ABN Production Truck produces On The Road programs. ⓱ The entrance of the 3ABN Evangelism Center in Nizhny Novgorod, Russia. ⓲ 3ABN Camp Meeting is a favorite for everyone.

❶ The 3ABN Sound Center creates "new sounds" to "make His praise glorious." ❷ Linda prepares to do a Bible segment on Kids Time. ❸ Operations Manager Theresa Boote conducts an interview at 3ABN Radio. ❹ Linda Shelton creates a new outreach at 3ABN: music videos. ❺ Danny, Linda & Fluffy.

the money!' Still, she was concerned about leaving her family in Canada for what, to her, seemed like a nebulous possibility. So, she canceled the first date to come down and then she canceled a second plan to come to 3ABN to discuss the matter. Finally, she sent a fax to my office apologizing and saying that she just didn't feel qualified to handle the job.

"I was disappointed in Theresa's response, but I knew God must have someone else that could step in. Then, three days later, my aide, Dee Hilderbrand, came into my office very excited and stated that we got a call stating that Theresa was on her way down from Canada. Theresa said that the Lord wasn't letting her sleep at night and that she had to check to see if He had something for her to do here. Apparently, He had.

"Even after she made the initial commitment, Theresa struggled because of her total lack of experience in this area. But I told her that in the early days none of us knew anything about television either. She decided to commute between the station and her home in Canada and leave it up to God whether or not she could get a Green Card to work here.

"On August eleventh, nineteen-ninety-nine, she began the application process for her Religious Worker's Visa and on April twenty-third, two-thousand, she received it. She responded positively and her presence represented a tremendous blessing ever since. It took us about a year to make it happen, but on February twenty-eighth in the year two-thousand, 3ABN Radio went on the air twenty-four hours-a-day, seven-days-a-week. And here's something else that's incredible:

"It's a rare occasion that the FCC opens a window to accept applications for low power FM stations throughout the United States. The very next month the FCC announced the first series of 'windows' for applications for low power FM radio stations. Yet, once again it was like the

Lord emphasized that He raised 3ABN Radio for such an hour as this, and His timing is always perfect.

"Since then we have been amazed to see God raising up workers from all walks of life to develop radio stations in their communities which will receive and rebroadcast 3ABN Radio. Let me emphasize here that these are not people with communication degrees, or even having experience with radio. These are people who just love Jesus and want to bring Him to their communities through this miraculous advent of 3ABN Radio.

"In fact, some of these people not only had no experience with radio but they were burdened with big obstacles to be overcome. They are undaunted by these hurdles and plunge ahead with great purpose. For example, there is a man and his wife in Colorado who are both hearing-impaired. They use a special phone to call 3ABN. The wife is also blind, but they were moved to develop a radio station in their community.

"There is another man who called me and said that he has a malignant form of cancer but he's going forward to build a radio station in his community because, in his own words, 'I want to do something big for Jesus while I can.'

"We have literally been in awe of what God is doing and with the people that God is bringing forward to work for Him.

"Let me say this. God is giving us something much better than a Pentecost today with all the technology that He has provided. He's giving us much more than evidence of His Blessing with tongues of fire on people's heads and three-thousand saved for the Kingdom in a day. He has provided us with a technology that can and does literally reach around the world. And He's also given us a technology that can reach into the hearts and homes in a pleasant and welcome manner. Through radio there's the potential of hundreds of thousands being saved in a day's time, just by hearing the message. And not only that, but radio can

178

continue to nurture and help people as they grow in the Lord.

"The God who parted the Red Sea so long ago is still demolishing seemingly immovable blocks today so His truth can march right into the hearts of those who are longing and searching for the truth."

Linda's excitement about radio is understandable and shared by many. There are some spectacular success stories. A prime example is the enthusiasm of Mr. and Mrs. Windell Borland, natives of Belize.

Several years ago they visited friends in Texas where, for the first time, they watched 3ABN. They were enthralled and were motivated to somehow bring the network broadcasting to their own country. They purchased a satellite dish in Texas and took it with them when they returned home. They gifted the dish to their local cable company who in turn immediately began airing 3ABN.

Awash with this success the dedicated Borlands began purchasing more satellites and giving them to other cable companies until all such entities in Belize were offered 3ABN. Most people would be thrilled and satisfied with such an accomplishment but the Borlands felt their quest was not yet fully realized. Their burden was that there were remaining small pockets of the population where cable, or even television did not reach.

But radio waves were all encompassing! With relish and great passion the Borlands built a three-hundred-fifty-watt radio station which reached approximately a thirty-five-mile radius from the transmitter. The station began broadcasting in nineteen-ninety-nine.

Quickly to follow were twenty-three baptisms as a direct result of this radio ministry and many more lives have been changed since. Because of the efforts of 3ABN listeners who held "high places," the Borlands were given a location for their radio transmitter on a tower at the highest point in Belize, as well as some neighboring countries and islands in

179

the Caribbean. Since nineteen-ninety-one and 3ABN's introduction to the country, it has been reported that the Adventist Church has grown by eighteen-thousand members.

Linda sums it up this way: "3ABN Radio is a marvelous way to saturate your community with the Good News of Jesus Christ. Local stations many times are seeking additional programming, programming that 3ABN Radio is happy to provide. Local stations amazingly go up for sale when prayer is involved. God wants his children to know the truth, 'which will set you free.' God opens doors where God's people really have an earnest desire."

Linda also pointed out that gathering the people to make 3ABN Radio happen at best delved into the most unlikely scenario.

Theresa Boote acknowledges that Linda was correct in describing her initial misgivings. She remembers that the proposition did seem ludicrous at the time.

"I immediately dismissed this as a no-way issue as I was not the least bit interested in radio in general, nor did I ever even listen to it. More significantly, I knew absolutely nothing about either radio or computer technology. Also, we were a hurting family at the time and I could not see my living apart from the family unit, especially my husband, Frank. This entire concept seemed contrary to scripture and therefore I thought God could not possibly be behind it," she said.

However once again, as it has done so often, 3ABN validated that God truly does work in mysterious ways. Something compelled Theresa to check it further and on May twenty-fourth, nineteen-ninety-nine, to travel to the station from her home in Canada.

"I was trusting in God to speak to me personally on location," she explained. The historical fact is that it was cut and dried from that point on. Theresa was a natural for the role even though bewildered with it all at first. As His drama unfolded, Linda's confidence in her was authenticated.

In the following comments, Theresa Boote describes the experience.

"The first week was very overwhelming with all the unfamiliar concepts and terminology so I felt the Lord had spoken to me. I packed my belongings on a Thursday night and prepared to return to Canada the next day. Later that evening, my husband encouraged me to hang in there, that I could get qualified help for all the technical issues. He had faith that I could provide leadership to make radio happen. He urged me to get the proper staff into place first and then come home.

"That advice calmed me because on my very first day 'on the job' I met a most interesting family who were visiting 3ABN from Walla Walla, WA. They were there to check out possible employment opportunities. They were Jay, Annette and Cari Christian. Jay had spent twenty-eight years in radio and two years in television while his wife, Annette, was a very creative and energetic marketing personnel. Cari had a willing spirit to work anywhere the Lord would lead. So I thought, great— I bet these people are sent by God to be the radio staff and, together with God's help, radio will be in place enough for me to return to my home and family within three to six months. And what an honor God has given me to play a role in this international ministry! So, yes, I can do this by God's grace."

Throughout June of nineteen-ninety-nine Theresa conducted the whirlwind of activities from lining up the technical staff, getting contracts for equipment, and making decisions on acoustics.

On July thirteenth, the first shipment of one-thousand CD's was ordered and on the twenty-ninth of that month, Beverly Seyer burned the first CD for radio (*"Help Yourself to Health,"* with Agatha Thrash) and (*"Bible Answers,"* by Doug Batchelor).

These offerings began the first audio library for 3ABN

Radio. Then, on Monday, August twenty-third, Jay Christian came on board the 3ABN Radio staff as a very welcome manager of production and handled the overall sound of radio. He was also to host a two hour live musical program called, 'Musical Meditations.'

Sandra Juarez, who was already on the 3ABN staff as Programming Director in television, was assigned to that same position for radio as well.

Theresa was encouraged to see a skilled and dedicated staff falling into place.

Excitement ran through the station (which is located at the site of the original television studio) on the final day of nineteen-ninety-nine when radio debuted with Danny and Linda in about a ten-minute segment on the 3ABN television New Year's Eve Special. Since then 3ABN Radio has become an integral part of the ministry.

Another milestone was on February twenty-seventh, two-thousand.

Theresa Boote shares a poignant thought she had at that time, "It is eleven-fifty-five p.m. Sunday evening, just five minutes before the birthing of 3ABN's new baby, 3ABN Radio. The radio staff has gathered for prayer and, having come through several weeks of serious birthing pains, we listen to B.J. Thomas' rendition of Amazing Grace.

"Then, as the countdown clock zeroes to midnight, the on-air button is pushed and 3ABN Radio launches the first of its twenty-four-hour-a-day, seven-day-a-week signal to Galaxy Three. A praise applause is rendered to the Lord and a new sound resounds in the earth. It is a sound that will shape the destiny of many for eternity. Praise the Lord!"

For this book, and in an openhearted manner, Theresa recalls those early days, revealing her thoughts and decisions and her interaction with Linda about 3ABN Radio.

"Pondering Linda's original request of me was agonizing. It literally cost me a lot sleep. I knew Linda was praying about all of this and maintained her faith in me, even though I had rejected a potential role for myself in the project. Then she told me that, miraculously, the money had been raised in advance, an unprecedented occurrence for a major project at the network. I took this as a sign, evidence that this must truly be God's project and it followed that perhaps there was a place for me after all.

"Also, Frank, my husband, (who is with Coast Guard Canada) was traveling a lot so I had a lot of time on my hands. I had a burning desire in my heart to work in the vineyard, to be a channel for God's blessing, for the saving of lost souls. From my own family's experience I knew the hurt, pain and grief that the darkness of sin inflicted. So I wanted to be an instrument in God's hands to bring hope and spiritual healing to others.

"So here I was, willing and eager to collaborate with Him, but there seemed to be no doors open for me. Also, at this same time Frank was away on business inside the Arctic Circle. I was lonely and a little confused because I was begging God to show me His plan for me.

"That night I had trouble sleeping because it suddenly struck me that He might already have been giving me the answer and I had been saying no. After a fitful night's sleep I awoke at eight a.m. and was quickly on the road. I decided that I would drive the seven-hundred miles to 3ABN and try it for myself. I decided I would stay at the network for a few days and pretend that I had accepted it and see how God spoke to me on site.

"After a few days I saw that my skills were inadequate for the task so I went to a friend at the network for prayer, fully intending to leave. My prayer partner told me to at least call my husband that night. Others, too, urged me to not make a hasty decision. They pointed out that I was taking on the weight of technical responsibility that was outside my area of strength and that I could hire professionals to help in that area.

"We pretty much decided that I would rely on Frank's

advice and comments and accept that as God's will speaking through Frank to me. When I talked to him that night Frank was very supportive and confident in me. He echoed the others' opinion that I was being unfair with myself to expect to have technical knowledge. My role was to offer overall leadership. This call and his reassurance helped me to carry on.

"At the beginning, when I first arrived in Thompsonville, David Turner, the 3ABN carpenter, was just beginning the process of converting the storage area into what would be the home of 3ABN Radio. It is located at the building that was the original television station. As the first person actually chosen for the radio operation I had to work with David on the simplest details.

"In the process I talked with Bobby Bradley, from Nashville, who is an expert on acoustics. What went into the walls, for example, was critical. I had visited other radio stations and observed that some were functional but unattractive while others were quite elaborate and expensive. I knew Linda would want our station to look attractive and be functional, but also be economical.

"It would have been easy to just order ready-made sound insulation material but the cost would have soared. We always handle 3ABN's money prudently so we shopped around the entire area for the best bargains and did most of the labor ourselves, thus saving much money.

"Doing the work ourselves was a real challenge but by working long days we did manage to make the February twenty-eighth advertised deadline. Other incredible challenges also faced me as operations manager at this time. Contracts for the purchase and installation of all radio equipment as well as proposals for a turnkey integration of our 3ABN Radio Network had to be solicited, studied and awarded. Decisions had to be made involving hundreds of thousands of dollars.

"For these decisions I had to rely on God to speak

through the valued television staff. But praise God, when the deadline arrived, we were ready to push the button to go on the air and we had two weeks of programming ready to go in advance.

"We hit a major snag on September tenth, nineteen-ninety-nine. I had been coming down on a volunteer basis to help out, but on this day I was halted at the border and denied entrance into the U.S. I was told I needed a religious worker's visa to continue to work in America. I was literally turned away at the border and had to go back home. This put me out of the picture temporarily, but Jay Christian was in place to continue work until I returned a few months later with the required visa.

"One of the early challenges was that Linda wanted a two-hour call-in talk show in the morning. We had no personality to host such a show and Linda wanted me to do it. I could not fathom that at all. That was more than I could bear to think about. But help arrived when pastor Samuel Thomas, Jr., and his wife, Karen, obliged us temporarily by voluntarily hosting the Monday, Tuesday and Wednesday programs originally called, 'Morning Watch Live.'

"Then, on August ninth, two-thousand, Pastor Richard O'Ffill and co-host Glenn Altermatt, from Orlando, Florida went on the air for their first live program and they would host the program each Wednesday. Cheri Peters, from Boise, Idaho, who hosted each Friday program, followed them on Friday, September twenty-second. Further changes resulted in the need to fill three days that suddenly became open.

"God impressed me that He was calling me to fill one of those openings. I felt overwhelmed by this assignment but knew that when God called, He also qualified, so I stepped forward as host on October eleventh, two-thousand. My programs would air each Thursday. Jo Peckinpaugh, from Hixson, Tennessee was then invited to host each Monday's program.

"She recorded her first program Monday, October tenth, two-thousand-one. God sent other incredible blessings for radio in the arrival of key staff members.

"In August, two-thousand, Gonzalo Adrian Santos, from Chicago, who worked with 3ABN television in the formative years of the network, joined the radio staff's engineering department. In September of that same year Nikki Anderson began as Administrative Assistant. Bryan Schaeneman joined the radio's production department to work with Jay Christianson. Further staff members included Michael Babb, a radio engineer from Gaston, Oregon, and in February of two-thousand-two, Jim Morris came on board as general and marketing manager of WBLC AM 1360, Lenoir City, Tennessee.

"To back up a little, a significant event took place in March of two-thousand. As Linda mentioned earlier, we had barely had our doors open when the FCC offered opportunities and invited people from around the United States to apply for a construction permit to build a low-power one-hundred-watt FM radio station (LPFM) and broadcast to their community. These stations had the option of doing eight hours of local programming a day but the rest of the time they could air programming of their choice. This created a tremendous opportunity for God's Word and Work to go forward.

"Amazed at God's incredible timing of getting 3ABN Radio on the air just one month prior, we realized that 3ABN could be a source of programming for these new stations. We went into high gear through television spots and mailings to let people know that this was a possibility for them and for individuals, young or old, to come forward and put in an application. It became a learning experience on our part to understand the rules and regulations guiding these applications so we could advise others. We found we could not own or operate them ourselves but it was perfectly all right to provide programs, to be their audio services source if they so chose!

"This ignited massive mailings on our part, between eight-hundred and one-thousand-five-hundred packets each window. We let churches and others know about the potential for them to apply for these permits and ultimately to obtain 3ABN programming. We assured them that we would be there for them and help them. It was neat. People told of how much work would be involved to undertake such a project and they were right. But they came to us for advice and the work of the Lord prevailed. It was such a rewarding experience and we came away from it inspired.

"We helped them do something in their communities that would greatly impact people, not just for a time, but for eternity. As of spring of two-thousand-two, at least ninety such stations wanted to carry 3ABN Radio, as much as sixteen-hours-per-day."

"The FCC is not generally known for working in tandem with God as a priority strategy, but their timing on letting opportunities for these new FM stations could not have been more opportunistic for sending 3ABN's radio messages out to the world. It was a massive project on the part of the government involving all fifty states, in groups of ten states at a time, five windows of opportunity over all.

"At 3ABN Radio, Nikki Anderson handled many of the contacts on promoting 3ABN's potential involvement with these new entities."

The experience affected her life deeply, as she explains in the following comments:

"It increased my faith. I was able to encourage them on taking on the technical issues, but most of them called to say that they didn't know anything about radio, but God was impressing them to get involved. I had no previous radio experience myself, but I kept encouraging them that this was doable, citing 3ABN's success as an example.

"Along the way, I encouraged them to step out in their faith and do this. Talking with them in this manner has impacted me and strengthened my personal faith. Through the process, I have made friends from one end of this country to the other. I love them like my own family. I have seen miraculous accomplishments.

"Many of these people, young and old alike, are fearful, but they want to do something for the Lord and they seize the opportunity. Their stories number in the hundreds."

Linda's dream of covering the entire world with 3ABN Radio has become a reality since early in the year two-thousand-one. Where television goes, so goeth radio. The station is constantly inundated with calls from around the globe giving thanks for the programming.

Some say that it has moved them deeply and emotionally and enriched their lives. Converts are constant and numerous. It has even expanded onto the Internet radio services where several thousand hits are made each week. E-mails arrive daily from around the world.

The 3ABN Radio and the television network, which led to it, have clearly established that there is an insatiable desire out there to hear The Word. It has become an integral part of the ministry and the two entities are intertwined.

Linda sys, "In conclusion, I just want to say a hearty 'Praise the Lord' because truly, I saw His hand over and over again in the development of 3ABN Radio. It's His! It was His idea. His plan and His miracle. To God be the glory!"

"As for Theresa Boote, she is an absolute jewel and God used her in a big way to make 3ABN Radio a reality. And it was Theresa who kept me in line when choosing the wallpaper and wall coverings. I have a notorious reputation for choosing furniture and wall coverings that are heavily saturated in flowers, and when it comes to color. . . it's heavy on the pink! Much to the dismay of our male workers.

"Dan and I say again and again that we are so thankful

that we were able to be a part of 3ABN at the grass roots level so we could grow with it. My early years at 3ABN of growing and learning and dealing with my own feelings of inadequacy rebounded to be an asset and a benefit in the early development of 3ABN Radio. From my point of view, God had hand-picked Theresa Boote to be a key person in the development of this new ministry. Yet Theresa struggled and stuggled with her feelings of inadequacy and inexperience, and almost went home to Canada on more than one occasion. Again and again (this is for Theresa . . and AGAIN!) I was able to encourage her and be her spiritual cheerleader in the development of 3ABN Radio. I was able to draw from my own painful experiences to be a blessing to my dear friend. Just as God demonstrated to me that He indeed could accomplish all things through me, if I was a willing vessel, God had demonstrated this to Theresa; that he can, will and now has done the same thing through her.

"And folks, I really believe these feelings of inadequacy and inexperience are a pre-requisite for everyone when beginning a ministry for the Lord. God loves to give us the seemingly "impossible" task so we can see and experience and know that it indeed is God that is using us as His tool to get the job done. And when we are weak, we are strong... through His strength alone! Think about Abraham, Moses, David, Esther, the apostle Paul and many more!

"It wasn't easy. We encountered the impasses, the brick walls, the questions, the doubting tongues and more. One day I was walking through the radio station when it was just a big pile of lumber and sawdust. Two others were with me. I was chattering to them about the wonders of reaching the world through radio and how terrific this new outreach was going to be. I was rather stunned when they both started to say things like, 'It will be a miracle if this thing happens,' and 'Are you sure you know what you're getting into?' They brought up problems and obstacles that I had never even thought about. My eyes saw an exciting, thriving, effervescent, Earth shaking ministry, but those with me only saw the piles of lumber and sawdust and a mountain of headaches. I knew these optimistic 'eyes' had to come from Jesus because I had not always looked through these kind of glasses in the past.

"When beginning a ministry, we desperately need eye salve! We need to see prosperity when there is an empty bank account. We need to see growth and movement when it seems like nothing is happening. We need to see light in the darkness. . . and in a nutshell, we need to look through the eyes of the Divine. Because without a vision, we perish!"

Chapter 15

The "van" story is extraordinary. Linda wanted to include it in the book but Danny didn't. Since I didn't know the story, I was neutral. The reason Danny was reluctant to include it here is because he didn't want the reader to misinterpret the story as some type of bragging about he and Linda, or 3ABN giving gifts. That is not the gist of the story at all. Actually the "gifts" involved went far beyond he and Linda helping people out. And the entire episode in the first place was triggered by presents that had been given to them, not the other way around.

The story, which transpired over a period of several years, had only been told publicly once prior to a rally in Grants Pass, Oregon, in nineteen-ninety-nine. In order to determine the value of the narrative for this book I decided to delve into the archives and view the Grants Pass VCR tape myself. I have never come across a better example of the old adage, "it is better to give than to receive."

Once I perused the tape I felt that it is an integral part of the 3ABN story. I sided with Linda in favor of its incorporation into the book and poor ole' Dan didn't have a chance after that. After pondering the best way to present it here I decided my interpretation and writing style might blur the magnificence of the fundamental message involved. Therefore, I decided only slightly to paraphrase it as Danny told it that day in Oregon, when it was taped.

He said, "I'm hesitant to tell you this story. I hope you will take it in the right vein. Don't think about us, or that we're bragging about what we did. Some time ago, before 3ABN even existed, my family and I traveled and sang some gospel music. I had been in an accident. While playing basketball I broke my wrist and I was going to be off work for several months. I was a carpenter and didn't have insurance. We lived from day to day and from one pay-check to another. We didn't have any savings. This was in the nineteen-seventy-nine through nineteen-eighty time period. I remember we had been asked to go to Berrien Springs (Michigan) to sing. We had an old Dodge that was in pretty bad shape, with a bad muffler. But the worst part of it was that in Michigan in the winter it really gets cold. It was about a four-hundred-mile trip and I knew the van would not make it.

"I had a friend, a nationally known songwriter who was giving a seminar about twelve miles from my home, at Marion, Illinois. So he invited me to come down to see him and say hello. I spoke to several people there and recognized a fellow who is on the radio several hours a day and he is always trading things. I thought that maybe he could help us out. We really wanted to go to Michigan. We'd had offers to sing in several churches where they would take up offerings for us and we could sell cassettes and minister and, at the same time maybe pay some of our bills.

"So I asked this man if he knew where I could get a motor home? I explained that I had to go to Michigan and the trip would be about a thousand miles round-trip. He asked if I had tried the trailer sales and I replied that they were too expensive and I didn't have any money. He finally shrugged and admitted that he didn't know any solution to the problem.

"At that point a man walked up right beside us. His name was Dale Smith, from Dale, Indiana. Dale had a smile on his face. It always kind of bothers you when people walk up with a knowing smile and you know that they know something that you don't know and they don't want to volunteer telling you right of way.

"He said, 'Excuse me, I didn't mean to eavesdrop on you but I couldn't help overhearing you saying you needed a motor home. You don't know me but I know you. I've heard your family sing a few times. I have a motor home and you can use it. All you have to do is to come over to Indiana to get it.'

I didn't know this man from Adam and I told him how far I was going to have to travel and he said not to worry, I could use it anyway. About that time his wife walked over and he introduced me and she said that she recognized me too. He told her that the Lord had impressed him to loan me the motor home. She was smiling but it seemed like a forced smile. She pointed out that the vehicle was not insured. He assured her that they would insure it. Her reaction was to again smile but I could tell she was upset at the whole idea. You can always tell that reaction in a woman. I know that one. She pointed out that the license plates had expired. Undaunted, Dale said they would license it. He also said that they could put bottle gas in it and clean it up like it was new.

"By now, sensing her opposition, I tried to back off but he simply asked when I'd need it and I replied, 'Next Wednesday.' He told me to just come over to his place and they'd have it ready for me. Praise the Lord! I went home and told my wife about it. When Tuesday rolled around, I didn't have the money for gas to travel the one-hundred-forty miles to Dale, Indiana, to pick up the motor home. I didn't know what I was going to do. But that night I got a call from Dale's parents who live about six miles from my house.

"They told me that they were driving over to see their son on Wednesday. They had heard we were going to use the motor home and said that if I'd like I could ride to his house with them. I accepted and we drove to Dale's house the next day, me with all of eleven dollars in my pocket, for gas for the motor home.

"It was beautiful! They had cleaned it shiny new and put towels and wash rags in it and I noticed it had new license plates. They also gave me a little certificate of insurance. I was still amazed because I didn't know this guy and this was a beautiful motor home. As I was ready to drive away I rolled down my window and told him I might be as long as a week away from home. He said, 'Danny, don't worry about it. Take this motor home and use it in your ministry. If I ever need it back, I'll call you. There is only one other condition. That is, if anything goes wrong with it, I'll pay for it. All you do is put gas and oil in it. The insurance and everything else, I'll take care of.' I thanked him for his generosity and I was even more moved by all of this later when I found out why his wife had been so reluctant. I discovered that Dale was an unemployed coal miner and they didn't know where their next pay check would come from. He had been out of work for weeks. That is why they had let everything expire, because they didn't have the money.

"I put about ten dollars worth of gas in the motor home. It already had some gas, so with the extra ten dollars of fuel, I knew I had enough to get home.

"After I returned home, I was showing my wife our new blessing when she asked, 'Do we have enough money to buy gas to get to Michigan?' I told her No, but we should pack anyway. As I was talking to her about it, a man from our church pulled up in our drive and came to the motor home. I invited him in and began telling him about our new miracle when he asked, 'Well, do you have enough money to buy gas to get to Michigan?' I told him No, but I wasn't worried about it because I knew God would provide. 'Well,' he said, 'That's why I'm here. The Lord impressed me to give you sixty dollars for gas to get you to Michigan.'

"Sure enough, the sixty dollars got us to Michigan, and once there as we began to sing in a few churches and sold our music cassettes, there was enough money to pay for the whole trip, plus enough to pay some bills.

"The story ended sadly for us because it was at the end of that trip when we were at home, the next day, driving our own vehicle, that Melody's mother, my first wife, Kay, was killed in an accident. We didn't need the motor home anymore after that and ended up giving it back. My daughter and I continued to travel and sing and we met Linda some time later and God blessed us in a marriage and I'm very thankful to have her.

"You know, Satan is out to steal kill and destroy. He's going to take what's good and try to make God look terrible. But God is a Creator. He can take these ugly things in your life, like the death of a loved one, sin, death, disease and sickness and He can turn those and make something beautiful out of it if you choose to allow Him to work through you. I've seen that happen in our lives and through our ministry.

"Several years ago, I was at 3ABN and some people came to the station to sing. The fellow is a blind person who plays the piano, and had previously been on national television. He also had Cerebral Palsy and was a genius who could hear anything and replay it perfectly. He could play classical music or any other style because of his unusual gift. They were in an old van almost exactly like the old Dodge van that I had been driving fifteen years before, the one I decided would never make it to Michigan. The vehicle was in bad shape and had no air conditioning to cope with the July heat. It broke down at the studio and the lady who was taking care of the singer came to me and asked if I knew anyone who could fix this engine or if there was a used van available at a low price. We walked outside and looked at it but the engine had been blown and it was hopeless. I'm reluctant to even tell this story because it might sound like, 'Danny's doing this,' and I don't mean it that way at all. If you hear the entire story I think it can be a blessing to all of us, because it has been to me.

"At that time Linda and I had been blessed with a new

195

conversion van. We traveled in it. It was very comfortable, with a high roof, a beautiful van. It was low mileage, at about thirty-five-thousand miles. So I walked outside to look at their vehicle, then I began to look at our new van, this beautiful Ford conversion van, and it was like I saw the name of this singer printed on the side of ours. I was thinking to myself, 'no way. I can't even entertain that thought. There's no way that we can do this.'

"I went ahead and talked to her for a few minutes and it's just like the Lord said, 'Why don't you give that van to them? They need it, give the van to them.' But I thought that we just couldn't do that. There is no way we can do that. And it was like the Lord was asking me, 'Danny, are you depending on that van, or Me?'

"So I asked the lady if a van like this one would help to satisfy their travel needs. She was overwhelmed, just by the idea. 'Oh, my goodness' she said. "It's so beautiful, but we could never afford something like that.' Well I told her a little grimly and gritting my teeth, 'I'm afraid you can.'

"I guess I have to confess to you here that I wasn't a very cheerful giver that day because I loved our van. Rick Odle (Seventh-day Adventist pastor) always says that 'confession is good for the soul but hard on the reputation.' But there was no question that God had impressed me to give them what they so desperately needed to continue their ministry. So I told them that I was impressed that they needed the van worse than we did. You see I hadn't realized it but the channel of blessing was beginning to kick in. God gives us opportunities from time to time to meet channels of blessings and if we're not faithful I think the blessings get cut. God doesn't cut them. We block up that channel with our selfishness. Finally I just told them, 'You take this van.' Obviously, they were thrilled and overwhelmed.

"It wasn't long after that that we had a motor home. We had used it, but not a lot. A singer, along with his family, came to perform at 3ABN. They had two teenagers and they were traveling in a van. It was in bad shape. The motor was knocking and sounded terrible. He wanted to know if we knew a good mechanic. 'What we really need is a motor home,' he said.

"He is a wonderful singer and a wonderful man and we are friends to this day. He has a great ministry that reaches tens of thousands of people. I won't give his name because that's not important, but it's probably somebody that you would recognize and love, who has appeared on 3ABN. He can tell the story if he wants to, and probably has. So he was telling about these problems as I walked outside and I looked over at that motor home and in my mind's eye I could see his name printed on it. Oh, no, I thought, not again!

"I knew that we could use that motor home occasionally but it was like the Holy Spirit told me to let him use it because he would use it every day and it would help him immensely. I asked him to come over and take a look at it. He walked inside and was so excited about what he saw.

"'It's beautiful,' he said. 'If only we could afford something like this.' I told him the Lord had impressed me to let him take the motor home and use it and if I ever needed it I'll call him. He was stunned and replied, 'What? You've got to be kidding.'

"I assured him I wasn't joking but there was one condition. He suddenly got a knowing look as if to say that, 'yeah, here it comes. I knew there would be a catch.' I told him the special condition is that we pay for the insurance and if anything goes wrong with the engine we pay to repair it.

"Again he was startled and asked why I would do such a thing. I told him to be honest with him I didn't want to. But the Holy Spirit was inside saying to do it. I think we have all experienced this when the voice inside us tells us what is right. It didn't take me long to realize that this motor home would be more of a blessing to him than to us. He could win over more souls if he had this vehicle to help his ministry and so he took it with him.

"It was only a matter of weeks before Dr. Raymond Moore, from Washington State, called me and said that he and Dorothy had a beautiful motor home. It was worth a lot more than the one I had just let this person use. He told me that they did not need it anymore and asked if I had a use for one. I told him that we had just in effect given one away and therefore we could use one. He told me to come and get it, that we could have it. He said they would just sign it over to us. I know these people and was convinced that they would have kept it in top condition.

"We had not even had a chance to go out and pick it up yet when a family which included four children, two teenagers and two younger ones, came to 3ABN to tape some music for us. Can you guess what happened to their van when they got to Thompsonville (Illinois)? That's right, the engine blew up. When I walked into the studio they were trying to put on their best face. They were trying to sing and be happy. Here were these people who travel around the country to perform and had been using a van to accommodate all of them, and their equipment and personal belongings. This situation was bad enough but to complicate matters, that inadequate vehicle was broken down. They asked me to pray for them. They knew that God had blessed Linda and me, and 3ABN and they hoped some of that might rub off on them. I told them that I would of course pray for them, and with them.

"When we were finished, I went to my office and was looking for something when I opened my desk drawer. The first thing that I spotted was a photograph of the motor home that Raymond had sent me. It jumped out at me and guess whose name I saw written on the side of it? That's right! I groaned and said to the Lord that we didn't even get this one yet, we haven't used it, haven't done anything with it. But then I began to think about it. This family could be a channel of blessing.

"So I gathered up the picture and took it out and showed it to them. Its beauty awed them. I told the Dad that we would fly him out to get it and he could drive it back. They could go ahead and use it and if I ever needed it, I would let them know. I made the same deal with them about our paying for the insurance, license and maintenance, just like Dale had done for me to begin this unusual chain of events... this 'channel.'

"Here we were. We were rid of the motor homes and rid of the good vans. All we had left was a little Minivan. This left us in a bit of a bind for space. We would make a short trip, or go to the airport and wouldn't have room for our entire luggage and equipment. It was extremely difficult to travel. We really needed a full-sized van. It didn't have to be the nice quality of those we had before and let go, but we definitely need something bigger.

"One afternoon I told Linda, 'Let's go down to the Ford dealer and see if we can trade in ours for a big van like we need.'

"She asked if we had the money and I answered no, but I just wanted to look. We did find one on the lot. It was full sized and was not the top of the line but it was far from the worst. I began to deal with the salesman and he finally said he'd make the deal for our van and fifteen-thousand-seven-hundred-fifty dollars. I told him no, that I wasn't ready right then to deal, so he told me it was a good deal, to go home and think about it.

"When we arrived home there was a blink on our answering machine indicating someone had called. When I pushed the play button a guy gave his name, a name I had never heard before. I didn't know him then and I still don't know him.

"He said, 'The Lord has impressed me with some urgency that you need fifteen-thousand dollars. I don't know why you need it, but you must know what it is so I sent it to you by overnight express.'

"I told Linda that this had to be for that van we had just looked at. That's all there is to it, it had to be for that purpose. The next day I went back to the dealer and told him I'd trade him for fifteen-thousand dollars even. I was more confident then because I had money. He said that deal would never happen but when I started to leave he asked me to wait, that he'd have another go at his boss. When he returned his rock solid position had moved downward to fifteen-thousand-two-hundred-fifty dollars. I told him no, that God had provided fifteen-thousand dollars and if He wanted me to pay a penny more, He would have given that much. The guy threw up his arms and said he wasn't going to argue with God, so we made the deal.

"So we acquired this beautiful van. A short time after that we had a couple visit 3ABN. They were from Texas. He was a former professional athlete who had made a lot of money before going into the ministry. We took them to a Bonanza Restaurant and he was dressed in a four-hundred dollar suit and his wife was also dressed very fashionably and expensively. Well, I buy my suits at Sears, and some even at discount stores and usually pay under one-hun-dred-fifty dollars. Linda usually buys dresses for seventy dollars or so.

"But here is this guy, a former pro athlete who had gone into a Seventh-day Adventist ministry who is now working to feed kids and work with kids on drugs and with other problems. Anyway, we're on our way to this restaurant with me driving and I hear her say in the back seat, 'If we only had a van like this for these kids.'

"No, not this time I was telling myself. Pardon this expression because I only use it when I'm at home and not on TV but I said to myself, 'There ain't no way!' Why not? Because they dressed better than we did. They made us look like Jack, the rag picker's kids. I love both of them, but I'm not giving them our van. And I didn't.

"They left and a few days later a man came to visit us. He is a wealthy Adventist who had visited us a few years before. He said during that previous visit that he had been thinking about donating a nice Suburban to 3ABN. On this visit, which was just a couple of days after the other couple had left, he told us, 'You know I had forgotten about it, but a couple of years ago when I saw you I told you I was going to get you a new Suburban.' I told him that yes, he had said that. But he left after the visit and went home and we never received that vehicle from him. He is very generous and had gone home and made a very generous gift to 3ABN instead of giving us a Suburban.

"Here's what happened. Let me tell you the principle of what happened. It is something that for me is very sobering.

"I asked the Lord, 'What is going on here?' I began to pray for an answer and He in turn began to deal with me. He told me what my problem was. He told me that I had given a van to a blind person 'because you saw that he really needed it. You also gave a van to that singer's family because you saw they really needed it. Then you gave a motor home to the other group because of their desperate need. You were giving out of your heart. And when I asked you to give to these folks, you didn't give because you didn't see a need.'

"You see, if it's God speaking, then I have to kick in to the faith mode, not the selfish mode or the Danny Shelton mode. God taught me a tremendous lesson by using this incident. You see, I wasn't really thinking. My eyes told me that these folks didn't really need it so I wasn't ready to give it. Suddenly I had shut off the Holy Spirit and justified it in my own mind because they dressed so much better than Linda and me. Do you see what I did wrong?

"And the Lord was showing me, and I'm sure to this date, that had I given that van which was worth about twenty-thousand dollars, that I would have received a Suburban worth about thirty-five-thousand dollars because that man

201

wouldn't have forgotten his commitment. That he did forget, was divine providence. The Lord was saying, 'See? Are you going to trust Me or not trust Me?'

A few weeks later we went to an ASI Convention and I saw this couple from Texas, the former pro athlete. We began talking and I asked them if they had ever acquired a van like they needed. They said no they had not. I didn't hesitate to tell them that we felt that they needed our van more than we did and it was theirs. They began shouting and getting excited right out in front of the hall where Sabbath Church was going on and I shushed them and told them to calm down or they would think we've gone Pentecostal.

"They said praise the Lord, do you mean this. I assured them that I did. But I was up front with them and told them the entire story, that had I rejected the idea first time around because they dressed so much better than us and seemed to have so much more money. I knew that God wanted them to have the van as a channel of blessing. I told them it was up to them now to decide how to use it. They did come and get the van and now kids are being hauled and young people are being taken to where they can get help. They are being ministered and being fed. The van is being put to much better use now than when it was with us. And guess what? A few months after this, the man who owned the Suburban called and donated it to us. We are still using it in the ministry!

"You see, what we have is not really ours. If we believe we are channels of blessing then God blesses us. The reason that He continues to bless 3ABN is because of the decision made years ago that the network was to be a channel of blessing. Don't ever make the mistake of holding things to your chest and saying to yourselves, 'No, this is ours, this is surely ours. God gave it to us, so He must have wanted us to have it.' He wants it to go where it will go best to further His Kingdom.

202

"Some time ago, a man drove up to 3ABN in this big motor home. It listed new for over two-hundred-thousand dollars and he had it appraised used shortly before coming to 3ABN at seventy-nine-thousand dollars.

"He pulled up on the parking lot and said, 'Where do you want me to park this? The Lord has impressed me to give it to you.'

"This time the Lord let us sell this one and put the money into operations. Shortly after we sold that motor home we received a call from Oregon from a couple who wanted to donate a beautiful motor home with a diesel engine. The Lord has allowed us to use this motor home to this day to travel to camp meetings, live 3ABN rallies, etc., to carry our 3ABN booth, as well as equipment and products throughout America. Al and Bernie Denslow are volunteers who spend months each year driving this motor home from place to place.

"A few months after this motor home was donated to 3ABN, we received a call from Hattiesburg, Mississippi from a brother who wanted to donate a nice motor home to us. Before we had even gone to Hattiesburg, I was talking to a woman involved in a singing ministry. They have several children and really need a motor home to travel in. The next week we were able to pick up the motor home and bring it to 3ABN and clean it up just in time for her to come and get it. Praise the Lord, it is now being used by this family to win souls for Jesus!

"A few months after that a family on the west coast donated a beautiful truck and thirty-one foot camper. We brought it back to 3ABN a couple of weeks later, and I was praying what to do with it when I received a call from Dale Smith. I had only seen Dale two or three times in the past twenty years since he loaned me his motor home back in 1982. He had lived away from the midwest a number of years and had now moved to southern Illinois.

"Dale told me that he had recently been called by the

Lord to be an evangelist. He had received invitations to speak over the course of several weeks in Wyoming. Though Dale belongs to a Pentecostal organization, he said the Lord had impressed him that he would eventually be speaking in SDA churches. He told me that he had never been in a SDA church, but that in every city that he was speaking in, he felt compelled to look up SDA churches. He told me the Lord had impressed him to call me to set up an appointment hoping that I might be able to shed some light on this situation. The Lord did give me a message for him, though I won't share it publicly at this time.

"After we talked for a couple hours, I asked Dale how he was traveling to Wyoming. He said that he and his wife and two kids were taking his crew cab truck. I asked him what he would live in for the next couple of months. He told me that he had looked at campers, but decided that the Smiths couldn't afford the one that he and his family really liked. I told him that someone had given 3ABN a thirty-one foot camper and invited him outside to look at it. As we drove up close to it, he looked shocked. I asked him if he wanted to go look inside, and he informed me that he didn't need to because that was the exact camper that he had wanted but couldn't afford to buy. I looked inside as he stayed outside and described in detail the exact layout of this camper.

"Dale had planted a seed twenty years before, with God's blessings, it now not only had blessed many others, but now even had come back to bless him! Yes, the Lord impressed me to tell him to take it and use it on his trip to minister for God's honor and glory.

"Only two weeks ago, God blessed us with another beautiful motor home, and the very next day the Lord told us where to place it. Now, even as I write this, we have yet another beautiful motor home, donated only yesterday. I have a feeling God already has a plan for it!

"It's my prayer that each of us can experience the joy of becoming a 'Channel of Blessing.' The Lord says in

Matthew 25:23, '...Well done, good and faithful servant; thou hast been faithful over a few things, I will make thee ruler over many things...' In other words, His desire for us is to be channels of blessings.

Chapter 16

To Russia, with love! Nowhere is the influence of 3ABN's vision seen more ardently and eloquently than in the former Soviet Union. We can quit skirting around the "M" word as we have in previous chapters and use it flat out here. What transpired in Russia, there in the heart of that bastion of atheism, is a miracle. And it happened in the blink of an eye, in God's time.

In all fairness I must confess that this writer was pessimistic about the Russian project in the early days. One morning I was talking to Danny Shelton after he had just returned from Russia and he said, "Oh, by the way, I think we have found a building and grounds that we can buy."

I had previously accompanied him on two trips to Gorky (after the fall of communism they later changed the name of the city to Nizhny Novgorod) and I was generally familiar with the city on the Volga River. During the communist years westerners were not allowed to visit Gorky because it was a strategic industrial area where they produced war materials. But since I'd been there a few times, Danny tried to describe the general location of the property within the city to me but I couldn't quite summon it up in my mind's eye. Nonetheless I was very excited about this prospect because private ownership by Americans in Russia is rare even today. Almost all property is owned by the state. At that time, in the early nineteen-nineties, private ownership was virtually nonexistent. Just how Danny was going to pull this off was beyond me, but I had learned enough about him by then that if he said it was going to happen, it would probably happen.

Danny was very excited about this location. It was a

building that the government had started and then, for whatever reason, had not finished. When he told me this fact I began to get enthusiastic because in Russia government buildings are magnificent. They are well built, ornate and immaculately groomed. Such structures stand out in stark contrast to private citizens' dwellings and homes, virtually all of which were in shambles, little if any plumbing, decrepit and unpainted for decades. Danny envisioned the location in question as a place where God could build a Christian cultural center. A location from where His Word could go out to people who had been suppressed and deprived of Christianity for over seventy years, and generally downtrodden for several hundred years. Danny's enthusiasm for this project was so pronounced that it was infectious and I agreed to go back to Russia with him to check it out first hand. That travel decision was a big mistake on my part, from an emotional standpoint. After all, what you don't see can't hurt you, and just going along with Danny's bright description, without personal verification, would have made me a most happy fellow.

Return to Russia we did though, and as we drove from the Gorky train station we passed several splendid government buildings and as we approached each one I was thinking, "is this the one?" But the answer each time was "no." Then we arrived at and pulled onto the property in question, Shelton's highly trumpeted future Russian branch of 3ABN. I was appalled, utterly devastated by the broken-down condition of the structure. Yes, structure. I wouldn't dignify it with the aesthetic description "building." It was horrible! Knowing Danny's keen sense of humor I even allowed momentarily for the possibility that this was an extravagant practical joke on me, that we would back the car out and drive to the real location. But no, this was indeed the "magnificent" grounds and building that he had been so excited about back in America. I had just traveled for twenty-four-hours straight through, flown across an ocean, taken a discomforting overnight train ride on a primitive railroad where the station houses at both ends were hangouts (at that time, they have since been modernized and cleaned up) for thugs, drunks and drug abusers. And then, in an exhausted state of mind and disheveled of dress, was transported by automobile to this site to observe what looked like a bombed out hulk!

As near as I could determine its history, the government had begun the building years before as an opera house of sorts but following some Russian logic they had simply abandoned it. The building was big, for sure, but all ground floors were dirt and mud inside the building. There were wooden planks to walk on to avoid most of the quagmire but where there were no such hastily devised walkways you were left to your own devises to negotiate the interior layout. Such as it was the building seemed endless, three floors high with cavernous areas in its bowels. The sky was visible from virtually every unfinished room in the structure. I wanted to just plop down (in the mud) and weep. I was certainly in no mood to patronize Danny. When I frankly expressed my disappointment and trepidation about the daunting technical problems of construction, not to mention the monumental cost of working in a foreign city where equipment and material were rationed only to government agencies and projects, he was not offended in the least. That is because he had worked out all of these problems and details and patiently explained it all to me.

As he looked around him, at his "magnificent structure," he said simply, "God will provide." I fervently wanted to believe him and Him. I really did, because by now I was forming a great fondness and admiration for 3ABN and what it stands for. After all, had I not already personally witnessed remarkable accomplishments by the network? Had not mountains been moved? Didn't I observe impossible accomplishments simply being reduced to the status of "impossible just takes a little longer?"

But this?! Tired and unkempt from constant travel, standing ankle deep in mud (inside the building), I simply could not share the dream. The indefatigable Danny however, was in his element. He roamed around from one room to another, eyes all aglow. "This will be…" he said, "and here we'll build…" He was listening to some inner voice that I couldn't hear, and seeing something unobservable to me. Apparently it was Him communicating, He, who was to become general contractor on this project.

Today, in retrospect, I am ashamed of my weak, pessimistic initial reaction upon viewing the Russian Center property for the first time. I, of little faith, could simply not capture Danny's vision when I first viewed the site. In the photo section of this book you will see the fruition of Danny's dream. Today it can arguably be described as one of the most magnificent privately owned buildings in all of Russia that is dedicated to improving the quality of the lives of Russian citizens. It is teeming with people who, through the center today, become educated in many skills, as well as learning good health habits. Healthful cooking and eliminating alcohol and drug abuse is taught. The latter of which is critical in Russia as much as it is in America, perhaps even more so. Young people can find sports and other healthy activities at the center and in the process many of these people find God, too. The Russian studios of 3ABN are located at the center with better programming than that provided the state network, and this message sweeps out in a constant ever-widening circle throughout Russia.

In two-thousand-two, Julia Outkina, director of the Russian Evangelism Center, along with other workers, attended the Euro-Asian Convention for Television and Radio Broadcasters, which was held in Moscow. Many broadcasters from throughout the former Soviet Union, including officials from the Author Regional Television (ART), visited the 3ABN booth set up there. The visitors viewed samples of the programming produced at the

Center and were so impressed that they verbally committed on the spot to carry some of it on their own networks in the future.

Soon after the convention, ART wrote and requested a catalog of the Russian programming. Outkina reported to 3ABN U.S.A. that ART ordered a large number of programs to be broadcast free of charge. ART made their debut in Russia in January of two-thousand-two to a potential audience of sixty-eight million viewers and thereafter continued to add new cable stations throughout the country. Another eventuality that resulted from the convention was a contract with a local station in Sergiev Posad (formerly known as Zagorsk), which is the main center of the Russian Orthodox Church. Finally, the Center is taking the audio portion of the television programs and making them available to radio stations throughout Russia. That radio ministry continues to grow in Russia.

In several follow-up trips to Russia since that less-than-impressive first visit I have watched the center grow by leaps and bounds. Through the incredible indomitable spirit of those that believed in the project from the start, and who were willing to lend backbreaking labor, an inspiring transformation has taken place. This all happened in a city of shortages where such basic items as light bulbs and toilet paper were unavailable, and the tools of construction and basic building materials were as rare as hens' teeth. If the workers wanted ten tons of sand from point A to point B, they formed a human bucket brigade. The elderly men and women who worked side-by-side with younger workers most often peopled these lines. Even to the get materials to the upper floors this ancient "human chain" method had to be used. One story especially accentuates the lack of available working tools and building materials. On one occasion Danny said he needed some brooms. A couple of workers started off toward the woods. They scoffed at the idea of simply "buying" brooms even though money was available. There were no such sweeping devices to be found in stores in the city and the workers, as they always did, were going to make their own.

Old men and women worked wherever they were assigned, from basement to rooftop, alongside the younger laborers because it was going to be their church too. There were so many touching individual stories. One seventy-eight-year-old woman told me that she had come to the site to work every day because she wanted to earn a few coins to give her gravely ill husband a better burial than would the state. During my last visit she told me she had accomplished that grim drudgery but had stayed on, for several years at that time, working full time as a volunteer at the center. She told me, "After seventy years I have finally found God, here. My life is so bright now. I have something to live for and I am happy."

Some workers, both paid and volunteer, came from hundreds of miles around. They worked in the heat of summer and continued through the freezing weather. The kind of brutish winters that have saved Mother Russia throughout her history by defeating invading armies, most notably the French and the Germans. The project has been ongoing for years now and it is ever expanding. It has been accomplished at a staggering cost financially, money that has been provided through the 3ABN channel of blessing. But build it they did. Against impossible working conditions and against all odds, they built it. Overcoming savage weather, they built it. Staving off a hostile political environment, they built it. Comprising over one-hundred-thousand square feet, they built it. God bless them, they built it. On subsequent visits to Russia I have stood in awe, witnessing and embracing the glory that so richly belongs to them. And to Him.

In the following passage Danny Shelton relates how he acquired the property and explains some of the difficulties involved in developing the Christian Cultural Center in

Russia. I was present when the described meeting with the Russian Adventists took place in the hotel lobby. An event where Danny tells about raising one-hundred-thousand dollars in a most unusual manner, money used to help build a new church. In Danny's words:

"In December of nineteen-ninety-one, Evangelist John Carter called me and told me he was going to Gorky, Russia, in the spring to hold an evangelistic series and he wanted me and 3ABN to participate. He explained that this was a city of over three million people located about two-hundred-fifty miles north of Moscow. I had never been to Russia before and it seemed like an exciting thing to do, to go into a communist country to spread the Word. Carter went over in January to set things up and in May of nineteen-ninety-two, we took our 3ABN crew and equipment to Russia and held our first series.

"We had no idea whether or not anyone would show up for the meetings but we rented an abandon indoor sports center with seating for about six-thousand people. The first night about twenty-thousand people showed up and we ended up filling the auditorium three times and instead of having one meeting a night we held three. We saw some six-thousand people come to Christ and over two-thousand-five-hundred baptized. We were thrilled about that.

"While we were there I met with the Russian Seventh-day Adventists' conference leaders. There have been Adventists in Russia for over one hundred years and they were persecuted during the Communist years. They only had one church in the city and it would hold about two-hundreed-fifty people. It was full to capacity and at the time, because of the Carter meetings, they suddenly had over two-thousand-five-hundred new members and no place to accommodate them. They had absolutely no money for a new building for evangelism and I felt impressed to help them if I could. We were staying at an old, run down hotel built on a bluff overlooking the Volga

River. These church leaders asked if they could visit us there for a meeting. While we were waiting for them in the lobby an American man, named Manny, walked up to me and began a conversation. He had paid his own way and come to Russia with the Carter group. He had already been there for a few weeks. He was restless and said frankly that he didn't even know why he was really there. He had just come to Russia to see if he could help in any way, by doing menial tasks like arranging chairs, passing out literature and so on. He had a tape recorder and asked me if I would tell him a little about 3ABN, which he had previously only heard of. I told him I only had a few minutes because I had to meet with these Russians. But we talked for awhile until the Russians we were waiting for showed up and we talked there in the lobby. When the local group did arrive I asked Manny if he would like to join us. He did so, reluctantly, not wanting to intrude, and again mumbling that he wasn't even sure what he was doing there in the first place.

"I began the conversation by getting right to the point and asking what it would cost to purchase a building and property, or to build a building that would seat three to four thousand people. They were taken aback by this question. 'Oh, no,' their spokesman said. 'That would be too much money, way too much money.' I posed the question again asking how much is too much. They looked at me as if I couldn't grasp the enormity, the sheer impossibility of what I was asking for. 'At least one hundred thousand dollars,' their leader replied. I made sure I understood them correctly through the interpreter and pressed the issue making it clear that we could build a church big enough for all those recently baptized, and to allow for growth, for the sum of one hundred thousand dollars. Suddenly a gleam of hope sprang into their eyes. 'Surely the impossible hasn't suddenly entered into the realm of distant possibility!' their facial expressions read. I told them that I would return to America, to 3ABN, and we would tell our viewers about all of this and we would pray. I added that we would do everything we could to raise the money for their church, God willing. I said if we were successful, we would purchase a building or build one. This almost sent them into shock. They were ecstatic just considering the prospect of such a miracle. There was no doubt that more than a few prayers in Russian would be answered here, if we could deliver. Their eager nods made it unnecessary for 'Da! Tyuank you Zhesus' to be interpreted for us. Of course, there was still room for doubt after all. From their perspective that amount of money was huge in America. In Russia, given the exchange rate, it was astronomical.

"After the meeting I got up and almost forgot about Manny who had been sitting there quietly observing throughout. I was trying to be polite to him and not make it appear that he was pestering me. I told him I would get on this project as soon as I returned to America. He looked at me with a big smile. He was beaming actually and he said, 'well, now I think I know why the Lord has brought me to Russia.' Again, to be polite more than anything, I said good, and why is that? I asked him if, after hearing the conversation, he wanted to make a contribution toward the project. 'Yes,' he said. 'I'll give you the one-hundred-thousand dollars you need!'

"Here, just when I thought I had figured out a game plan, to return to 3ABN and raise the money, it turned out that God had already come up with a better way. He had impressed this man who had traveled half way around the world, and who had hung around for several weeks seemingly without purpose by his own admission, to provide the vital means to build a church for our Russian brothers. He did give the money as promised. God is good.

"We began a search and a few months later they found a building so I went back to Russia to look at it. It was all grown up in trees. It was only a shell of a building and you could see right through it. It was intended originally to be an opera house that they had started fifteen or twenty years previously. Some of the roof was done but most of it was unfinished. Our advisor there thought the one-hundred-thousand dollars would buy it and it would take fifty-thousand dollars more to finish it.

"Of course, as a construction person myself I knew it would cost much more than that to convert this site into a viable center. And as I envisioned, the eventual cost to do the building, television studios, air time, continued Evangelistic, about forty employees and literature such as Russian Bibles, has run the cost into several million dollars. But I felt the Lord would provide and, after many international legal entanglements, He has, to the extent that 3ABN in the former Soviet Union is now seen in more than one-hundred-ninety-five cities."

Construction

"As a person who has worked in construction myself and was part of my own construction company at one time, I know that building can be difficult even under the best of circumstances. Working under the conditions that existed in post-communism Russia was extremely tough. Everything in the country had come grinding to a halt. Material was scarce and equipment lay rusting on job sites. More importantly the people themselves, at all levels, were confused and aimless in their everyday lives. At best, working conditions were confused. A case in point was a situation where they needed to drill some holes through the concrete on the roof to hang rods through. Workers were up there with hammers and chisels assaulting this thick concrete like they would have a hundred years ago. That was an enormous task to attempt to accomplish but here were eight people up there trying to drill through seven inches of concrete by hand. I asked them why they didn't buy a drill. A spokesman said that drills were too expensive. When I asked if a drill could be found, he replied that they could be located, but he repeated that the cost was prohibitive. I asked if they could buy one at a lumber yard and they were totally confused, having no idea of what a lumberyard was. I explained a typical lumber yard back home with all that could be purchased there. They looked skeptical like perhaps this was some kind of American joke. Surely no such places existed. No, when they needed something they would just go look around the city and when they found it, they would haggle over the price.

"Finally, they assured me that they could probably find the type drill and bit that was needed but the cost would be prohibitive, as much as ten or fifteen dollars. I gave the drill hunter fifteen dollars and he took off across the field to the road to hitch a ride. After a few hours he returned. He had found an electric drill at another construction site for ten dollars and brought the five dollars change back, a remarkably honest thing to do when there was no tracing the purchase and no receipt, and considering that these people were hungry.

"Because of the shortage of back-saving equipment, at first every task was done by the sweat of the brow. For example, there was a need for tons of dirt inside to fill in the floors prior to pouring concrete. They would have thirty people form a human chain and pass dirt and sand to where it was needed. I asked them if they had a 'dozer' or a crane to lift heavy stuff to the roof. Always the answer was the same, 'It is much too expensive.'

"They worked on the assumption that we simply could not afford to acquire the needed equipment. They would move piles of bricks one at a time, sometimes throwing them upward from floor to floor, one at a time. Of course, they needed thousands of them for a building of this immense size. I asked about hiring a crane and got the same old song and dance about too much money. But we overcame that and negotiated the needed equipment (for an average of three dollars per day) which took a tremendous work load off those gallant people who were prepared to do the back-breaking labor because they so much believed in the cause.

"All of this was a result of an incredible paradox. There was construction equipment everywhere but it belonged to no one. The government had owned everything and soldiers ran the equipment under Communism. It was the same with food. People were going hungry despite the fact that there were bumper crops, but no one to harvest or transport them. The government had always done that before. The entire system of their society had been jerked out from under them, like a rug. And there was no workable structure replacing it. And nobody knew how to do anything for himself or herself because they had previously been taken care of and told what to do from cradle to grave.

"Strong leadership was called for here. I returned to America and talked to my cousin's husband, John Kantor, who has had considerable experience in construction work. I asked him if he would go to Russia for a few months to oversee this project. John said he would do this and he threw himself into the job with professionalism and enthusiasm.

"The 'few months' extended into about three years, but after those three years the Lord has blessed us and we have the largest Protestant facility in all of the former Soviet Union. It is impressive in size. As far as worship is concerned, it has an auditorium that will hold one-thousand-two-hundred people and another one for Youth Church that holds over five-hundred. Our 3ABN Russian studios are also located in one wing of this huge building. Also, Sabbath Schools and it houses a small clinic area. It is truly a massive project by any standard.

"The spirit of the people was inspiring. When I first arrived there were eight people on the roof drilling holes by hammer and chisel, like I mentioned. They were elderly folks and they had gotten to the roof by a ladder that was made of saplings they had cut down and tied together with ropes. They would climb the final thirty feet to the roof using this precarious method. The elders were so enthused.

"They were members of the church and they were excited about building a place for God. By my second and third trip they had already been working as volunteers for months before we had a chance to eventually hire them. They just wanted to help. We had fifty or sixty church members that would come out every Sunday and weekdays to do menial tasks and basic labor, many of whom had been baptized through our meetings there. They supplemented Kantor's hired crew of construction workers that sometimes reached more than one-hundred people.

"Along with the standard problems of construction found under the best of working conditions, and the unique situation of the scarcity of equipment and materials, came the legal entanglements. Because of the progressive thinking of Boris Nemptsov, governor of the Nizhny Novgorod area, privatization of property was allowed and encouraged.

"I was introduced to Nemptsov through his sister, Julia Outkina, a woman who attended our early meetings and was converted. Julia was to eventually become an integral part of 3ABN's explosive growth in Russia. The governor opened the door to private ownership long before most other areas of the former Soviet Union and as a result, brought Western and foreign money into his city. There were still major hurdles.

"One was the fact that you didn't really know who to deal with on such matters as land title, building codes, zoning and a multitude of other legalities. Various groups would claim authority and jurisdiction and most of them were only concerned about getting money from you. People in America mostly believed that free enterprise stepped in with the fall of communism. That was simply not true. At virtually every level communists were still in places of authority. They had run the country for seventy years and things were not about to change over night. Where non-communists stepped in, they mostly did not know how to govern. The Lord blessed us though and Boris Nemptsov turned out to be a caring person who had been anti-Communist in the previous regime and therefore somewhat of an outcast during Red rule. He eventually rose in the political ranks to become very important in government under Boris Yeltsin.

"There were also other problems that impeded progress. The language barrier was always there and no matter how many interpreters we hired, communication problems arose. Kantor learned to speak Russian to develop rapport with his workers. There was also the attitude of the Russian worker. In the final years under communism the system was slowly disintegrating. Workers wandered without direction or leadership. A Russian joke was, 'the government pretends to pay us and we pretend to work.' The average worker did not want to take orders from another Russian because they had been told exactly what to do all of their lives. That's why I brought in Kantor who proved to be an able leader. But it all came together over a period of about three years. Through the ministry of John Carter and the support of 3ABN about eighteen-thousand people had been baptized into the Seventh-day Adventist Church by two-thousand-two, and the network was seen in one-hundred-ninety-five cities in the former Soviet Union. It has been a rewarding experience to watch God's will unfolding in a land where He was often rejected in the past.

"I mentioned Dr. Julia Outkina and her contribution to the project, which has been profound. If I had to name people in my life who I respect the most, Julia would be close to the top of that list. She has a Ph.D. in linguistics with a specialty in English. She taught English which has become widespread in the Russian educational system. She only came to our nineteen-ninety-two meetings with John

Carter just to hear the English language spoken. She hadn't had a chance prior to nineteen-ninety-two to meet Americans and practice their language because until them, Gorky had been a city closed to westerners. We were among the first Americans to go there after the communist ban was lifted.

"There were aircraft manufactured there and work on nuclear submarines. Thus, no outsiders were allowed. Julia had never spoken to an American to hear our language first hand and therefore the meetings provided her an excellent opportunity to hone her English. As it turns out, she was to gain much more in the bargain.

"After several weeks, she began to feel a new spirit moving within her and she was overwhelmed with the presence of God. She accepted Jesus Christ and was baptized into the SDA Church. She worked with the center project from day one and played a vital role in its construction and development. She also became the director of the 3ABN in Russia. The year two-thousand-two marked a decade of dedicated service from Julia and she in turn has moved many Russians toward accepting God in their lives. I would be so bold as to say that without her, we wouldn't even have started this project.

"Originally, Julia traveled to our Illinois studio to tape programming in Russian, but the center is so well established there now that they have state-of-the-art equipment as sophisticated as any in Russia and they create their own programming taped and live.

"Ongoing now, the center has a church that will hold about one-thousand-two-hundred people. Also, one of the major Seventh-day Adventist Conferences has offices there. It holds a youth chapel where young people come to practice music and hold church. A major program is to bring American doctors to the center to work on peoples' teeth and give them other medical examinations. For some Russians, they have never had the benefit of this level of professional treatment.

"And, as far as communists are concerned, we have had numerous individuals who were high-ranking members of the party who have since converted and given their lives to the Lord.

"A major problem in the early days consisted of dealing with the legal issues. We attempted at every turn to comply with all of the rules put forth. This was new legal ground being broken and often 'officials' of varying degrees of authority would show up with demands that needed to be satisfied along with the inevitable 'fees' that accompanied these requirements. Sometimes it amounted to little more than bribes. However in recent years things seem to be better, perhaps because the center has had such a positive effect on the city and an ever-widening area of Russia.

"I'm sure that Julia still encounters daily problems with officialdom, but the powers that be seem to understand now that we are good for the Russians. Not only in winning of souls and giving them a better way of life, but also from a financial standpoint because 3ABN has employed as many as one-hundred-twenty people at a time, all of whom earn a fair wage by Russian standards. We certainly bolster the economy by bringing money into the area rather than taking money out, which has been the goal of some western businesses. Over all the Russian experience has been one of the most rewarding at 3ABN."

Mending Broken People: Part Two

There you have it then. In summing it up, I have been deeply moved by my association with 3ABN. As a journalist I was caught up in an exciting story. As a person I was touched by all that I surveyed and wanted to share it. Hopefully, this account will convey that message.

Throughout this book the various views and religious perspectives of Danny Shelton have been reflected. The author deems it proper to expand on that creed. The following, final two chapters were written by Danny Shelton himself and published independently. These viewpoints are fundamental in portraying Shelton and his beliefs. They are reprinted here with the permission of Shelton and Pacific Press Publishing Assn.

223

Chapter 17

CAN WE EAT ANYTHING?
WHAT DOES THE BIBLE SAY?
By Danny Shelton

I don't claim to be either a Republican or a Democrat. Why? Because I see so much disunity in both parties, so many inconsistencies, so many people using the political system to get what they want without regard for the good of the vast majority of citizens. It seems to me that too many politicians have their own agendas.

"So, how do you vote?" someone may ask.

I vote for the person who most favors my personal convictions. For example, if a particular is pro-abortion, then I don't vote for that person. As an American, I'm grateful for the privilege of voting. In the history of the United States, thousands have given their lives that I might have the right to vote as my conscience tells me to. Yet I rarely vote a straight party ticket. It's kind of like a smorgasbord; I pick and choose from a variety of parties and candidates.

Many people look at religion the same way. For some time I've believed that the reason a lot of people don't become Christians is because they see so much disunity among us. At times it seems that, like politicians and politics, we Christians can hardly agree on anything. But I have to ask: Should it be this way? The difference between Christianity and politics is that Christians have a guidebook to follow – the Holy Bible, inspired by the Holy Spirit Himself. The inspired guidebook should settle disagreements shouldn't it? Yet, even though the Bible is consistent with itself throughout the sixty-six books, many people treat it as though it, too, is a smorgasbord. They pick and choose whatever seems to fit their religious appetite and plate.

I've never doubted that God's thread of truth runs true and consistent throughout the Bible regardless of the subject matter. Scriptures on salvation, for instance, line up perfectly from Genesis to Revelation. Since the beginning of time, humanity's only chance of salvation has been through Jesus Christ. Men and women have never been able to work their way into the kingdom of heaven. Yet, many times our tendency is to believe that people were saved by keeping the law in the Old Testament, and that in the New Testament we're saved by grace. The fact is, people have always been saved by the grace. The fact is, people have always been saved by the grace of God – in the Old Testament as well as in the New. But a closer inspection of the Old Testament law of God reveals that it is a transcript of His own character. God is love – always have been and always will be – and since the first sin in the Garden of Eden, He has been in the "business" of restoration and salvation for the human race.

The Old Testament points to the cross of Calvary in the New Testament. No longer is there a need to shed the lamb's blood for forgiveness of sin because the spotless Lamb of God shed His blood on the cross to cover our sins and to give us eternal life. Many Christians and Jews are still haggling over the "do's" and "don't's" of how to keep the Sabbath. Some are still haggling over the feast days and ceremonial laws that Christ's death nailed to the cross (see Colossians 2:14-16). Others of us ignore portions of God's Word, and no matter whether we do so intentionally or unintentionally, in either case we are robbed of many blessings such as good health and long life because we don't embrace all of His counsel.

The Lord has said that He wants to heal all of our diseases (see Psalm 103:3), but in order for Him to do so we have to abide by His laws and precepts. One could easily surmise that God just wants to preside over people and make them do what He says – or else. Or we can believe that since God created us and loves us too much, He has left instructions in His Word that will help us live long, happy, and healthy lives. After all, who would know more about what food we need to take into our bodies to stay healthy than the Creator who made us? He wants us to "prosper and be in health, even as [our] ... soul prospereth" (3 John 1:2).

The intention of this little book is not to condemn and criticize those who don't participate in the truth that lies within. Its only intention is to bring to the surface the fact that God loves us to much that He left us a road map that, when followed, will lead us not only to a longer, healthier, and happier life here on earth, but will also prepare us for the kingdom of heaven.

Our minds and our hearts are very capable of deceiving us. The Bible says, "The heart is deceitful above all things, and desperately wicked: who can know it?" (Jeremiah 17:9). It also says, "There is a way which seemeth right unto a man, but the end thereof are the *ways of death" (Proverbs 14:12). As Christians, we often become so comfortable in our relationship with God that we depend on "impressions" from* God to guide us – even if those impressions may not line up with the Word of God. But in reality, His Word, the Bible, is the only source of truth that God has entrusted to us to lead us to Jesus and, ultimately, to heaven.

Much of what you are about to read here may go against generations of teachings, traditions, and lifestyles. It's my sincere prayer that as you read this little book about "eating," the principles of good health will ring clear in your mind – not the tones of legalism and "salvation by works." This book is not about bondage to an old law, but about freedom. Freedom of choice, both physically and spiritually, to enjoy the benefits of a long, healthy, and happy life – now and forever.

The Struggle Over Appetite

And speaking of appetite, the purpose of this little book is to examine one of those areas where Christians seem to pick and choose the most – *eating!* After visiting hundreds of churches over the last thirty years or so, and eating at dozens and dozens of church potlucks, I almost always come away with the same question: "Do Christians really believe it's all right to eat anything that doesn't eat them first?" It seems that the temptation over appetite – the one that Eve yielded to in the Garden of Eden – is still prevalent today. Let's look at the Scriptures.

> Now the serpent was more subtil than any beast of the field which the Lord God had made. And he said unto the woman, Yea, hath God said, Ye shall not eat of every tree of the garden? And the woman said unto the serpent, We may eat of the fruit of the trees of the garden: But of the fruit of the tree which is in the midst of the garden, God hath said, Ye shall not eat of it, neither shall ye touch it, lest ye die. And the serpent said unto the woman, Ye shall not surely die: For God doth know that in the day ye eat thereof, then your eyes shall be opened, and ye shall be as gods, knowing good and evil. And when the woman saw that the tree was good for food, and that it was pleasant to the eyes, and a tree to be desired to make one wise, she took of the fruit thereof, and did eat, and gave also to her husband with her, and he did eat (Genesis 3:1-6).

God said to Eve, "Thou shalt not eat…," and yet Eve ate and convinced Adam to eat as well. God says to us, "Thou shalt not eat…," and yet we do eat – whatever doesn't eat us first, without regard to God's instructions in the Bible.

When Adam and Eve disobeyed God, it was sin. In fact, it was the very sin, the sin which opened upon the earth

228

the floodgates of sorrow due to disobedience. What is sin, and what are the consequences of sin? The Bible says that "sin is the transgression of the law" (1 John 3:4). What law? God's law – His will as expressed in the Bible and specifically as expressed in the Ten Commandments.

Many Christians seem to feel that this matter of appetite – what we eat or don't eat – is a little thing. They agree that Christians ought to take seriously what God says about lying or stealing or adultery, but they don't feel that this matter of diet is important in the Christian life. Yet, the apostle James declares, "Whosoever shall keep the whole law, and yet offend in one point, he is guilty of all" (James 2:10). Each commandment is a link in the chain that makes up God's law. If you break a single link, the entire chain is broken. We may think that the matter of what we eat is of little importance, but the issue isn't what we think. The issue is: What does God say? If God has given us instructions, rules, laws about our diet – then if we disregard His will in this matter, it becomes sin. All sin, whether great or small, breaks the perfect, complete chain of God's will for our lives just as breaking a single link in a chain, spoils the entire chain.

And what are the consequences of sin? Paul gives us the answer: "The wages of sin is death" (Romans 6:23). To their sorrow, Adam and Eve found the truth of that statement. Satan had assured Eve, "Ye shall not surely die" (Genesis 3:4). But that was a lie. Death came to them as a result of their sin – and to all their descendants.

Satan's first attack against humanity centered around appetite, and he's still using that same temptation today.

God's Original Diet for Human Beings
When God created Adam and Eve, He designed their bodies and planned what they should eat in order to maintain them in perfect health and strength. Let's see what that original diet was that God gave to our first parents.

> So God created man in his own image, in the image of God created he him; male and female created he them .... And God said, Behold, I have given you every herb bearing seed, which is upon the face of all the earth, and every tree, in the which is the fruit of a tree yielding seed; to you it shall be for meat (Genesis 1:27-29).

So God's original diet for mankind was a vegetarian diet – fruits, nuts, grains, and vegetables. I look at God's words here in Genesis regarding diet as something like the owner's manual to a new car. When you buy that new automobile and drive it out of the dealer's showroom, there is a booklet in the glove compartment called the owner's manual. It tells you all about your new car – where all the controls are and how they work, and how to service and care for your new possession. It tells you the kind of gasoline to use and how often to change the oil, the correct tire pressure, and all the other things you need to know in order to keep your new car running smoothly and trouble free for as long as possible.

Now, you can disregard that instruction if you want to. You can throw away the owner's manual and put in the cheapest gasoline you can find. You can never change the oil or use the wrong kind. You can put brake fluid in the gas tank – if you want to. But that doesn't make a lot of sense, does it? The manufacturer doesn't tell you how to care for your car just to be bossing you around. The manufacturer knows what your car needs because he made it. He's giving you this information so that you can keep your car operating at its peak performance for as long as possible.

There is another reason, too, that God has given us rules about what to eat and other health principles. It's found in 1 Corinthians 6:19, 20. "Know ye not that your body is the temple of the Holy Ghost which is in you, which ye had of God, and ye are not your own? For ye are bought with a price: therefore glorify God in your body and in your spirit, which are God's."

Our bodies belong to God. He lives in us through His Holy Spirit. If that is true, then shouldn't we want to put into our bodies only food that is healthful and pleasing to God?

Have you ever thought about how you are able to know anything about God – to understand spiritual things and respond to His love? It is through your mind – the ability to think and reason and understand. And that ability depends on your brain – a physical organ that is part of your physical body. Our spiritual relationship to God depends, to a large extent, on our physical condition. If our bodies are healthy and our minds are clear, we are able to understand God's love for us and His will for our lives. We can respond to love to Him and follow Him. But if our bodies are not healthy, if our diet and other habits are causing us to have poor health and clouded minds, then it is much harder for us to respond to spiritual things.

Clean and Unclean Meat

We've seen that God's original diet for men and women at Creation was vegetables, nuts, grains, and fruit. Later, He allowed humans to eat the flesh of certain animals – but not all animals. And He is very clear about which may be eaten and which may not. The Bible refers to these groups as "clean" and "unclean" meat. Let's see what God has to say about this distinction:

> These are the beasts which ye shall eat among all the beasts that are on the earth. Whatsoever parteth the hoof, and is cloven footed, and cheweth the cud, among the beasts, that shall ye eat....These shall ye eat of all that are in the waters: whatsoever hath fins and scales in the waters, and in the seas, and in the rivers, them shall ye eat (Leviticus 11:2, 3, 9).

There is more detailed instructions in this chapter, as

231

you can see if you read the whole section. But this is the general rule that God has given – animals that are both cloven hoofed and who chew the cud, and fish with both fins and scales are allowed. But both characteristics must be present. God specifically says,

> The hare, because he cheweth the cud, but divideth not the hoof; he is unclean .... And the swine, though he divide the hoof, and be cloven footed, yet he cheweth not the cud; he is unclean (Leviticus 11:6, 7).

With such a clear word from God – the original diet from Eden and the detailed instructions found in Leviticus 11 – how is it that there is such a difference of opinion among Christians about what should be eaten and what should not? Why is it that some Christians believe one should eat only a vegetarian diet (or at most only clean meat) while others seem to feel that they can eat anything that doesn't eat them first?

Texts That Aren't Easy to Understand

Well, to be perfectly fair, there *are* some texts in the Bible on this topic that are not easy to understand at first. And some Christians point to these texts to prove that they can eat anything they choose with God's blessing.

Does the Bible contradict itself? Is it possible that these health laws were nailed to Jesus' cross as part of the ceremonial law? Let's find out by turning to the Bible itself. We want to look at what it says about the Christian and his diet and see if we can find a harmonizing thread that runs through the whole Word of God.

Acts 10

Some believe that the story of Peter's vision in Acts 10 is evidence that God has changed His mind about some food being unclean – that it proves we can eat whatever we want.

Here is the story.

Cornelius was a centurion in the Roman army who lived in Caesarea. He was a godly man who wanted to follow God's will for his life as far as he understood it. One day, God told him in a vision that he should send servants to Joppa, to a house by the seaside, and ask for a man named Peter who would tell him more about God's will for his life. You can read all this in Acts 10.

So Cornelius told his servants to go to Joppa and find Peter. He wanted to know and follow all the light Peter could give him. As the servants drew near to Joppa, Peter was on the rooftop of the house by the sea, praying. He became very hungry and wanted to eat. But while food was being prepared, God gave Peter a vision. Let's pick up the story from the Bible at this point. In his vision, Peter

> .... Saw heaven opened, and a certain vessel descending unto him, as it had been a great sheet knit at the four corners, and let down to the earth: Wherein were all manner of four footed beasts of the earth, and wild beasts, and creeping things, and fowls of the air. And there came a voice to him, Rise, Peter; kill, and eat. But Peter said, Not so, Lord; for I have never eaten anything that is common or unclean. And the voice spake unto him again the second time, What God hath cleansed, that call thou not common. This was done thrice: and the vessel was received up again into heaven. Now while Peter doubted in himself what this vision which he had seen should mean, behold, the men which were sent from Cornelius ... stood before the gate (Acts 10:11-17).

Some Christians believe that this vision God gave to Peter means that He has cleansed all unclean food and animals, making them acceptable as food. After all, didn't He show Peter a great sheet filled with all kinds of unclean animals and then told Peter not to call unclean what He had cleansed?

Is that what Peter understood the vision to mean? Peter was horrified to think that God would tell him to eat these unclean animals! He had never eaten anything like that before. Peter "doubted in himself what this vision he had seen should mean" (verse 17). But he wasn't to remain in doubt very long.

The men from Cornelius were at his door. They told him of the vision God had given their master and begged Peter to come with them and explain God's truth more completely. The Holy Spirit told Peter to accompany these men for He had sent them.

The next day, Peter and some others went to Caesarea to Cornelius's house. Now that may not seem particularly amazing to us, but for Peter, it was an extremely unusual and extraordinary thing to do.

Why?

Because Jews didn't associate with non-Jews. They felt that Gentiles were unclean and so to enter the home of a Gentile – and certainly to eat with Gentiles – would make them unclean. Listen to how Peter explained it to Cornelius and his household:

> Ye know how that it is an unlawful thing for a man that is a Jew to keep company, or come unto one of another nation; *but God hath shewed me that I should not call any man common or unclean* (verse 28, italics supplied).

Did you get that? What had Peter come to understand that this vision meant – the vision that God had given him of the sheet with all the unclean animals in it? Did Peter decide that God was telling him it was all right to eat anything he wanted because God had made all foods clean and healthful? No. Peter realized that the vision meant he wasn't to look upon any person as unclean or common. God was showing him that he should be willing to take the gospel to the Gentile Cornelius and his household. Peter continues, "Of a truth I perceive that God is no respecter of persons: But in every nation he that feareth him and worketh righteousness is accepted with him: (verses 34, 35).

So you see, this vision isn't talking about food at all. It is talking about people and how God accepts anyone who will turn to Him – no matter his or her background or life. That's what Peter came to see the vision meant. Peter didn't start eating anything he wanted to as a result of this vision – at least we don't have any record that he did. But we do have his own words explaining what Peter understood God's vision to mean – and that understanding had nothing to do with what Peter was to eat or not eat. God was showing him that he should not consider the Gentiles unclean, but that he should go to Cornelius's house and preach the gospel to him.

Romans 14

Romans 14 is another chapter of the Bible that many point to as evidence that no food is off limits to the believing Christian. Here is what Paul says in this chapter about food and eating:

> Receive one who is weak in the faith, but not to disputes over doubtful things. For one believes he may eat all things, but he who is weak eats only vegetables. Let not him who eats despise him who does not eat, and let not him who does not eat judge him who eats; for God has received him .... He who eats, eats to the Lord, for he gives God thanks; and he who does not eat, to the Lord he does not eat, and gives God thanks .... I know and am convinced by the Lord Jesus that there is nothing unclean of itself; but to him who considers any thing to be unclean, to him it is unclean. Yet if your brother is grieved because of your food, you are no longer walking in love. Do not destroy with your food the one for whom Christ died .... for the kingdom of God is not eating and drinking, but righteousness and peace and joy in the Holy Spirit .... Do not destroy the work of God for the sake of food. All things indeed are pure, but it is evil for the man who eats with offense. It is good neither to eat meat nor

drink wine nor do anything by which your brother stumbles or is offended or is made weak (verses 1-3, 6, 14, 15, 17, 20, 21, NKJV).

At first glance, Paul certainly seems to be saying in these verses that anything is good for food and mature Christians may eat whatever they want to eat. But let's look at this passage more closely. We need to understand what is going on in the church that caused Paul to write these words. Only a few months earlier, Paul had written this to the Christians in Corinth:

> Therefore, concerning the eating of things offered to idols, we know that an idol is nothing in the world, and that there is no other God but one .... However, there is not in everyone that knowledge; for some, with consciousness of the idol, until now eat it as a thing offered to an idol; and their conscience, being weak, is defiled. But food does not commend us to God; for neither if we eat are we the better, nor if we do not eat are we the worse. But beware lest somehow this liberty of yours becomes a stumbling block to those who are weak. For if anyone sees you who have knowledge eating in an idol's temple, will not the conscience of him who is weak be emboldened to eat those things offered to idols? .... Therefore, if food makes my brother stumble, I will never again eat meat, lest I make my brother stumble (1 Corinthians 8:4, 7-10, 13 NKJV).

This puts Paul's advice in Romans 14 in a whole new light, doesn't it? He isn't talking about clean or unclean foods, as outlined in Leviticus 11. He's talking about food offered to idols. You see, in Paul's day, the people worshiped many different gods. They brought animals to their temples and presented them as an offering to the idol of their god. The animals were killed and the meat prepared. Now, the god didn't eat the meat! So what happened to it? The priests of that god would eat some of it. And some of it was sold in the marketplace. Buying this food and eating it was considered an act of worship to the god to whom it had first been offered. Sensitive Christians, especially those who had recently been pagans and had worshiped these gods, didn't feel right eating this food that had been offered to an idol. For them, it was like repudiating Jesus and worshiping their old pagan god.

But mature Christians, who didn't necessarily have the same background, didn't feel that way at all. They could eat food that had been offered to an idol with a clear conscience. They knew that an idol was just a piece of stone or wood. It didn't mean anything to them in the least. It didn't make any difference if the food they ate had been offered to an idol. It was still good food. For them, it didn't mean that they were worshiping that pagan god. But a sensitive, "weak" Christian would see the stronger Christian eating this food and think, "Look at Brother So-and-So! Look what he's doing!" And his faith would be damaged.

Paul's whole argument in Romans 14 and 1 Corinthians 8 is that Christians ought to be sensitive to each other's feelings. The mature Christian shouldn't eat food offered to idols – even though he could do so with a clear conscience – if it was going to be a stumbling block to a weaker brother.

Paul isn't saying that those who are strong in faith can eat anything they want to eat regardless of whether it is healthful food or not. He isn't ignoring or doing away with the laws God gave in Leviticus about clean and unclean foods. In fact, he isn't talking about the matter of clean or unclean food at all. He's talking about good, wholesome food, that happens to have been offered to an idol – and what eating such food may do to the faith of someone who is weak and sees eating food that has been offered to an idol as an act of worship to a pagan god.

Paul had already told the Christians at Rome that they should take care of their bodies so that they could present themselves to God as "a living sacrifice, holy, acceptable unto God, which is your reasonable service" (Romans 12:1). He says, too, "Whether therefore ye eat, or drink, or whatever ye do, do all to the glory of God" (1 Corinthians 10:31). How can we eat something that God has pronounced unclean and told us not to eat – and still eat to His glory?

1 Timothy 4 and Mark 7

The apostle Paul, writing to the young pastor Timothy, warned him that some individuals would depart from the true Christian faith and teach that we should

> ... abstain from meats, which God hath created to be received with thanksgiving of them which believe and know the truth. For every creature of God is good, and nothing to be refused, if it be received with thanksgiving: For it is sanctified by the word of God and prayer (1 Timothy 4:3, 4).

"This clearly teaches," say some Christians, "that anything is good for food and we can eat whatever we want to eat. The apostle Paul himself says that everything God made is good and shouldn't be refused." And these individuals turn, then, to a similar text in Mark 7 in which Jesus says,

> There is nothing that enters a man from outside which can defile him; but the things which come out of him, those are the things that defile a man .... Do you not perceive that whatever enters a man from outside cannot defile him, because it does not enter his heart but his stomach, and is eliminated, thus purifying all foods? (verses 15, 18, 19, NKJV).

What do we do with such Bible texts? Are all foods now clean? Can the Christian eat anything he wants? It might seem so – unless we take the time to understand what these verses are actually teaching.

Let's look first at Paul's words in 1 Timothy 4:3, 4. Does the apostle here really teach that God's clear distinction between clean and unclean foods has been abolished?

Notice that Paul is talking about food which "God hath created to be received with thanksgiving" (verse 3). Did God create the pig as food to be received with thanksgiving – when He has specifically said elsewhere that the pig is unclean and unfit to be eaten by humans (see Leviticus 11:7)? Does thanking God for a pork roast – or even saying a prayer of blessing over it – change the fact that God has said that pork is unclean and not to be eaten?

So if Paul isn't talking here about abolishing the distinction between clean and unclean foods, what *is* he talking about?

He's talking about false teachers in the church who will come along making up rules that aren't in the Bible – such as no marriage (verse 3) or not eating certain wholesome foods. They will insist that others need to follow these rules. And in fact such individuals did come along in the early church. Some taught that the physical body was evil and that all physical desires, such as marriage or taking pleasure in eating, should be avoided. Others taught that Christians should avoid certain wholesome food for ritual or ceremonial reasons. Paul wants Christians to know that God is the Author of marriage. He's also the One who created our bodies and provided good food to nourish us and to give us pleasure. He created these things for us to receive with thanksgiving. And because He is the Creator, He knows what we should eat in order to keep our bodies healthy, strong, and spiritually alert.

Our bodies haven't changed since Bible times in terms of what is required to keep them healthy. The nature of unclean foods hasn't changed; the pig, for example, is still the same animal it was in Bible times. And God hasn't changed His mind about what we should and should not eat as He has outlined it in His Word.

But what about Jesus' words in Mark 7 – that it isn't what we take into our bodies from the outside that defiles us, rather it is what comes out of our hearts that defiles? How do we explain that?

Let's look at the context of this statement. If you look at the beginning of this chapter, you'll see that the conversation began when the religious leaders saw Jesus' disciples eating without first washing their hands. They were upset at this, because they had all kinds of special rituals that spelled out how they were to wash before eating. Not to wash meant that they would be "unclean" ritually. It really didn't have anything to do with getting the germs off their hands or their food before eating. It was all about following the ritual so that they wouldn't be *ceremonially* unclean.

So they challenged Jesus, "Why don't your disciples follow the 'tradition of the elders' (verse 5) and wash in these special ways?" But at the very time they were so careful to wash before eating, they were plotting the murder of Jesus Himself! They were taking advantage of the ordinary people and exploiting them for their own gain. They were doing away with the Scriptures by their traditions. So Jesus said, "Look, it isn't what you eat – what comes into your body from without – that you need to be worrying about. You need to be worrying about the defilement that comes from within. The evil thoughts of your heart come out in your words and actions. They are what defile you. The food you eat goes into the stomach and is eliminated and done with. But the evil that is in your hearts stays there and festers."

Once again, the discussion wasn't about clean or unclean foods at all. Jesus wasn't talking about what foods a person should or should not eat. He wasn't declaring that the food God had pronounced unclean in Leviticus was now clean and suitable for food. He was talking about spiritual things.

If you don't think that is true, just consider this. If this text really means that nothing that we take into our bodies can defile or harm us – then we should be able to eat strychnine if we want to and it wouldn't hurt us! Or we should be able to eat spoiled food without getting sick! If we really believe these texts mean that we can eat or drink anything we want to, then good Christians should be able to drink alcohol or chew tobacco or even snort cocaine – and not worry about being defiled physically or spiritually. We could be eating dogs and cats or horses or snakes or spiders – maybe even each other! All we have to do is to be thankful for it and ask God to bless it.

You say, "Brother Shelton, that's absurd! That's going too far! Of course, the text doesn't mean that we can eat anything at all without hurting ourselves. " And I agree. That is my point. The text isn't talking literally about what we eat and take into our bodies. It's talking about spiritual values and following useless rituals while at the same time disregarding God's clear instructions about how to live.

Glorifying God in our Lifestyle

You see, God has made it quite plain in His Word that we are to glorify Him in all things – even in what we eat and drink and the health habits we follow (1 Corinthians 10:31). He has spelled out what foods we should be eating – and what foods we should not eat. He created us and knows what is best for our physical health. Yet, so often we decide that we will eat what *we* want to eat – even if God has said, "Thou shalt not eat of it."

God knew way back there in Leviticus of the disease and heartache and pain that human beings would bring on themselves by eating those things that He said not to eat. For example, He explicitly commanded us to stay away from the blood and fat in meat. "No soul of you shall eat blood .... For it is the life of all flesh; the blood of it is for the life thereof: therefore I said unto the children is Israel,

Ye shall eat the blood of no manner of flesh" (Leviticus 17:12, 14). "It shall be a perpetual statute for your generations throughout all your dwellings, that ye eat neither fat nor blood" (Leviticus 3:17).

You've heard the old saying, "We become what we eat." Well, I believe it is more than just an adage. When we continually eat animal fat, it will either show up on the outside of our bodies in the form of extra weight, which overworks our heart, or it will show up on the inside of our arteries, eventually clogging them to the point of a heart attack or stroke. Sometimes, it shows up both on the outside *and* the inside, doubling our risk for a heart attack or stroke!

It's interesting to me that the vast majority even of those Christians who believe that we shouldn't eat animals described by God as "unclean," will still go to the nearest fast food restaurant and order a hamburger that contains both fat and blood – believing that they are eating "clean" food. But according to the Bible, even "clean" meat must be prepared properly in order to remove the fat and the blood before it is eaten. After all, the same God who outlined what is "clean" meat and what is "unclean," also says, "It shall be a perpetual statute for your generations throughout all your dwellings, that ye eat neither fat nor blood" (Leviticus 3:17). When the fat and blood is completely removed from meat, it is commonly called "kosher" meat. Many Jews today still eat only "kosher" meat. It is not considered very succulent to the taste; in fact, many years ago, I tasted some "kosher" meat myself. To me, it was kind of like trying to eat leather. I never went back for seconds!

In the Garden of Eden when God was the "dietitian," meat of any kind was not on the menu. Even 2,500 years later when the children of Israel had to depend on God for their food in the wilderness, His provision of choice didn't include meat. Instead, He supplied them with "manna" every day. The Bible says, "And the manna was as coriander seed, and the color thereof as the color of bdellium. And the people went about, and gathered it, and ground it in mills, or beat it in a mortar, and baked it in pans, and made cakes of it: and the taste of it was as the taste of fresh oil" (Numbers 11:7, 8).

When the children of Israel grew tired of the manna and complained, God allowed them to have meat. But even then He sent only "clean" meat as outlined in this same chapter of Leviticus – chapter 11. He sent them quail to eat – not pigs! Once again this shows us the consistency of God's Word. God wouldn't tell us to eat only what He defines as "clean" meat – and then provide unclean meat.

Today medical science confirms the wisdom of God's prohibition against eating the fat and blood in meat. Cholesterol (found particularly in fat and red meat) is a prime culprit in heart disease – one of the primary causes of death, along with cancer, in the western world today. Satan must be rejoicing when he sees all the heart attacks and cancer and strokes that we bring on ourselves by our unhealthful diets. He knows that he has an entrance into our hearts as long as we don't control our appetites and choose to put food in our mouths that God has forbidden us to eat. The very first sin in the Garden of Eden involved appetite and choosing to obey God's commandment regarding what to eat and what not to eat. The results were disastrous for Adam and Eve. Satan was able to come into their lives and bring sorrow, destruction, and death upon them and their descendants.

And the same is true today. If we disregard what God has to say about what we should and should not eat, then we given Satan an opportunity to work in our lives. The Bible says, "To him that knoweth to do good, and doeth it not, to him it is sin" (James 4:17). We need to reach the point that we serve God – not from feelings, but from faith. It isn't a matter of what *we* think, of what we feel or believe or want. It's a matter of what *God* has said. It's a matter of trusting and obeying Him. It's a matter of believing and following what God has said for our own good in His Word about clean and unclean food. And to tell the truth, I believe that all of us would be very disappointed if we believed that our Creator God loved the people of the Old Testament enough to guide them away from foods that would be harmful to them and then told us in the New Testament not to worry about our health – to go ahead and eat anything that doesn't eat us first. That now it's all right to eat unclean foods that will shorten our lives through heart attacks, strokes, cancer, etc.

I have heard Christians say, "It's not about what you eat or what day you keep, it's about people." While I agree that Christianity is about loving people – it's also about loving God enough to be obedient to His commandments. Although it is true that Christ died to save people, we must be willing to die to self to obey God. As I was thinking about this, a friend was asking the Lord how to reply to that statement. The Lord flashed this thought into his mind: *The commandments on the second table of stone deal with people, but those commandments on the first table deal with Me.* You see, the last six of the Ten Commandments are about our relationship to our fellow man – lying, stealing, committing adultery, coveting, etc. But the first four of the Ten Commandments are about our relationship to God – putting Him first and honoring His name, keeping His Sabbath holy, etc. And although we certainly don't want to downplay the value of the last six commandments, at the same time, we must walk in the light of the first four.

Lip Service vs. Obedience

We honor people by respecting them – not just saying that we love them, but *showing* our love. If I love my neighbor, for example, then I won't steal from him, will I? No.

I will respect his property. If I love my neighbor, I won't just tell him I love him, but I'll respect and honor him enough to never kill him or anything that is his. We could continue with examples of adultery, lying, coveting, etc.

It's the same with God. If we truly love God we will not just say that we love Him – we will *show* it by the way we live. God wants us to honor Him with our obedience. He says plainly that "To obey is better than sacrifice" (1 Samuel 15:22). The sacrifice of praise that we bring to God when singing praises, praying, or giving testimonials, etc. is very good; it is our lip service, and we should be doing that. But God does not honor *lip* service alone if it isn't accompanied by obedience to His commandments. Jesus said, "If ye love me, keep my commandments" (John 14:15).

We see this principle of lip service versus obedience illustrated in the lives of Cain and Abel just shortly after their parents had been expelled from the Garden of Eden. The Bible tells us that

> Cain brought of the fruit of the ground an offering unto the Lord. And Abel, he also brought of the firstlings of his flock and of the fat thereof. And the Lord had respect unto Abel and to his offering. But unto Cain and to his offering he had not respect (Genesis 4:3-5).

Why did God not accept Cain's offering? Because Cain was doing what *he* wanted to do rather than what God had asked him to do. Cain and Abel both knew that they were to sacrifice a lamb as an acknowledgment of their sin and their acceptance of the Savior that would come. So when Cain brought his fruit sacrifice before God, he brought the highest form of insult. To someone looking on, it might seem that Cain was bringing a nice offering to God. But he was really bringing an offering to himself – because he was disregarding God's will and following his own. Cain enjoyed and loved gardening; he actually was guilty of worshiping the fruit rather than the Creator of the fruit by making a sacrifice of it. He appeared to be piously obedient, but he was actually disobeying God's commandment to bring a blood sacrifice representing the sacrifice Christ would offer at Calvary. And the scriptures tell us that God rejected Cain's sacrifice – not because there was anything wrong with the fruit, but because Cain chose to offer what he wanted to offer and not what God had commanded.

In the same way, many Christians love the feeling they get from singing praises, lifting up their hands, praying, etc. – but they do not obey God by keeping His laws and commandments. Just as God rejected Cain's offering (man's offering) back in Genesis, He is also rejecting multitudes today who honor Him with their lips, but who are not willing to obey His commandments. Jesus told us this would happen among Christian people. He said, "This people honoureth me with their lips, but their heart is far from me" (Mark 7:6). How do I know Jesus is talking here about Christians? The answer is simple – only Christians honor Jesus with their lips. People following Satan don't honor Jesus with their lips. Atheists don't. Muslims and Hindus don't honor Jesus with their lips. Although they may honor God with their lips, they don't honor His Son, Jesus, as Christians do. Jesus knew that in the last days there would be Christians – a movement, if you will – that would encourage great lip service to Him, but that would ignore His commandments, especially those dealing with our relationship to Him.

It happened in Christ's day, and it's happening today. He tells us "In vain do they worship me, teaching for doctrines the commandments of men" (Mark 7:7). Once again, Jesus is describing a group of Christians who worship Him, but whose worship He rejects because they teach and keep only the commandments of men – not the commandments of God. Since the fall of Adam, we human beings are inherently selfish. So, it would make sense that we would teach "do not steal," because we don't want anyone taking something that is ours. It's easy for us to teach "thou shalt not kill." This commandment, of course, keeps anyone from killing me or mine. Teaching the adultery commandment is a no brainer for us Christians because we don't want anyone fooling around with our husband or wife. "I'll leave yours alone if you'll leave mine alone."

I recently saw a special on television about a primitive tribe in Brazil. Only twenty years ago they were advocating free sex among the men and women of the tribe. But because this custom caused so many problems, they finally changed their tribal rules to allow only one wife. I find it interesting that they made this change without any missionaries being involved or teaching them about God's commandments. They did not change their customs to please God, but to please themselves. Yet, technically, it appears that they are fulfilling the letter of God's law, aren't they? – at least as far as the seventh commandment is concerned.

In reality, the last six commandments are by nature easier to keep than the first four because the last six are really all about "us." The first four commandments, on the other hand, are all about our relationship to God. Here, God gives us the opportunity to leave the physical realm and go to the spiritual realm, which after all, is the key to everlasting life. If we live only in the physical world, we will eventually die. It is through our spiritual relationship with God that we can live forever.

In Leviticus 11:7, 8, for example, God not only says do not eat the pig, He also tells us not even to touch its carcass. The physical nature says to us, "But pork tastes good! Why would God create something that tastes so good yet deprive me from eating it?" The physical nature rationalizes that God couldn't have really meant what He said about unclean foods. One can even rationalize that this train of thought reeks of legalism.

Spiritual Infants or Mature Christians?

A man once told me, "We're not saved by what we eat or drink; we are saved by the blood of the Lamb. So as long as I acknowledge that fact, I can eat or drink whatever I want." I've even heard people say, "If the Lord wants me to quit eating unclean foods, He'll impress me when to quit." Human nature leads us to depend on our feelings – or as some may term it, "our hearts." But the Bible says "The heart is deceitful above all things, and desperately wicked: who can know it?" (Jeremiah 17:9).

I cannot believe that the Lord could possibly take delight in our continually remaining "spiritual infants," that is to say, that we actually expect the Creator God of the universe to follow us around constantly telling us every move we can or cannot make. God gave us His Word to read and study for ourselves. In it, He has given us His will for our daily lives. When we study it, we find, for example, that He says not to eat unclean foods. Yet because our physical senses tell us that some unclean foods taste good, we decide we will eat them until we're "impressed by the Lord" not to eat. That's what I'm talking about when I refer to "spiritual infants." God has given us all the resources necessary to know that the "hog" was never intended to be taken internally. Medical science agrees and confirms what the Bible has said for thousands of years, and even records these findings for us to study so that we can make intelligent decisions. The choice is left up to us. We can ignore the findings of medical science and eat – or we can learn from these findings and abstain, improving our chances of a longer, healthier, and, consequently, a happier life.

I believe all of us are "spiritual infants" in certain areas of our walk and relationship with God. For instance, I know Christians who are consistent in their giving of tithes and offerings, and I've yet to talk to one who doesn't tell me how God has blessed him as a result of his financial giving

– and goes on to make statements such as, "I've learned that I can't afford *not* to give to God." In essence, these individuals are saying that the 90 percent that they have left after paying tithe always seems to go much further than when they kept 100 percent for themselves. This is definitely true in my own experience. In fact, I have friends whose businesses have been so blessed by their giving 10 percent back to God that they have begun to give 20 percent. They soon realized that the 80 percent they kept began to be much more than their original income of 100 percent! Now they are giving 30 percent of their entire income to the Lord's work.

On the other hand, I know Christians who say they cannot afford to give 10 percent of their income to the Lord's work. For years they seem to live "hand to mouth" – just barely making ends meet, always enduring one financial crisis after another, as well as constantly fighting the depression that comes from financial stress. They have not matured in the area of financial giving. They are still "spiritual infants" and therefore not enjoying the benefits and blessings and joys of giving. It's not for me to judge these folk as "sinners" because they do not pay tithe, but rather to share with them the benefits of God's blessings on those who do.

In the same vein, this book is written not as a judgment of those who eat "unclean" foods as described in the Bible. It's written to encourage people to enjoy the physical and spiritual benefits associated with obeying God's law of health.

While driving down the highway, I stop every time I come to a stop sign. When I was very young and learning to drive, I was taught that drivers are to stop at stop signs. But when I first received my driver's license, I didn't always stop at all the stop signs. "After all," I reasoned, "I don't think it's really necessary to stop at all these signs." I was in my infancy of driving at that time. I hadn't seen first hand the results of not obeying the law about stop signs. Now, after more than thirty-five years of driving, I stop at all stop signs. Why? Because I've seen what happens when a driver doesn't stop. I've seen the pain and death that can happen as a result of not obeying the stop sign. In fact, my first wife's life was taken many years ago by a young driver who didn't see the necessity of stopping at every stop sign and obeying the rules of the road.

When it comes to eating unclean foods, human nature doesn't want to read the "signs" in the Bible or the "signs" when medical science tells us some foods are bad for us. Our lust for the physical enjoyments blinds our eyes to the "stop signs" all around us. Instead, we say, "Well, if the Lord doesn't want me to eat this food, He'll impress me when to quit."

The Lord has given us food "stop signs" for our benefit. He wants us to be healthy and happy. He wants us to prosper and be in health, even as [our] ... soul prospereth" (3 John 1:2). We are simply talking about health principles, not legalism. Many Christians don't accept the Bible's health principles about not eating unclean foods. Yet, they follow and teach the same concept when it comes to smoking, drinking, or using drugs.

When a person is "saved," most church members will tell him that he needs to quit smoking, even though there is no scripture in the Bible telling him not to smoke. They also will tell him he needs to get off drugs, even though the use of drugs is not mentioned in the Bible. My question to these folks is: "Why isn't this attitude against smoking and drugs considered legalism?" Why would they tell someone to stop doing something that the Bible says nothing about directly, but they never encourage him to quit eating unclean foods that the Bible specifically says not to eat?

When it comes to smoking, drugs, and drinking alcohol, many Christians are willing to abide by and teach Bible

principles of a healthful lifestyle because they know these habits not only destroy a person physically, but they can impair one's relationship to Christ. The same is true with eating unclean foods. They not only cause strokes, heart attacks, cancer, and much more, but they can also impair our relationship with the Creator. Why? Because disobedience to God's laws spawns sin, and "the wages of sin is death" (Romans 6:23).

All humanity fell from perfection into a sinful world because Adam and Eve trusted their own understanding and thought they knew better than God what was good for them. Satan lied to Eve, telling her that even if she disobeyed God she would "not surely die" (Genesis 3:4). And he lies to us today, telling us the same thing – disobedience in this matter of appetite will not lead to death. And all the while, like Eve, we are swallowing his lies hook, line, and sinker.

Is it possible to break the first commandment by what we eat? I believe that it is. In the first commandment God says, "Thou shalt have no other gods before me" (Exodus 20:3). I believe that many of us today have made a god out of food. We're going to eat what we want to eat even if it kills us. And you know what? It is. In many cases the food choices we make are killing us.

Modern Research Confirms the Bible's
Health Principles

Today modern medical science and research studies are backing up what the Bible says about a healthful diet with an impressive array of scientific evidence and statistics. A vegetarian diet – God's ideal diet for human beings as given in Genesis – is becoming more and more popular as increasing numbers are making the switch to a flesh-free lifestyle. And no wonder. The benefits are enormous.

USA Today (December 7, 2001) interviewed Neal Barnard, president of Physicians Committee for Respon-

sible Medicine (PCRM), a nonprofit organization focusing on preventive medicine, and reported:

> Studies have found that vegetarians actually get far better nutrition than nonvegetarians, Barnard says. And vegetarians get larger amounts of fiber, iron, many vitamins and other cancer-fighting compounds than meat eaters.

The article went on to point out a study of Seventh-day Adventists in California – a group that is made up of mostly vegetarians – showing that on average Seventh-day Adventists live ten years longer than the general population.

The same *USA Today* article cited Barnard as stating,

> Vegetarians have a 40 percent less risk of cancer and much less risk of heart disease, diabetes, hypertension, kidney disease, and other problems that are common among meat eaters ... Vegetarians also live several years longer and enjoy better health (USA Today, December 7 2001).

These statements are backed up by research from the Adventist Health Study in which more than 20,000 California Seventh-day Adventists were used as a control group in studying the health benefits of a vegetarian, nonsmoking, nonalcohol lifestyle. Seventh-day Adventists were selected for research because they follow closely the diet and health principles given in the Bible. Many, although not all, are vegetarians, the Church has three major health-related requirements – nonuse of tobacco in any form, total abstinence from alcoholic beverages, and excluding from the diet any "unclean" meat that is prohibited by the rules we have already looked at in Leviticus. In addition, Adventists are encouraged to follow other good health habits, including the liberal use of fruits, nuts, vegetables, and whole-grain cereals, moderation in fat and salt intake, avoid tea, coffee, and other drinks containing caffeine, and lim-

ited use of refined sugar.

And what did researchers find when they compared the health of Seventh-day Adventists to the general population?

They found that California Adventists had significantly less coronary heart disease than Californians as a whole. They found that Adventists had less strokes, bronchitis, emphysema, diabetes, peptic ulcers, cirrhosis of the liver, and many types of cancers. They found that Seventh-day Adventists tend to live longer than the average population. Specifically, the study showed that compared to the general population:

- Adventists had a 79 percent *lower* rate of death from lung cancer.

- Adventist men had a 40 percent *lower* death rate – and Adventist women had a 24 percent *lower* death rate – from all types of cancer.

- Adventist men had a 34 percent *lower* death rate from coronary artery disease.

- When deaths from *all* causes were considered, Adventist men had a 34 percent – and Adventist women had a 12 percent – *lower* rate than the general population.

These are impressive statistics for the health benefits of the diet that God originally gave to human beings. But there is more. The same study showed that eating nuts and whole-wheat bread significantly reduces the risk of both fatal and nonfatal coronary heart disease. Individuals who ate nuts from one to four times per week reduced their risk of dying from heart disease by 27 percent compared to those who ate nuts less than once a week. But those who ate nuts five times a week or more reduced their risk even more – by 48 percent compared to those who ate nuts less than once a week!

Dr. Hans Diehl, director of the Lifestyle Medicine Institute in Loma Linda, California, and Dr. Aileen Ludington, write this in their book, *Dynamic Living:*

> Seven out of 10 Americans suffer and die prematurely of three killer diseases: heart disease, cancer, and stroke. In his comprehensive report to the nation titled *Nutrition and Health*, C. Everett Koop, M.D., stated unequivocally that the Western diet was the major contributor to these diseases. He confirmed that saturated fat and cholesterol, eaten in disproportionate amounts, were the main culprits. He reminded people that animal products are the largest source of saturated fat as well as the only source of cholesterol. To compound the problem, Dr. Koop pointed out, these foods are usually eaten at the expense of complex-carbohydrate-rich foods such as grains, fruits, and vegetables.
>
> The average risk of heart disease for a man eating meat, eggs, and dairy products is 50 percent. The risk for a man who leaves off meat is 15 percent. However, the coronary risk of a vegetarian who leaves off meat, eggs, and dairy products drops to only 4 percent. An editorial in the Journal of the American Medical Association commented on these advantages, stating that a total vegetarian diet can prevent up to 9 0 percent of our strokes and 97 percent of our heart attacks (pages 149, 150).

The *Journal of the American Dietetic Association* has gone on record that:

> Scientific data suggest positive relationships between a vegetarian diet and reduced risk for several chronic degenerative diseases and conditions, including obesity, coronary artery

disease, hypertension, diabetes mellitus, and some types of cancer...

> Studies indicate that vegetarians often have lower morbidity and mortality rates from several chronic degenerative diseases than do non-vegetarians. Although nondietary factors, including physical activity and abstinence from smoking and alcohol may play a role, diet is clearly a contributing factor (Position Paper, adopted by the ADA 1996).

What are all these medical studies and this scientific research telling us? They are confirming that God knew what He was talking about when He told us in the Bible what to eat – and what not to eat. His original diet of nuts, fruits, grains, and vegetables is still the most healthful for human beings. And wouldn't that make sense? After all, God created our bodies. He knows how they operate. Shouldn't He know what foods will keep our bodies healthy and vigorous?

A Choice to Make

Jesus said, "I am come that they might have life, and have it more abundantly" (John 10:10). Now I know that this verse is talking primarily about our spiritual well-being. Jesus came to give us abundant spiritual life. But I also believe that He is speaking about *all* aspects of our lives – including our physical health. The Bible says in 3 John 2, "Beloved, I wish above all things that thou mayest prosper and be in health, even as thy soul propereth."

God is concerned not only about our spiritual health; He's concerned about our physical health as well. He has told us how to eat to have abundant, healthy lives. Now you and I have a choice to make. Are we going to disregard what God has said and follow our own wishes in this matter of eating? Or are we going to listen to the Creator, believe that He knows what is best for us, and follow His wishes in what we eat?

The Lord had Paul write something very important in 1 Corinthians 6:19. "What? know ye not that your body is the temple of the Holy

Ghost which is in you, which ye have of God, and ye are not your own?" I believe that when we continually take foods into our bodies that we know are harmful – as spelled out in the Bible and supported by modern medical science – we are indeed making an idol of our bellies and therefore defiling God's temple. Remember, Paul says that our bodies are not our own; they belong to God. Paul also says, "Know ye not that ye are the temple of God, and that the Spirit of God dwelleth in you? If any man defile the temple of God, him shall God destroy; for the temple of God is holy, which temple ye are" (1 Corinthians 3:16, 17). And 2 Corinthians 6:16 ASKS, "what agreement hath the temple of God with idols? For ye are the temple of the living God."

Like all the other issues of life we face, what we eat really comes down to a matter of choice. Are we going to follow God's will or our will? Do we really believe it's all right to eat anything that doesn't eat us first? Are we going to choose our food based solely on what tastes good? The Bible talks about those "whose God is their belly" (Philippians 3:19). It calls them "enemies of the cross of Christ" (verse 18).

God has a better plan in mind for us. He has spelled it out in His Word. He has told us plainly what to eat – and what not to eat – in order to have the best possible health and to be able to serve Him to the best of our ability. He calls on us to glorify Him through our bodies and by what we eat and drink (see 1 Corinthians 6:19, 20).

Jesus makes the choice we face clear in John 14:15. "If ye love me, keep my commandments." How shall we respond? If we love Him, won't we want to follow His will for our lives?

Chapter 18

The Forgotten Commandment
A Battle for Our Loyalty to Christ or Man
By Danny Shelton

The purpose of this book is to find out from the Scriptures, "is there a forgotten commandment?" If there is, then these questions need to be asked, "Which one is it?" and "Should those of us who claim to be Christians be keeping this commandment?"

God gave Moses the Ten Commandments, yet most Christians today obey just nine. Why?

Let's first read the Ten Commandments from the King James Version of the Bible:

I am the Lord thy God, which have brought thee out of the land of Egypt, out of the house of bondage. Thou shalt have no other gods before me.

Thou shalt not make unto thee any graven image, or any likeness of anything that is in heaven above, or that is in the earth beneath, or that is in the water under the earth. Thou shalt not bow down thyself to them, nor serve them: for I the Lord thy God am a jealous God, visiting the iniquity of the fathers upon the children unto the third and fourth generation of them that hate me; and showing mercy unto thousands of them that love me and keep my commandments.

Thou shalt not take the name of the Lord thy God in vain; for the Lord will not hold him guiltless that taketh his name in vain.

Remember the Sabbath day, to keep it holy. Six days shalt

thou labour and do all thy work; but the seventh day is the sabbath of the Lord thy God; in it thou shalt not do any work, thou, nor thy son, nor thy daughter, thy manservant, nor thy maidservant, nor thy cattle, nor thy stranger that is within thy gates; For in six days the Lord made heaven and earth, the sea, and all that in them is, and rested the seventh day; wherefore the Lord blessed the sabbath day, and hallowed it.

Honour thy father and thy mother; that thy days may be long upon the land which the Lord thy God giveth thee.

Thou shalt not kill.

Thou shalt not commit adultery.

Thou shalt not steal.

Thou shalt not bear false witness against thy neighbour.

Thou shalt not covet thy neighbour's house, thou shalt not covet thy neighbour's wife, nor his manservant, nor his maidservant, nor his ox, nor his ass, nor anything that is thy neighbour's (Exodus 20:3-17).

In examining these texts, we find that according to the fourth commandment, God set aside, or made holy, the seventh day of the week – the day we call Saturday. In fact, Genesis 2:2 says that at creation God "rested on the seventh day from all his work which he had made." Now, from everything I've ever learned about God or even heard about Him, nothing even remotely suggests that He gets tired! He must have rested for a reason, as an example to us. We find right in the middle of the fourth commandment, God" instruction to us to keep holy the seventh day of the week – to worship Him on that day and to rest from our regular work. The fourth commandment leaves no question about it – we are to obey Him in this matter just as much as we are to obey Him in the other nine commandments.

Can we be sure which day of the week is the seventh day?

The big question we might have after reading the fourth commandment is: "Which day of the week is the seventh day?" Is Saturday really the seventh day of the week? How do we know? Maybe our calendars are all wrong. Maybe time has been lost or gained. I've heard that many calendars in Europe today say that Monday is the first day of the week, making Sunday the seventh day. Let's examine these questions.

First of all, let's see what the United States Naval Observatory in Washington, D.C. has to say about this matter of time being lost or gained. In a letter dated March 12, 1932, the director, James Robertson, stated:

...We have had occasion to investigate the results of the works of specialists in chronology and we have never found one of them that has ever had the slightest doubt about the continuity of the weekly cycle since long before the Christian era...There has been no change in our calendar in past centuries that has affected in any way the cycle of the week...

As you can see, according to this source, the weekly cycle is still the same as it was 2,000 years ago when Christ walked the earth. Also, from Scripture we can see that Jesus had no trouble knowing which day of the week was the seventh day – the day for weekly worship. Luke 4:16 says, "As his custom was, he (Jesus) went into the synagogue on the sabbath day." The whole Jewish world in Jesus' day kept holy God's seventh-day Sabbath. In fact, the Jews have continually kept the seventh-day Sabbath.

If we question whether Saturday is really the seventh day of the week, the Sabbath, we have to stretch our imaginations to decide that all the Jewish people around the world could have somehow gotten the days mixed up in the weekly cycle since Jesus was on earth. And if this were so, then Jews in different places around the world would probably be keeping any number of different days. Instead, we see them unified all over the earth on the matter of which day of the week is the seventh day Sabbath.

We have Bible evidence, too, that Saturday is the seventh day of the week, God's holy Sabbath. Luke 23:54 says that the day Jesus died "was the preparation, and the Sabbath drew on." Then Luke 24:1 says that the day Jesus rose from the grave was "the first day of the week." So from the Bible we have this three-day sequence: the day before the Sabbath (the day Jesus died), the Sabbath, and the first day of the week (the day Jesus rose from the dead). All the world recognizes Good Friday as the day Jesus died. All the world recognizes Easter Sunday as the day He rose to life. And the day between Friday and Sunday is which day? Saturday. And the New Testament calls this day "the sabbath" (Luke 23:54). I believe we have enough information available to us to know without a doubt that the Saturday of today is the same day that the Bible calls the seventh day of the week – God's holy Sabbath.

It is also interesting to note that the cycles of time marked on earth are determined by astronomy. A day is measured by how long it takes the earth to rotate, a month is determined by the cycle of the moon, and a year is measured by how long the earth takes to revolve around the sun. Only the weekly cycle has no anchor in astronomical time. That traditional measurement of time can only be traced back to God's creation when the seventh day was set aside as the Sabbath.

Is the Sabbath still part of God's will for Christians?

I think it would be timely here to look at why God commanded His children to keep holy the seventh day of the week. Why did God place such a seemingly unimportant matter right in the heart of the Ten Commandments? And further, why is the fourth commandment the only one of the ten to begin with the word, "Remember"? If God were going to change or do away with the fourth commandment at a later date – and many Christians believe He did – would it make sense for Him to begin the fourth commandment by saying, "Remember"? In fact, it would seem that the other nine commandments should have started with the word "Remember" even more so than the fourth – since most Christians agree that these nine are still binding today and will be binding throughout all eternity, while they feel that the fourth commandment was done away with. *The word "Remember" tells us that God knew people were going to have trouble with that commandment – that they would be tempted to forget it.*

God says that the Sabbath is a "perpetual covenant" and that it is "a sign between me and the children of Israel for ever" (Exodus 31:16, 17). How, then can some Christians today say that the Ten Commandments were part of the old covenant and no longer valid for God's people?

It reminds me of the time when my family and I sang one Sunday morning at a big, popular, Sunday-keeping church in Tennessee. After the service, the pastor came to me and said, "Someone just told me that you're a Sabbath keeper. Is that true?"

"Yes," I replied.

The pastor continued, "Do you mean to tell me that you live under that old covenant? I'm glad to say that I'm not under that old law anymore; I'm under grace!"

I remember looking at him and saying, "OK, that sounds good to me. You've convinced me." Then I picked up the Sunday offering plates that were close by and began to leave.

"Oh, excuse me, Brother Shelton," the pastor said, "but that's not your offering! That's the church's offering. We'll send you a check for your part."

"No," I replied. "I'll just take all of it."

As I started out to my van, the pastor quickly followed

to let me know again that this was his church's offering — not mine.

"I understand," I assured him. "But if the Ten Commandments were done away with at the Cross, then I'm not really stealing your money because there isn't anything now that tells me it's wrong to take something that doesn't belong to me!"

As I handed back the offering plates, the pastor understood my point and had to reconsider his idea of not being "under the old law." Let's look now at the Bible definition of sin. "Sin is the transgression of the law" (1 John 3:4). This is one of the easiest texts to understand in the whole Bible. If there were no law, there could not be any sin.

Did Jesus' death on Calvary nail the Ten Commandments to the cross? Again, let's see what the Bible has to say on this subject. Jesus said, "Think not that I am come to destroy the law, or the prophets: I am not come to destroy, but to fulfill" (Matthew 5:17). It's amazing that so many people, including many Bible scholars, try to make this verse say something that it just doesn't say! You cannot make this scripture say that Jesus' death on the cross did away with the Ten Commandment law. No. Jesus says, "I am not come to destroy, but to fulfill [or make complete]."

Now Jesus *did* do away with the ceremonial laws when He died. Paul says that Jesus was "blotting out the handwriting of ordinances that was against us, which was contrary to us, and took it out of the way, nailing it to his cross" (Colossians 2:14). How beautiful to know that the death of Jesus means we no longer have to look at the blood of lambs, the table of stone, or try to be perfect by our own works! Now that Jesus has taken our sins on Himself at the cross of Calvary, His righteousness atones for our sins if we simply confess that we are sinners and ask for His forgiveness. The Bible says that "all have sinned, and come short of the glory of God" (Romans 3:23). It also says that "if we confess our sins, he is faithful and just to forgive us our sins, and to cleanse us from all unrighteousness" (1 John 1:9).

Now let's see what actually is going on when a pastor makes an altar call. What I his intention? Whether he is a Baptist, Presbyterian, Pentecostal, Methodist, or whatever, his intention is to get one to confess his sins to God and then ask Jesus into his heart so that he might be "saved." Are you starting to get the point? If God's law was nailed to the cross, then there really is no need to encourage someone to ask for forgiveness because there is no longer any sin to be forgiven.

Why? Remember the Bible definition of sin is "transgression of the law" (1 John 4:3). Follow this line of thinking now. If there is no more law, then there is no more sin. And if there is no more sin, then there is no reason to repent of our sins. If there is no reason to repent of our sins, then there is no need for a Savior. And if there is no need for a Savior, then there is no need for pastors. And if there is no need for pastors, then there is no need for churches—and so on and so on. Now that's deep! Think about it for a moment, and go back and re-read that paragraph and let it soak in for a bit.

By now you are probably beginning to ask, "Since the Bible is so clear that the Ten Commandments are still valid today, then why do so many churches try to explain them away?"

Again, the answer is very simple. If we acknowledge that the Ten Commandment law of God, the Decalogue, is still valid today, then we have to accept and keep the fourth commandment, recognizing that Saturday, the seventh day of the week, is the Sabbath that God, the Creator of the universe, blessed, set apart, sanctified, and made holy as His day of worship.

Who dares separate what God has joined together? (See Matthew 19:6). Whether it be marriage (which is what

Matthew 19:6 is talking about) or the only thing God ever wrote with His own finger in stone—His Ten Commandments—we are warned not to try to separate what God has joined together. Yet Christians everywhere would have us believe that only nine commandments are valid today. They believe it is wrong to kill, commit adultery, lie, steal, but insist that the fourth commandment, containing the seventh-day Sabbath, has been separated from the other nine and nailed to Jesus' cross.

Actually, there are some interesting comparisons between marriage and the Sabbath. Both were instituted by God in Eden during Creation week. God sanctified both marriage and His holy Sabbath day. And just as no one can separate a husband and wife united in holy matrimony, neither can one separate God's fourth commandment from the rest. Both marriage and the Sabbath are founded on the same principle—the blessing and authority of the Creator who gave both institutions to humanity.

I have found that no matter what subject I'm dealing with in life, I always make the best decisions when I base them on principle. What do I mean by "principle"? Operating on the basis of principle means not getting caught up in feelings, sensations, emotions, wants, or desires. It means basing my life on what is right and what is wrong according to God's Word.

Let me give you an example. Many Christians say that God is not particular about which day a person keeps as the Sabbath—even though God has specifically designated the seventh day of the week as the day of worship. Let's compare that same principle to the idea of marriage and see how it turns out. Suppose you have gone to prayer meeting one evening, and after the service is over, you look for your spouse. He or she happens to be standing next to six friends. You say, "Honey, it's time to go home, but tonight I think I'll take one of your six friends home with me to spend the night with me in our bed. I know we're married and that our marriage has been sanctified by God, but since you are there with six of your friends, I don't think it really matters to you which of them I sleep with, just as long as it's one of them!"

I think you get the point. If you want to stay married, I wouldn't encourage you to try something this foolish! In the first place, you wouldn't even want to do this because you love your spouse. Secondly, you know, according to God's Word, that sleeping with someone other than your spouse is sin. You would be breaking the seventh commandment, the one that says, "Thou shalt not commit adultery." (Exodus 20:5)

In the same sense, we are committing spiritual adultery by willfully breaking God's fourth commandment and keeping another day that has not been instituted or sanctified or made holy by God. God says, "I the Lord thy God am a jealous God." (Exodus 20:5)

A look at some puzzling texts

Although there are no texts in the Bible showing that God changed the Sabbath day, there are a few texts we want to look at that on the surface may seem confusing. We know that the Bible was written under the inspiration of God and never contradicts itself—"All scripture is given by inspiration of God" (2 Timothy 3:16). But some texts have confused some sincere Christians a they studied this matter of the Sabbath.

For example, in Colossians 2:13, 14 the apostle Paul says of Jesus: And you, being dead in your sins. . .hath he [Jesus] quickened [made alive] together with him, having forgiven you all your trespasses; blotting out the handwriting of ordinances that was against us, which was contrary to us, and took it out of the way, nailing it to his cross.

Many Christians point to this text as evidence that God's Ten Commandment law was nailed to Jesus' cross and came to an end at that time. But we have already seen that God's

265

Ten Commandment law will last for eternity. So what law is Paul talking about? What law was nailed to Jesus' cross?

The next few verses help us to answer that question:

Let no man therefore judge you in meat, or in drink, or in respect of an holy day, or of the new moon, or of the Sabbath days: which are a shadow of things to come, but the body is of Christ (verses 16, 17).

So the laws, or ordinances, that Paul says were nailed to Jesus' cross were those that foreshadowed the work that Jesus would do when He came to live on earth—His sacrifice as the Lamb of God. These, Paul goes on to say, are the ceremonial laws God gave His people in the Old Testament dealing with meat and drink offerings, new moon festivals, and ceremonial "Sabbath days" such as the Day of Atonement, Pentecost, Feast of Tabernacles (see Leviticus 23:4-38). In fact, Leviticus 23:39, specifically shows that these ceremonial "sabbaths" (which could fall on any day of the week in different years) are distinct from the weekly seventh-day Sabbath of the fourth commandment.

Another text that has puzzled some Christians is 1 Corinthians 16:1, 2. Paul wrote to the Christians at Corinth:

Now concerning the collection for the saints, as I have given order to the churches in Galatia, even so do ye. Upon the first day of the week let every one of you lay by him in store, as God hath prospered him, that there be no gatherings when I come.

Some have thought Paul was talking about taking up offerings in church on the first day of the week and that this text, then, showed that Christians in Paul's day were worshiping on Sunday, the first day of the week. But if you read the text carefully, it becomes clear that Paul was telling the believers at Corinth to figure up at home on Sunday what they could give to the collection he was gathering for the believers in Jerusalem. They were to "lay by...in store" this offering so that it would be ready for

Paul to pick up when he came through Corinth on his way to Jerusalem. There is no hint here that God has changed the day of worship to Sunday.

Acts 20:7 is another text some people use to try to prove that the early Christian church worshiped on Sunday:

Upon the first day of the week, when the disciples were come together to break bread, Paul preached unto them, ready to depart on the morrow.

Again, if you read the entire passage, you discover that this was a special meeting that had been called because Paul was passing through the area and wanted to see the believers he had brought to Jesus on his earlier missionary journeys. Some have said that they were holding a Communion service because it says they "were come together to break bread." Most likely it was a common meal, and at any rate, Acts 2:46 says that the early Christian believers broke bread together "daily." Once more, we find no hint of Sunday sacredness in the early Christian church.

Why do most Christians today ignore the seventh-day Sabbath?

Now that we have shown from the Bible that God's Ten Commandment law, including the fourth commandment, is still valid today, you may rightfully be wondering, "Why don't most Christians—Protestant and Catholic—keep God's holy seventh-day Sabbath?"

Before examining this question, I want to make it clear that I believe God has sincere followers in every church. We are not saved by the denominational name over the door of our church building. I believe God judges each believer's heart individually. I love people of all faiths—or even no faith. Jesus says, "Love one another, as I have loved you" (John 15:12). So when we are talking about God's Sabbath, we have to deal with church doctrines and creeds and systems—in both Protestant and Catholic churches—but we are not judging individual hearts.

267

When we look at the fact that most Christian churches are not keeping God's seventh-day Sabbath, the big question is: Why? This seems to be the only commandment of the ten that is under attack by Christian church organizations. There must be a reason. There must be something about the fourth commandment that Satan really hates. What is it? Let's read the fourth commandment once again:

> Remember the Sabbath day, to keep it holy. Six days shalt thou labor and do all thy work: but the seventh day is the Sabbath of the Lord thy God: in it thou shalt not do any work, thou, nor thy son, nor thy daughter, thy manservant, nor thy maidservant, nor thy cattle, nor thy stranger that is within thy gates: for in six days the Lord made heaven and earth, the sea, and all that in them is, and rested the seventh day: wherefore the Lord blessed the Sabbath day, and hallowed it.

Notice that there is something very important contained in the fourth commandment that is not found in the other nine. The fourth commandment identifies who is the author of all ten of the commandments—the Lord who "made heaven and earth, the sea, and all that in them is." Now we know who it is who wrote the Ten Commandments. It is the Creator God, the God of the universe, the great I AM! Now follow closely with me for a minute.

If we examine the Ten Commandments, we will find that they are divided into two parts. By obeying the first four commandments we show our love to God. When we obey the last six, we show our love for our fellow man. For example, we show our loyalty to God by not having any other gods before Him, by not bowing down to any other gods, and by not taking His name in vain. And when we keep the fourth commandment—the Sabbath commandment—we show our loyalty to the one and only Creator God.

The fourth commandment is the only one that tells us which God we serve—the God who "made heaven and earth, the sea, and all that in them is" (Exodus 20:11). If we try to do away with the fourth commandment, we don't even know what God we're loyal to. I was in India some time ago and found out that thee are millions of gods worshiped in that country. The God we serve created us; He's our Creator. That fact—more than any other—distinguishes Him from all those manmade gods.

The last six of the Ten Commandments show our love for others. For example, if we don't steal from our neighbor, if we don't commit adultery with his wife, if we don't lie about him, etc. we are demonstrating our love for our neighbor.

The fourth commandment, you see, contains the seal of God. Without the fourth commandment, we wouldn't know who had written the other nine. Imagine for a moment that you read in the newspaper that the United States has just declared war on another country! The first questions that would probably come to your mind would be, "Says who?" After all, there are nearly 300,000,000 Americans. Any one of them could have declared war on another country, but that means nothing unless someone with the authority to do so actually declares war. The president of the United States is the only one who has the authority to sign a declaration of war after Congress has taken that step. His seal consists of several parts: (1) his name—George W. Bush; (2) his title—President; (3) his territory or domain—the United States of America. Be assured that if George W. Bush, president of the United States of America, signs a declaration of war, then America is indeed engaged in war!

Our Creator God has His seal contained in the fourth commandment: (1) His name—"the Lord thy God"; (2) His title—Creator; (3) His territory or domain—"heaven and earth, the sea and all that in them is."

Remember, the Bible says that war broke out in heaven. "And there was war in heaven: Michael and his angels fought against the dragon; and the dragon fought and his angels, and prevailed not" (Revelation 12:7, 8). Why did war break out in heaven? Because Satan was jealous of God. He said, "I will be like the most high" (Isaiah 14:14). He was able to convince one-third of the angels to follow him (see Revelation 12:4).

The great controversy between Christ and Satan continues today—except that now Satan is working to get human beings to give their allegiance to him instead of God. Satan knows that he and his unholy angels are lost, but he wants to make a mockery of God before the whole universe by destroying us, God's creation (see John 10:10). He still wants to be like the most high God. So he is stealing the allegiance of the human race by having his human agents change God's Ten Commandments and thereby deceive the nations to follow him instead of the Creator God of the universe.

Brothers and sisters, the issue is not only about a day; it's about allegiance. The question is: Whom are we going to serve? Do we love God enough to serve Him and keep His commandments fully—including the fourth? Or are we going to serve Satan and worship on his counterfeit day as instituted by man? Is this possible? Let's see what the Bible has to say. "In vain do they worship me, teaching for doctrines the commandments of men" (Mark 7:7). In fact, if you read this verse closely, you'll see that Jesus is predicting this will happen. Again, it's not just about a day; it's about allegiance.

Notice, too, James 2:10. "For whosoever shall keep the whole law, and yet offend in one point, he is guilty of all." What law is James talking about? The Ten Commandment law that God wrote on tablets of stone with His own finger; notice the next verse: "For he that said, Do not commit adultery, said also, Do not kill. Now if thou commit no adultery, yet if thou kill, thou are become a transgressor of the law" (James 2:11). Think about this. I think we can all agree that Jesus is the "cornerstone." All creation hinges on the cornerstone. The stone that God wrote His law on represents Jesus Himself—the Cornerstone. The Ten Commandment law is nothing more than a transcript of Jesus' character. The Ten Commandment law is God's own Word. John says, "The Word was made flesh, and dwelt among us" (John 1:14). Imagine this!

Jesus, the Cornerstone, gave to Moses the Ten Commandments on tablets of stone representing Himself. The Bible records that Moses became angry when he saw the wickedness of the people, and he threw down the tablets of stone and broke them (see Exodus 32:19). But did that do away with the law of God? No. The Bible records that God gave him another set of stone tablets containing the Ten Commandments. These were placed in the ark of the covenant in the sanctuary and eventually were hidden when Israel went into exile. There are some indications that these tablets of stone with the law written on them by God Himself will be revealed to the world at God's appointed time.

In the same way, Jesus' body was broken for us when He died on the cross (see 1 Corinthians 11:24). Like the broken tablets of stone, Jesus' broken body didn't destroy the law of God, but fulfilled it (see Matthew 5:17). Then, after His death, Jesus ascended to heaven to intercede on our behalf until the appointed time when He will return and all the earth will see Him and know that He is King of kings, and Lord of lords. Praise God!

Isn't it wonderful that God loved us enough that He would set aside a twenty-four-hour day every week that we can spend with Him? It's a weekly reminder that He loves us and hasn't forgotten us. A friend of mine refers to the Ten Commandments as the "Ten Promises." What a wonderful way to describe them! The Bible says that we should put on the whole armor of God (Ephesians 6:11).

When we put on—or wear—the character of God, His Ten Commandments, He promises us victory over the devil. We won't lose control and kill someone, for example. We won't lose control and kill someone, for example. We won't fall into stealing or committing adultery. He promises us victory over lying or coveting. What love! An old hymn says, "A wonderful Savior is Jesus my Lord, a wonderfully Savior to me." Truer words were never spoken.

What the Sabbath means to me personally

We've seen something of what the Bible says about God's seventy-day Sabbath and its importance. Now, before we go on to look at other aspects of this subject and their significance for the times in which we are living, I would like to explain briefly what the Sabbath means to me from a personal standpoint.

For me, the seventh-day Sabbath of the Lord is the highlight of every week. It's my escape from all my everyday problems in this life. During the Sabbath, I seem to be lifted up into heavenly places in close communion with God. Every seven days the Sabbath reminds me that Jesus loves me and that He hasn't forgotten me. It reminds me that Jesus is coming back to this earth very soon to redeem me from this sin-sick world. The seventy-day Sabbath is God's covenant—or agreement—with me that I am His and He is mine though all eternity. Notice what God said back in the day of Israel: "Verily my Sabbaths ye shall keep: for it is a sign between me and you throughout your generations; that ye may know that I am the Lord that doth sanctify you" (Exodus 31:13). Verse 17 says that the Sabbath is a sign between God and His people "for ever."

On the Sabbath I can leave my daily cares behind. All my business affairs—whom I owe money to, who owes money to me, how much is (or isn't) in my bank account, all these things can just go away for twenty-four hours. I don't have to worry about them or deal with them. Let me tell you, it's wonderful to be able to get away from all the business of buying and selling. The Lord knows we can't concentrate on our relationship with Him if we're concerned with carrying on the usual daily transactions of life. That's why He tells us to avoid working on the Sabbath, or buying and selling things.

Thus said the Lord unto me; go and stand in the gate of the children of the people, whereby the kings of Judah come in, and by the which they go out, and in all the gates of Jerusalem;

And say unto them, Hear ye the word of the Lord, ye kings of Judah, and all Judah, and all the inhabitants of Jerusalem, that enter in by these gates: Thus saith the Lord; Take heed to yourselves, and bear no burden on the Sabbath day, nor bring it in by the gates of Jerusalem;

Neither carry forth a burden out of your houses on the Sabbath day, neither do ye any work, but hallow ye the Sabbath day, as I commanded your fathers. But they obeyed not, neither inclined their ear, but made their neck stiff, that they might not hear, nor receive instruction. And it shall come to pass, if ye diligently hearken unto me, saith the Lord, to bring in no burden through the gates of this city on the Sabbath day, but hallow the Sabbath day, to do no work therein;

Then shall there enter into the gates of this city kings and princes sitting upon the throne of David, riding in chariots and on horses, they, and their princes, the men of Judah, and the inhabitants of Jerusalem: and this city shall remain for ever (Jeremiah 17:19-25).

The Lord knows, too, that we need physical rest as well as mental rest on the Sabbath. I'm thankful that He tells us in the fourth commandment to stop all our usual labor and work for the twenty-four hours of the Sabbath. Medical science will confirm that anyone who works seven days a week will burn out much faster than someone who works six days as God has commanded—and rests on the Sabbath.

Sometimes people get hung up on what is, or is not, work on the Sabbath. In my opinion, these kinds of discussions end up splitting legalistic hairs. It's very easy to sort out, as far as I can see. God set the example for us.

> Thus the heavens and the earth were finished, and all the host of them. And on the seventh day God ended his work which he had made; and he rested on the seventh day from all his work which he had made. And God blessed the seventh day, and sanctified it: because that in it he had rested from all his work which God created and made (Genesis 2:1-3).

What work is it that God rested from? The work of creating the world, of course. But let me ask you another questions: Does God quit working in our behalf on the Sabbath? Does Jesus quit interceding for us during the Sabbath hours? Of course not! The Bible tells us that "the Sabbath was made for man, and not man for the Sabbath" (Mark 2:27). Did God rest on that first Sabbath at the end of Creation week because he was tired? No. He rested to set an example for us to follow. In the same way, on the Sabbath we are to abstain from our daily work in the sense of doing the job that we do the other six days of the week. But we should never let the Sabbath stop us from doing God's will during its hours. We shouldn't be like some who are so afraid they won't keep the Sabbath correctly that they won't drive a car, walk a mile, or help a neighbor in need on the Sabbath.

I've found great peace of mind in keeping the Sabbath when I concentrate on my relationship with God and my relationship with other human beings. In other words, I try to dedicate the Sabbath to service. I don't just pull up an easy chair and sit all day on the Sabbath. Neither do I spend the Sabbath in bed. I try to focus on helping others.

You may ask, "How do you do this in actual practice?" Here are some suggestions that have worked for me.

Sabbath evening (Friday night) is a good time to spend in family worship, reading the Bible, and restful fellowship. Begin Sabbath morning with prayer and devotions, then go to church and worship God. We want to spend time in worship and holy convocation (church service or holy assembly) with God. As the Bible says:

> Six days shall work be done: but the seventh day is the Sabbath of rest, an holy convocation; ye shall do no work therein: it is the Sabbath of the Lord in all your dwellings (Leviticus 23:3).

> And on the seventh day ye shall have an holy convocation; ye shall do no servile work (Numbers 28:25).

But don't go to church expecting everyone to serve *your* needs. Plan to be a blessing to those around you. Take part in the Sabbath School. If you can't teach a class, then help the teacher by taking part in the discussion of the lesson. If you can't sing, you can give your personal testimony during the praise time. If you're too shy to do that, you can take up the offering, help run the audio system, or help in some other behind-the-scenes way. You can bring some food for the church potluck dinner after the service. If your church doesn't have a potluck dinner, then invite someone home with you for lunch—especially someone needy. To me, it's important that I go to church not only to *receive* a blessing, but to *be* one.

God's seventh-day Sabbath is also a great time to spend with your family—both during church and the rest of the day. Current statistics show that the average parent spends only a few minutes a day with his or her children. Sabbath afternoon is a great time for the whole family to take a hike in nature. Look around you and take time to enjoy the outdoors. I'm very fortunate to have been raised by parents who taught me the truth about God's seventh-day Sabbath. Some of my fondest childhood memories always seem to revolve around the time my family spent together on God's holy Sabbath.

Passing out gospel literature is another great way to spend the Sabbath with your family. Remember, the Sabbath isn't about us. It's about our relationship with God. It's an opportunity to serve others. Scripture tells us that Jesus spent much of the Sabbath healing the sick and serving others. I believe there will be many, many people in heaven because someone cared enough to take the time and effort to introduce them to Jesus through literature. And, of course, the Sabbath is a wonderful time for personal prayer and study because the closer we are to Jesus, the more we will want to share Him with others.

Is God really particular?

No wonder the devil wants Christians to forget the Sabbath commandment—the only one that God specifically said for us to "Remember." Disregarding the fourth commandment takes our eyes off the only true God who can give us victory over sin and make it possible for us to defeat that old serpent, the devil.

Very simply put, it's like this: By trying to change the Sabbath from the seventh day of the week, that our Creator God instituted, to Sunday, the first day of the week. Satan takes away God's "seal," His authority on earth. By keeping a false Sabbath, we are paying the homage to Satan that he has wanted since sin began in heaven some 6,000 years ago.

Is God really particular? Does the day really matter to Him? Let's look at 1 John 2:4. "He that saith, I know him (Jesus) and keepeth not his commandments, is a liar, and the truth is not in him." The word for "commandments" in the original language *(entolai)* refers to the precepts or laws that Jesus taught and lived by and certainly includes the Ten Commandments. The Bible gives several examples of God rejecting those who failed to follow His commandments. Let's look at just a few.

Cain and Abel both brought sacrifices to God. Abel brought a lamb as God had directed. But Cain brought fruit and vegetables from the ground. He failed to follow God's instructions. God accepted Abel and his offering, but He rejected Cain and his offering (see Genesis 4:3-5).

Likewise, Uzzah reached out his hand to steady the ark, knowing that God had commanded that no one touch the sacred furniture associated with the sanctuary. He must have reasoned that God wasn't that particular. But Uzzah paid with his life for his presumption (see 2 Samuel 6:6, 7). God means what He says?

Even Moses himself, man of faith that he was, had times of weakness and failure. When the Israelites were dying of thirst in the desert, God told Moses to speak to the rock and water would gush out freely for the people and their animals. But Moses became so frustrated with the complaints of the people that he hit the rock with his rod—just as he had done the first time. Water poured out, but God was displeased that Moses hadn't done what He told him to do. Moses had to pay for his sin by not getting to enter the Promised Land (see Numbers 20:7-12).

It seems like such a little thing—striking the rock instead of speaking to it. But it wasn't really a matter of whether Moses hit the rock or spoke to it. It was a matter of obedience. Would he obey God or not? Will we obey God or not? That's the issue. Saturday or Sunday—the seventh day of the week or the first. It isn't a matter of days, really. It's a matter of obedience. Will we obey God or not?

How the change came about

If God's Sabbath is really Saturday, the seventh day of the week, then how did a change come about? Why would the Christian world institute Sunday in place of God's seventh-day Sabbath? That's a fair question—one that most people ask when they first discover that Saturday is the Bible Sabbath.

First we should note that if Sunday is not the bible Sabbath, then it is an error. And Paul warned the Christian leaders in Ephesus that errors would creep into the church:

> I know this, that after my departing shall grievous wolves enter in among you, not sparing the flock. Also of your own selves shall men arise, speaking perverse things, to draw away disciples after them (Acts 20:29, 30).

Church history records that, unfortunately, this came to pass. Very quickly, the early church found itself caught up in a number of doctrinal errors. Paul told the Thessalonian church that a spirit of hatred against God's laws would arise in the church, and that, in fact, it was already at work (see 2 Thessalonians 2:3-7). The Sabbath was one of the god's laws that suffered during early church history and through the following centuries. Although some Christians always remained faithful to the day that God had so clearly set apart in His Word, the majority of Christians gradually gave up the biblical seventh-day Sabbath for the first day of the week. What led them to make such a change in spite of god's specific commandment? Two factors especially caused the church to substitute the first day of the week for the seventh.

Anti-Judaism. There was intense debate in the New Testament church about whether Gentile Christians should be required to observe all the rituals and ceremonies of Judaism. This was the first factor that moved the church away fro God's Sabbath. The first Christians were Jews. Naturally, the continued many of the Old Testament practices they had been accustomed to following. One group in the church demanded that Gentile converts follow these

278

same practices, while another group insisted that this wasn't necessary—and of course, it wasn't.

Eventually, the church decided in favor of freedom for the Gentiles. But the strong arguments used against the Old Testament rituals—such as circumcision and the sanctuary sacrifices—were apparently misunderstood as time went on. *Everything* connected with the Jews became suspect. And since the Jews kept the seventh-day Sabbath, Christians came to look down upon this day as they did other practices considered to be especially Jewish. As the Christian church grew, it increasingly wanted to distance itself from the Jewish community from which it had sprung.

Evangelism. The second factor was a desire to attract pagans to the church. As pagans were converted, they brought with them some of their former ideas. A great many of the pagan religions already honored the sun on the first day of the week. In fact, that's how it got the name *Sunday!* Church leaders began to think that it would be easier to win pagan converts to the church if they could continue to worship on the day they had been used to honoring.

So the desire to avoid identification with the Jews, coupled with the desire to make Christianity more appealing to the pagans, made it easy for the early church to assign a special prominence to the first day of the week. The resurrection of Jesus on that day provided a ready reason.

These are some of the factors that we see in the history of the early Christian church for Sunday to become more prominent and Saturday to fall into disfavor. As the early Christian church—the organization that we know today as the Roman Catholic Church—grew in popularity and power, it united itself with the state. Under the influence of the church, the Roman emperor, Constantine, in 321

A.D. issued the first law requiring people to cease their labors and worship on Sunday.

Who claims to have changed the Sabbath to Sunday?
Actually, God foresaw that this change would happen right within the church. Did you know that through the prophet Daniel, the Bible predicts that a religious power would actually think to change God's law? The prediction was written down centuries before Jesus was born in Bethlehem. Let's look at this prediction and see how this "change" happened.

Speaking of the power he saw in vision, Daniel says, "He shall speak great words against the most High, and shall wear out the saints of the most High, and think to change times and laws" (Daniel 7:25). Notice that this power Daniel is talking about will go against God, "the most High," and try to change His "times and laws." How do we know that Daniel was saying this power would change God's "times and laws"? Notice that this phrase appears in the list of charges God brings against this power: it's guilty of blasphemy, persecution, and *changing "times and laws."* Human authorities have a perfect right to change man-made practices and laws. So, since God considers what this power has done terribly wrong, *it must be God's times and laws—rather than man-made ones—this power has attempted to change.*

Now, what law of God deals with time? Only one of God's Ten Commandments is concerned with time—the fourth commandment that specifies the seventh day of the week as God's holy Sabbath. Daniel said that this power would try to change God's law about time, the Sabbath. Is there any religious power on earth today that claims to have changed the Sabbath day of the Lord? Actually, there is. Let's look at some quotations by this power that claims to have done just that?

The Catholic Church for over one thousand years before the existence of a Protestant, by virtue of her divine mission, changed the day from Saturday to Sunday. . . .The Christian Sabbath is therefore *to this day* the acknowledged offspring of the Catholic Church. . .without a word of remonstrance from the Protestant world. *(The Christian Sabbath,* 2nd edition, "The Catholic Mirror," Baltimore, 1893.)

Q. *Which is the Sabbath day?*
A. Saturday is the Sabbath day.

Q. *Why do we observe Sunday instead of Saturday?*
A. We observe Sunday instead of Saturday because the Catholic church transferred the solemnity from Saturday to Sunday (Peter Geiermann, *The Convert's Catechism of the Catholic Doctrine,* St. Louis, 1957).

Q. *Have you any other way of proving that the Church has power to institute festivals of precept?*
A. Had she not such power, she could not have done that in which all modern religionists agree with her;—she could not have substituted the observance of Sunday, the first day of the week, for the observance of Saturday, the seventh day, a change for which there is no Scriptural authority (Stephen Keenan, *A Doctrinal Catechism,* New York, 1876).

You may read the Bible from Genesis to Revelation, and you will not find a single line authorizing the sanctification of Sunday. The Scriptures enforce the religious observance of Saturday, a day which we never sanctify (Cardinal Gibbons, *The Faith of Our Fathers,* p.111).

Of course the Catholic Church claims that the change [of the Sabbath from Saturday to Sunday] was her act. . .And the act is a mark of her ecclesiastical power (Letter by H. F. Thomas, chancellor of Cardinal Gibbons).

Please remember that these are not my statements. These are quotations from publications and spokesmen of the

Catholic Church, admitting without hesitation that the act of changing god's Sabbath commandment was carried out by the authority of the Roman Catholic Church alone. Now please don't misunderstand. We are not talking about individuals here; we are talking about religious institutions and systems. God has faithful followers in every church and every denomination—including the Roman Catholic Church. But when God's Word says that a religious power will arise that will try to change divine laws regarding time, and when the Catholic Church states clearly and without stammering that she has made just a change, then I believe those who want to remain faithful to God have to stand up and look at the evidence. Again, it's not an issue of two days; it's an issue of loyalty to God. It's a matter of deciding whether we will be faithful to what God says and obey Him or whether we will turn away from His commandment and follow another way.

Let's go back and look at that verse in Daniel again—the verse in which the prophet predicted that a power would arise change Gods laws about time. Notice that Daniel says that this power will *"think* to change times and laws" (Daniel 7:25, emphasis added). It's interesting that the bible would say it just that way. Can any church or institution or power actually change a commandment of God unless God Himself makes a change? Not really. We can try to change God's law. We can *think* we have changed God's law. We can *claim* we have changed God's law. And we can even get people to follow us in disobeying God's law. But we can't really change one of God's commandments, can we? The Catholic Church admits there is no Bible authority—no text anywhere in Scripture—for worshiping on Sunday, but she claims to have made the change anyway.

Why is this issue so important?
"But why make such a fuss over this?" someone asks.

"Why is it so important?"

It's important, as we've pointed out already, because the issue is really "Whom are we going to serve? Are we going to be loyal to God and obey Him? Or are we going to obey the power that has turned away from His plain commandment?" It's really that simple. It's a matter of serving and obeying God. Jesus said, "In vain do they worship me, teaching for doctrines, the commandments of men" (Mark 7:7).

And there is another reason this issue is important. The Bible indicates that as we get nearer and nearer to the end of earth's history, this matter of loyalty to god will become even more pronounced and more important. Revelation 14 pictures God's last message to men and women as being spread across the heavens by three angels. These angels are symbols. They represent God's last-day message that is being carried by men and women to the entire world. Let's look briefly, then, at the three-fold message God has for us here at the end of time just before Jesus comes.

The message of the first angel is a call to worship the Creator God. In fact, the language reminds us of the wording of the fourth commandment. The first angel says:

> Fear God, and give glory to him; for the hour of his judgment is come: and worship him that made heaven, and earth, and the sea, and the fountains of waters (Revelation 14:7).

Likewise the fourth commandment tells us to worship God because He is the Creator of all things in heaven, earth, and the seas. It tells us that the special day God has set aside for worship is the seventh day of the week—His holy Sabbath day (see Exodus 20:8-11).

The message of the second angel is:

> Babylon is fallen, is fallen, that great city, because she made all nations drink the wine of the wrath of her fornication (Revelation 14:8).

Babylon was the nation in the Old Testament that attached Israel, God's people, and carried them into captivity. Babylon was the nation that tried to destroy the worship of the true God of heaven and substitute its pagan gods. And so Babylon became a symbol for all the forces that would oppose God's people in the last days. So when the second angel says that Babylon has fallen because it has made all the nations of the world drink the wine of its fornication, that's a way of saying that the forces fighting against God in the last days will try to force everyone to give allegiance to these forces rather than to God. It's represented as "fornication," or adultery. Disloyalty to God is pictured in the Bible as spiritual adultery. Once again, it all comes down to an issue of loyalty.

Finally, the third angel declares:

> If any man worship the beast and his image, and receive his mark in his forehead or in his hand, the same shall drink of the wine of the wrath of god which is poured out without mixture into the cup of his indignation; and he shall be tormented with fire and brimstone in the presence of the holy angels, and in the presence of the Lamb (Revelation 14:9, 10).

These few words are the most urgent warning God has given anywhere in the Bible. He warns us against worshiping this power that is opposed to Him, and He warns us not to receive its mark. Who or what is this power and what is its mark?"

The "beast power" that we are warned against is the power that is pictures in Revelation 13. There a power is represented that opposes God's law at the end of time and demands the world's loyalty in the place of god. And Revelation says "all that dwell upon the earth shall worship him, whose names are not written in the book of life of the Lamb" (Revelation 13:8). In contrast, Revelation 14:12 says, "Here is the patience of the saints: here are they that keep the commandments of God." So on one side, we have a small group of those who remain faithful to God and His law. And on the other side is most of the world giving loyalty to this power that puts itself in God's place.

What is the mark of this power's authority? Do you remember that when we looked at quotations from the Catholic Church, we saw that the church pointed to its attempt to change God's Sabbath day from Saturday to Sunday as the "mark" of its authority?

Standing at a crucial crossroads

The world stands at a crucial crossroads today. We believe that Three Angels Broadcasting Network has been called into existence to help counteract the counterfeits that Satan is trying to palm off on the world today. He is deceiving the people and the religious organizations of the world to pay homage to him by observing his counterfeit to God's holy Sabbath. He has influenced religious people and organizations to substitute Sunday, the first day of the week, for God's true Sabbath, Saturday, the seventh day of the week.

As we have said several times before, the question isn't just a matter of Sunday versus Saturday. The question is: Do I want to give my allegiance to human institutions by ignoring God's instructions and following man-made traditions instead? I believe this little book you are reading has proven beyond doubt that worshiping on Sunday is based on nothing more than human tradition as instituted by the Catholic Church as long ago as the fourth century after Jesus. We saw earlier that the system of the papacy fits the description of the power brought to view in Daniel 7 and Revelation 13 and 14—the power that will attempt to change God's law. (Note that several times Revelation clearly specifies the keeping of God's commandments as a distinguishing characteristic of His people in the last days. See Revelation 12:17; 14:12.) Much of the information on this point as presented in this little book isn't new. It's been known and understood as far back as the days of Martin Luther and the Reformation.

But what may not be so well known is the meaning of the *image* of this power. Revelation 14:9 speaks of an "image" of this power and warns us against worshiping it as well. Let me explain.

When I look in a mirror, I see a reflection of myself—of what I look like. The image isn't actually me; it's a copy that reflects me perfectly. The image in the mirror is under my control and direction; it does nothing on its own. It's the same with the image to the beast mentioned in Revelation 14:9. The image is under the control of the beast itself. When this power tries to change the seventh-day Sabbath of the Lord, as Daniel prophesied (see Daniel 7:25), then the image to the beast automatically does the same.

We've seen statements from the Roman Catholic Church clearly admitting its efforts to change God's law and the Sabbath. Protestants, by virtue of their very name, claim to protest—or oppose—the mistakes of the Catholic Church. But by keeping Sunday as the Sabbath, which rests on nothing more than Catholic tradition, Protestants have become an image to that power.

God says that those who receive this image or mark of the beast's power "shall drink of the wine of the wrath of God, which is poured out without mixture into the cup of his indignation." (Revelation 14:10).

These are very solemn words. Clearly, we don't want to follow the beast power or its image or receive its mark. We want to be among those pictured in verse 12—those who faithfully "keep the commandments of God." One of the very last verses in the Bible emphasizes again the importance of remaining faithful to god in spite of all the pressure Satan may bring to bear on us. Revelation 22:14 says, "Blessed are they that do his [God's] commandments, that they may have right to the tree of life, and may enter in through the gates into the city."

You may wonder: Does anyone have the mark of the beast now? Is it too late for me already?

The answer is, No. No one has the mark of the beast today. Not until the issues are clearly drawn at the end of time and a person makes a conscious decision to follow the beast in this matter of Sunday versus God's Sabbath, will anyone receive the dreadful mark that God warns us about. A great controversy has been going on between Christ and Satan for the last 6,000 years That struggle is still going on today. The controversy is over our souls—who will claim them? Will we spend eternity with Christ in heaven or be lost forever?

Do you see the picture? Increasingly, as we draw nearer and nearer to the coming of Jesus and to the end of the world, the issue will become one of loyalty to God—as demonstrated by our obedience to Him. Will we obey His commandment to keep holy the seventh-day Sabbath or will be accept the mark of the power that puts its will in the place of God—by observing its authority to change the Sabbath to Sunday, the first day of the week? On the one hand we have a power that demands people show allegiance to it by disregarding God's law and receiving its mark. On the other hand are those who insist on remaining faithful to God and keeping His commandments—including the seventh-day Sabbath of the fourth commandment. That's why this matter of the Sabbath is so important—and why it will become even more important as we move closer to the end of time.

Once again, I want to stress that we aren't casting doubt on the sincerity of individuals or other Christians. We're talking about institutions and systems and organizations and the stands they take. We're talking about what God's Word says the situation is and how it will intensify. We believe a closer look at the prophecies of Daniel and Revelation show us that the powers opposed to God in the last days will attempt to do away with God's holy Sabbath and force everyone to recognize the authority of a substitute day. Yet from Genesis to Revelation, not a single line of Scripture authorizes a change of God's original seventh-day Sabbath to any other day. Revelation predicts that this issue of the Sabbath will become a litmus test for the whole world—and the issue is simply: Will we obey God or won't we?

The short sixty or seventy or eighty years that we spend on planet Earth is just a testing period during which we decide where we want to spend eternity. The Lord has created us with freedom of will. We can choose; we can decide for ourselves. We can ask God to forgive our sins and serve Him. Or we can serve the devil. There is no in-between.

Someone might ask, "What about my mother? She was a wonderful Christian woman, but she never kept the seventh-day Sabbath. Will she be lost?"

You can be assured that no one will be accidentally lost. God holds us responsible only for that which we have had an opportunity to learn and understand. The Bible says, "To him that knoweth to do good, and doeth it not, to him it is sin" (James 4:17). Remember the Bible definition of sin—"sin is the transgression of the law" (1 John 3:4). Willful disobedience to God's law is sin. Once again, keep in mind that the issue isn't so much concerned about a day as it is about loyalty to God. It's about loving and obeying God to the best of our ability. That's all we can do. When we honestly make mistakes because we don't know any better, God's blood covers us. We cannot work our way to heaven. We are saved by grace and grace alone—not by our Sabbath keeping or any other act of obedience. We obey God because we love Him. Jesus said, "If ye love me, keep my commandments" (John 14:15)

No, mother will not be lost because she didn't obey something she didn't understand. We can be lost only when we ourselves choose to reject God and stand on the side of Satan.

Sunday laws and the future

Earth is fast coming to an end. Satan knows that his time is short, and he "as a roaring lion, walketh about seeking whom he may devour" (1 Peter 5:8). Right now he is waging war against the faithful saints of God as never before. He is determined to gain the allegiance of everyone that he possibly can. And we humans are playing right into his hands. Let me explain.

In America today, there is a religious movement underway to make Sunday a holy day. In fact, this effort has been going on for more than three hundred years. It began with the Puritans who settled New England. They believed they were establishing God's kingdom on earth. So they enacted laws that enforced religious practices, including the observance of Sunday as they believed it should be done. For instance, they forbade even married couples to kiss on Sunday. Of course, they excluded working on Sunday too, taking that provision directly from the fourth commandment. Some states in America still enforce these laws. For instance, in Illinois, car dealers are not allowed to see cars on Sunday. The list of prohibited activities varies from state to state, and even local governments can make their own policies in many case. For example, in the community in which I live, public school children are allowed to practice their school sports on Saturday, which is not a regular school day, but not allowed organized school practices on Sunday.

Many of these religious laws and those who promote them seem to be politically motivated. There seems to be an effort to promote Christians to run for government office. Many religious leaders are encouraging Christians to run for local, state, and federal offices. For what purpose?

The answer seems obvious to me—to change the government.

Now, that doesn't seem like a bad idea at first. "After all," say many Christians today, "look at the mess most of our school systems are in. God has been taken completely out of the schools. Evolution is taught instead of creation. Teachers are no longer allowed to start the school day with prayer. The Ten Commandments have been taken down from the classroom walls. Anyone can see that the cumulative effect of all these things is one reason we have so many problems in schools today—everything from poor learning to school shootings."

So the reason many religious leaders are urging Christians to run for government offices, including school boards, is simply to be able to gain a majority and be able to influence laws and policies. Their motives may be good, but once this happens, the potential for abuse is everywhere. Change becomes easy. All that has to happen is to vote in new Bible-based laws.

For example, if enough Christians were on a local school board and if they had the authority to do so, they could reverse the ban on school prayer, put the Ten Commandments back in the classroom, start teaching Creation. This would not suddenly reduce crime and violence. . .and all the students would not start loving Jesus and going back to church. Just imagine if a Christian with such an agenda were to become president of the United States! Or what if a coalition of such Christians had enough members to truly influence government officials. Could this be happening already? Some may say, "If it is, so what? It sounds better than what is currently in place."

But I see a major problem with this kind of thinking. My mother used to say, "A man convinced against his will, is of the same opinion still." Franklin, local, state, and federal governments can pass all the moral laws they want, and it won't change the sin problem in the human heart.

Only Jesus can do that!

Many religious leaders may mean well; I certainly can't judge their motives. But religion should not be forced on people by passing laws designed to impose moral beliefs. We know this already. We have seen this kind of thing happen in history during the Dark Ages. Many millions of people were killed because church leadership became more powerful than secular leadership. The governments of church and state were combined. As a result of the persecution that resulted, people fled to America where a constitution had been drawn up that guaranteed religious persecution would never happen again.

This issue not only occurred in the past. Today there are leaders who continue to urge the uniting of church and state. Charles Malik, President of the General Assembly of the United Nations, Ambassador to the United States and Guest Lecturer at Harvard said:

> The only hope for the western world lies in an alliance between the Roman Catholic Church which is the most commonly, influential, controlling, unifying element in Europe and the Eastern Orthodox Church. Rome must unite with Eastern Orthodoxy, because the Eastern Orthodox Church controls western Middle East, [the east end of the Mediterranean] and if they don't solidify that control, Islam will march across Europe. Islam is political. The only hope of the western world lies then in a united Europe under the control of the Pope. And then all Protestant Christians around the globe must come into submission to the Pope so we will have a unified Christian world.

Satan is all about control. It doesn't make any difference to him whether he uses church leaders or secular officials. He has been most successful through the ages when he has been able to mix church and state, and that is exactly what he is trying to accomplish again in our day.

I believe that very shortly we are going to see Sunday lifted up as a day of worship and an effort made by church and state to pass a national Sunday law declaring that business as usual on Sunday is to be closed down. The thinking behind such a move is simply this: the morals of our society are crumbling rapidly, especially among the youth, our leaders of tomorrow. We all know that God appears to be withdrawing His blessings from the United States because of our disobedience to Him. So people reason that as a nation, we must do something drastic to show God that we are still a Christian people. They think that if we pass a national Sunday law, then our nation will once again be inviting God's Holy Spirit back into our government, and we will become a much more spiritual nation again.

This is the reasoning that will be used to justify laws promoting Sunday observance. Any number of events could trigger this national Sunday law—disasters like the recent World Trade Center destruction. Look at how people reacted to this recent disaster: they panicked, oil prices jumped, and immediately there were prayer sessions and calls for the national to return to God. The restoration of Sunday laws are a natural extension of this scenario.

And let me tell you that I believe we haven't seen anything yet! When this great nation begins to dictate to people—through legislation—regarding the day on which they should worship, then we will see a time of trouble like never before. In fact, when the United States passes a national Sunday law prohibiting people from doing business as usual on Sunday, then we will see God withdraw His Spirit. Why? Because instead of showing our allegiance to God by worshiping Him on His holy seventh-day Sabbath, we will be pledging our allegiance to Satan instead by honoring Sunday, his counterfeit sabbath. May I repeat? It's not just about a day, it's about whom I am going to serve.

If you look closely at this scenario, you'll find that it isn't the papacy that is directly legislating such religious laws. In fact, today it is mostly Protestants—whose faith is built upon the Bible, and the Bible only—who make up the religious coalitions that are attempting to influence political leaders. Yet Satan is using such groups as pawns in his attempt to institute his order of government. Protestants, unwittingly carrying out the dictates of the beast power, become an image of this power. Let's look at Revelation 14:9 once again: "The third angel follows. . .saying with a loud voice, If any man worship the beat and his image, and receive his mark in his forehead or in his hand, the same shall drink of the wine of the wrath of God, which is poured out without mixture into the cup of his indignation."

Question: How does one worship the beast and its image? Answer: By knowingly ignoring God and His commandments—including the fourth—and observing the counterfeit sabbath instead of God's seventy-day Sabbath.

By now, you may be wondering why I am so sure that thee is going to be a national Sunday law implemented by the United States government before Jesus comes. Let's read Revelation 13:3. "And all the world wondered after the beast." This power obviously is one whose authority the whole world—every nation—follows. Is there anything so far on which the whole world agrees enough to follow the lead of such a power? After traveling much of the world, it's my opinion that Sunday sacredness and closing businesses on that day is one of the few things most of the world could agree on.

What should we do?

Let's read another text—Revelation 13:17. "No man might buy or sell, save he that had the mark, or the name of the beast, or the number of his name." I think we can agree that if this prediction in God's Word of restrictions on commerce are true, there must be something that the world will be able to use to determine who will be able to buy and sell. It will be something that will signify our allegiance to this power. Suppose a Sunday law were to be passed forbidding people to work or buy or sell on Sunday. What would happen if a person didn't comply with the law, but instead, worshiped God on the seventh-day Sabbath? What if he opened his store on Sunday as usual in spite of the law. Do you think that business would be shut down?

Yes, Sunday sacredness could easily become the mark spoken of in Revelation 13 and 14. Remember, this mark will be something of such huge magnitude that the whole world will know about it. And in order for this mark to be enforced by prohibitions on buying and selling, there will have to be laws passed. We are not there yet, but I believe that this time, predicted in God's Word, is fast approaching.

Shouldn't we pledge our allegiance today to the great Creator God of the universe and begin preparing now to keep all His commandments?

God Himself wrote the fourth commandment on tablets of stone, commanding us to keep holy the seventh-day Sabbath. In Isaiah, God tells us that we will keep the Sabbath throughout eternity in heaven. "It shall come to pass, that from one new moon to another, and from one Sabbath to another, shall all flesh come to worship before me, saith the Lord" (Isaiah 66:23)

My question to you is this: Why wouldn't a Christian want to honor God by keeping His Sabbath now in preparation for keeping it in heaven through all eternity? Christians don't feel they can disregard God's other nine commandments until they begin keeping them in heaven. In fact, virtually all Christian churches teach that if we kill, steal, commit adultery now, we will be lost and never go to heaven—unless we confess these sins and, by God's grace, quit doing them. Can you imagine using the same reason for continuing in these sins that Christians give for breaking God's fourth commandment?

Yet many Christians try to reason that it isn't important to keep God's fourth commandment. Would any Christian dare say, "It's OK to murder people because that isn't a very important commandment"? Of course not! We all agree that it's wrong to kill. We all agree that it's wrong to steal. We all agree that it's wrong to commit adultery.

Can you see how the devil is deceiving the whole human race and how he is orchestrating the world now to pledge their allegiance to him by lifting up Sunday as the mark of obedience to him?

In closing, let me ask you this question: How do we decide what is truth?

Do we determine truth by majority vote? We determine a lot of things by voting and then following the majority vote. But we can't do that with truth. We don't determine truth by a majority vote. Right is right even if no one is right. And wrong is wrong, even if everyone is wrong. In spiritual things, truth is what God says it is in His Word. It isn't what we *believe* to be true. It isn't what we want to be true. It isn't what most people *agree* is true. *It is what God says that is truth!*

Does it really matter—this question of God's seventh-day Sabbath? Not if it's only a matter of Saturday versus Sunday. But if it's a matter of Jesus versus self—His way versus our way—then it matters, doesn't it? If it's a matter of loyalty to God or loyalty to the powers opposed to God, then it matters, doesn't it? Jesus says, "If ye love me, keep my commandments" (John 14:15). The issue, then, is not one day or another. The issue is love and loyalty. Jesus has told us His will concerning the Sabbath. Do we love Him enough to obey?

It's my prayer that each of us will be among those who

keep His commandments and "have right to the tree of life, and may enter in through the gates into the city" (Revelation 22:14).

Epilogue

I feel privileged to have had the opportunity to write this book. I ran into some extraordinary incidents during trips to Russia and Romania in the course of observing 3ABN "in action." Probably enough to fill another book.

The first trip to Romania was just after the revolution that ousted Nicolae Ceausescu. He had ruled brutally for decades, plundering and murdering, and he and his wife were summarily put to death by the revolutionary tribunal. Church members were treated especially harsh during his rule. Some church buildings were bulldozed and members went underground during most of that period. Times were extremely difficult. Food was desperately scarce, yet the church people we met tried to share their meager rations with us. There was still a strong military presence with troops patrolling Bucharest streets, and electricity was dispersed to various parts of the city intermittently, a few hours at a time. They actually turned on the runway lights for our plane to land and then off again after we were down. It was so cold in the rundown hotel we stayed at that I slept in all of my clothes, including overcoat, hat and gloves. The front doors of the hotel had chains wrapped around them all night. I didn't know whether that was to keep them out or us in. But the people literally wept with joy to see Danny Shelton and despite the handicaps (the communists were still very powerful) he laid the groundwork to help them help themselves with a Christian ministry.

In Gorky (later changed to Nizhny Novgorod) Russia, we also encountered strong resentment from local hardliners. They broke windows in cars and tried to sell "protection" to the Americans, much like in the Chicago of the 1920s. The 3ABN crew was there televising the crusade of California pastor John Carter. He had rented an abandoned sports arena to hold religious meetings. The communists tried to shove the 3ABN cameraman around and to threaten local citizens to stay away. Despite all of this Carter packed the arena three times a day. The crowd trying to attend was so intense that military trucks came in with dogs to disperse them. Some of the door glass was broken in the crunch as people were turned away and told, "Attend the next meeting in a few hours!" In response to this I saw one elderly man crying and he said, "I've waited 70 years for this. Don't make me wait any longer."

In the crowding I was cut off from Danny and our group and waved for them to go on into the building. I continued to take photos for my newspaper. The Russian soldiers took a dim view of this but didn't attempt to stop me. As the crowd dispersed I walked around the back of the building hoping to find a way in and there I saw a most astonishing sight. Not to be denied "The Word," a group of people had broken out a basement window and in an orderly single file were climbing down into the arena. They were well dressed and smiling men, women and children.

Of all the accomplishments of 3ABN, though, to me the building of the religious and cultural center in Russia is the most awesome. At a time when the country was crumbling, this magnificent building rose from the rubble. It was a miracle, in my eyes.

I will move on now to other projects. After my enthralling ten-year journey with 3ABN, still formally unattached to any church or religion. Still longing. But my experiences with 3ABN and Linda and Danny Shelton have changed my life for the better. I have observed them first hand mending broken people. And it is good.

Bob Ellis
November 2002